AFRICAN-AMERICAN POLITICAL PSYCHOLOGY

AFRICAN-AMERICAN POLITICAL PSYCHOLOGY
IDENTITY, OPINION, AND ACTION IN THE POST-CIVIL RIGHTS ERA

Edited by

Tasha S. Philpot and Ismail K. White

First published in 2010 by
PALGRAVE MACMILLAN® in the United States – a division of St. Martin's Press LLC,
175 Fifth Avenue, New York, NY 10010.

Where this book is distributed in the UK, Europe and the rest of the world, this is by
Palgrave Macmillan, a division of Macmillan Publishers Limited, registered in England,
company number 785998, of Houndmills, Basingstoke, Hampshire RG21 6XS.

PALGRAVE MACMILLAN is the global academic imprint of the above companies and has
companies and representatives throughout the world.

Palgrave® and Macmillan® are registered trademarks in the United States,
the United Kingdom, Europe and other countries.

ISBN: 978–0–230–62355–2

Library of Congress Cataloging-in-Publication Data

African-American political psychology : identity, opinion, and action in the post-Civil
Rights Era / edited by Tasha S. Philpot, Ismail K. White.
    p. cm.
  ISBN 978–0–230–62355–2 (hardback)
    1. African Americans—Politics and government—Psychological aspects. 2. African
Americans—Psychology. I. Philpot, Tasha S. II. White, Ismail K.
  E185.615.A59245 2010
  320.97301'9—dc22

                                                                    2010012509

A catalogue record of the book is available from the British Library.

Design by MPS Limited, A Macmillan Company

First edition: November 2010

10 9 8 7 6 5 4 3 2 1

Printed in the United States of America.

For Natalie and Khalil

CONTENTS

TABLES

Figures

ACKNOWLEDGMENTS

Many of the papers compiled in this volume were originally presented at a conference held at the University of Texas at Austin, March 3–5, 2005. The conference, entitled "African-American Political Psychology," brought together sociologists, political scientists, and psychologists deeply committed to claiming a space in social science for the study of African-American political behavior. We would like to thank the various departments and institutes at the University of Texas at Austin that made the conference possible: the Department of Government, the Center for African and African-American Studies, and the College of Liberal Arts. We are especially grateful to the Public Policy Institute at the University of Texas at Austin for its generous financial contributions. We would also like to thank Curt Nichols and Ernest McGowen for their invaluable assistance in helping organize the conference. Finally, we must thank the support staff in both the Department of Government and the Center for African and African-American studies for helping us navigate through the very extensive bureaucracy at the University.

Notes on Contributors

Ray Block, Jr.
Ray Block is an Assistant Professor of Political Science at Florida State University. He has a long-term fascination with the study of mass-level political involvement. His ongoing research looks at racial differences in expressions of political interest (an important but understudied form of psychological engagement, which refers to a person's desire to "follow" or "pay attention to" politics). More generally, he seeks to understand how political engagement relates to political activism, and is working on several projects that examine the mutually reinforcing properties of interest in politics and political participation.

Roy Eidelson
Roy Eidelson is a psychologist who studies, writes about, and consults on the role of psychological issues in political, organizational, and group conflict settings. He is the former executive director of the Solomon Asch Center for Study of Ethnopolitical Conflict at the University of Pennsylvania and is a licensed clinical psychologist.

Kyle Endres
Kyle Endres is a doctoral student in the Department of Government at the University of Texas at Austin. His research interests include political participation, campaigns and elections, and the media.

Kenneth Foster, Sr.
Kenneth Foster is an Assistant Professor of Psychology at Texas Women's University. His research interests include Social Identity, Substance Abuse and HIV/AIDS, Adolescent Violence, School Reform.

Vincent L. Hutchings
Vincent Hutchings is a Professor and a Research Associate Professor at the Center for Political Studies in the Institute for Social Research at the

University of Michigan. His general interests include public opinion, elections, voting behavior, and African American politics. He recently published a book at Princeton University Press entitled *Public Opinion and Democratic Accountability: How Citizens Learn about Politics*, that focuses on how, and under what circumstances, citizens monitor (and consequently influence) their elected representative's voting behavior.

John Iadarola

John Iadarola is a graduate student in the Department of Government at the University of Texas at Austin. His research interests include fundamentalist religion's impacts on political beliefs, psychology, and behavior, ethnic and religious war, and the origins and development of terrorist groups.

Mikhail Lyubansky

Mikhail Lyubansky is a Lecturer in the Department of Psychology at the University of Illinois at Urbana-Champaign. He is interested in exploring factors and conditions associated with changes in beliefs about race, ethnicity, and nationalism. To that end, he has been studying how acculturation strategies and cultural involvement affect psychological adjustment and core beliefs in immigrant and minority populations. His work has been published in the *Journal of Black Psychology, Journal of Child and Family Studies,* and *American Journal of Community Psychology.*

Harwood K. McClerking

Harwood McClerking is an Assistant Professor of Political Science at The Ohio State University. He has research interests in group politics, group identity and heuristics, and race and representation in the U.S. Congress. He is completing a book manuscript, with the working title "A Common Fate: Group Identification in Black Americans," that examines how groups maintain identification through political means. He has an article in the May 2004 *Journal of Politics* on the effect of Black racial composition and media attention on the representation of Black substantive policy issues in Congress.

Eric L. McDaniel

Eric McDaniel is an Associate Professor in the Department of Government and an affiliate of the Department of Religious Studies and the Center for African and African American Studies. He specializes in the study of political behavior, with an emphasis on racial and ethnic politics, and religion and politics. His book, *Politics in the Pews: The Political Mobilization of Black Churches* (2008, University of Michigan Press), provides a discussion of how Black religious institutions choose to become involved in politics.

Ernest B. McGowen

Ernest McGowen is a doctoral candidate in the Department of Government at the University of Texas at Austin. His interests include political participation and race and ethnicity. In particular, he is interested in how and why African Americans in low-density black areas incur higher costs to participate politically in high-density black communities, often at the expense of participating in more local politics.

Tasha S. Philpot

Tasha Philpot is an Associate Professor of Government at the University of Texas at Austin. She is affiliated with the Center for African and African American Studies and the Center for Women's and Gender Studies. Her work has been published in the *American Journal of Political Science, Political Behavior, Public Opinion Quarterly, National Political Science Review*, *Journal of Black Studies,* and the *Journal of Politics*. She is the author of *Race, Republicans, and the Return of the Party of Lincoln* (2007, University of Michigan Press).

Jas M. Sullivan

Jas M. Sullivan is an Assistant Professor of Political Science and African & African American Studies at Louisiana State University. His research and teaching focuses on African American politics, political psychology, and racial identity & stereotypes.

Nicholas A. Valentino

Nicholas Valentino is an Associate Professor of Political Science and Communication Studies at the University of Michigan. His research interests focus on the impact of mass media during political campaigns on the attitudes and political behavior of citizens. In particular, he has focused on the impact of political advertising on the criteria citizens use during candidate evaluation. His work has appeared in the *American Political Science Review, the Journal of Politics, Public Opinion Quarterly, Political Behavior, Political Communication, Political Research Quarterly, Journalism and Mass Communication Quarterly, Urban Affairs Review,* and in several edited volumes on mass media and political communication.

Hanes Walton, Jr.

Hanes Walton, Jr. is a Professor of Political Science and a Senior Research Scientist at the Center for Political Studies in the Institute for Social

Research at the University of Michigan. His books include *African American Power and Politics; The Political Context Variable; Reelection: William J. Clinton as a Native-Son Presidential Candidate; Liberian Politics: The Portrait by African American Diplomat J. Milton Turner;* and *The African Foreign Policy of Secretary of State Henry Kissinger: A Documentary Analysis.*

Ismail K. White

Ismail White is an Assistant Professor of Political Science at The Ohio State University. He studies American politics with a focus on African-American politics, public opinion, and political participation. His current research projects include a study of the effects of racial cues on political evaluations, an investigation into the racial origins and consequences of felony disenfranchisement provisions, and a study examining Americans' beliefs about the genetic origins of race and gender. Work from these projects has appeared in the *American Political Science Review, Public Opinion Quarterly, Journal of Black Studies,* and *Virginia Journal of Law and Social Policy.*

Kristin N. Wylie

Kristin Wylie is a doctoral candidate in the Department of Government at the University of Texas at Austin, with an emphasis on comparative politics and methodology. Her research explores the causes and implications of political underrepresentation of women in democratic Brazil. Her broader research interests include representation of and participation by marginalized groups in the neoliberal era, and the intersection of capitalism and democracy in developing countries.

DEFINING AFRICAN-AMERICAN POLITICAL PSYCHOLOGY

TASHA S. PHILPOT AND ISMAIL K. WHITE

RECENTLY, POLITICAL SCIENCE HAS EXPERIENCED AN UPSURGE in the number of volumes devoted to the study of political psychology. Bridging theories of cognition, personality, and intergroup relations with the study of the way individuals interact with the political world, this line of research has furthered our knowledge of the psychology of political decision-making, socialization, opinion formation, and behavior. Nevertheless, most of the findings yielded from extant studies are based on White Americans. Decades of research in both political science and psychology have demonstrated that external, environmental factors influence individuals' mental processes, especially as they relate to politics. Inasmuch as such factors vary systematically across racial and ethnic groups, the political psychology of these groups warrants study. Thus, we begin the extension of the current literature by applying it to African Americans.

The experience of the African in America is unique. From the arrival of the first Africans in the 1600s through slavery and Jim Crow to the present, the legal, social, and political reality of Blacks remains unparalleled to any other group in American society. How this experience has resonated in the political psychology of Blacks and what that means for how Blacks think about the political world, however, remains largely unexplored. While there have been a few attempts to study this topic, such studies have been sporadic and disconnected from one another and currently do not constitute a cohesive subfield of either political science or psychology. Hence, this is the objective of this volume.

We have assembled a number of papers from both psychologists and political scientists in an effort to combine both disciplines' understanding of this phenomenon. Our goal is to take lessons learned from previous research and incorporate them into new theories and utilize new data sources in an effort to create a unified study of Black political psychology.

We begin by defining African-American political psychology. African-American political psychology finds its primary roots in two fields of study—Black psychology and political psychology, although aspects of Black political psychology can also be traced to history, sociology, economics and Black studies. Baldwin (1986) offers this definition of Black psychology: "African (Black) Psychology is nothing more or less than the uncovering, articulation, operationalization, and application of the principles of the African reality structure relative to psychological phenomena" (243). Political psychology can be thought of as "the study of mental processes that underlie political judgments and decision making" (Kuklinski 2002, 2). By marrying these two definitions, we posit that African-American political psychology is the study of how the distinctive experiences of African-Americans in the United States have shaped the way Blacks think about politics and how that, in turn, impacts their political behavior. This differs from general understandings of political psychology in that here, we contend that the central feature of how Black's view and respond to the political world is based on experiences and perceptions of racism that have their origins in slavery, Jim Crow segregation as well as more subtle forms of racism and segregation in contemporary America. It is important that we make clear that we are *not* arguing that there is any inherent difference between Blacks and non-Blacks in their fundamental ability to process political information. Rather, we are interested in exploring how political context—in this case, race relations in the United States—interacts with universal theories of psychological mechanisms.

We offer a model of how Black political psychology should work in Figure 1. Based on previous research, we argue that the process of developing a distinct African-American political psychology begins with understanding that the historical and contemporary political, social, and economic structure of the United States has shaped Black life and that these structures have limited the life chances of African-Americans (Walton 1985; Massey and Denton 1993; Walton and Smith 2003). As a result of this social, legal, and economic ghettoization, Blacks have developed group-centered identities and ideologies (Cross 1991; Gurin et al. 1980; Gurin et al. 1989; Harris-Lacewell 2003; Dawson 2001). Consequently, these ideologies and identities serve as resources for navigating through the political world (Dawson 1994; Conover 1984;

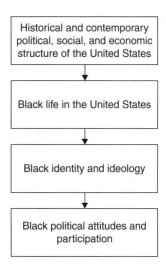

Figure I.1   Model of African-American political psychology.

Tate 1993; Gurin et al. 1989). Evidence to support our proposed model and its implications are provided in the chapters included in the volume.

Understanding the mental processes that underlie Blacks' orientation toward politics has largely been ignored by both mainstream political science and mainstream psychology. The shift in focus of political scientists from the study of institutions to the study of individual-level political attitudes and behavior gave rise to the reliance on large n probability sample surveys. These surveys, however, did not yield subsamples large enough to make reliable inferences about Black public opinion. It has only been within the last few decades that surveys have featured large enough samples of African Americans to conduct meaningful analyses. Even with data limitations, however, scholars have uncovered large differences in Black and White political attitudes—even on issues that have nothing to do with race. Nevertheless, viewed as a monolithic group, much of the work on the racial divide focuses on Whites, ignoring the role of Blacks in this division.

For psychologists, we argue, the over reliance on White undergraduates as research subjects has greatly inhibited the ability to make reliable inferences about African-American behavior—to the extent that we are not willing to assume that everyone that walks into a lab has a blank slate, or at least the same slate; there are good reasons to believe African Americans may respond differently to a number of well-established behavioral stimuli developed using White undergraduates. Because of their tenuous position in American society, racial considerations factor heavily into how a majority of African Americans see the world. Thus, the reliance on predominantly White undergraduate subject pools may reduce psychologists' ability to "develop new constructs, to focus on new variables, and especially to identify new interactions: conditions under which effects occur and classes of people among which effects are most likely to occur" (Krosnick 2002, 196). Consequently, the political psychology of Blacks within psychology is also an understudied area.

The omission of African Americans from the study of political psychology can be seen in published research on the subject. Looking at the journal *Political Psychology* as well as the 3 periodic handbooks on political psychology—Knutson's (1973) *Handbook of Political Psychology*, Hermann's (1986) *Political Psychology*, and Sears, Huddy, and Jervis's (2003) *Oxford Handbook of Political Psychology*—the discussion of race (let alone a focus on African Americans) is nearly absent.[1] For instance, of the 646 articles included in this analysis (omitting forums, comments, presidential addresses, or research notes) published in the journal, *Political Psychology*, from 1979–2006, only 56, that is 9 percent, of the articles touch on some aspect of race. Of these, 13 articles focus on aspects of Black life, most of which occur within the last decade. Looking at the handbooks on political psychology, the landscape is even more barren. It is not until the 2003 *Oxford Handbook of Political Psychology* that race is introduced into the discussion. With respect to Blacks, we see only a superficial treatment of Blacks within a larger discussion of group identity.

Why is this omission problematic? If context is important to understanding the political psychology of individuals and African Americans experience a reality much different than that of other groups in society, then it is necessary to explore the boundaries of broad, general psychological and political concepts previously assumed to be applicable to all. To be sure, Black scholars in both fields have pioneered the study of African Americans, which has led to the carving out of a separate space for Blacks in both disciplines. We argue, however, that Black politics, Black psychology, and the intersection of the two should be moved from the margin to the mainstream. Doing so provides a check on the external validity of what we think we know about these fields.

In addition to presenting an in-depth analysis of Black political psychology not provided elsewhere, this volume sets itself apart from other books in this area by creating a conversation between two groups who have previously been at odds with one another. Currently, there is a disjointed discussion between political scientists and psychologists with respect to how to approach the study of African-American political psychology. Generally speaking, political scientists have provided a framework for understanding political phenomena while psychologists provide the framework for fully understanding mental processes. Few studies from psychologists examine how these processes underlie political beliefs, attitudes, and behavior. Increasingly, political scientists have incorporated extant psychological theories into their research but this integration is still limited. Finally, political scientists typically treat political outcomes as dependent variables and mental processes as independent variables. In contrast, psychologists treat mental processes as dependent variables while political outcomes are treated as the independent variables. Viewed individually, studies in the area of Black political psychology seem disparate and conflicting with one another, with disagreement over which direction the causal arrows go. By applying our model of Black political psychology, we illustrate that the relationship between politics and psychology is cyclical and reinforcing.

As we explore this process, we argue that research in this area should address the following questions:

- How does the Black experience shape Blacks' political outlook and attitudes?
- Do these experiences resonate differently with different segments of the Black community?
- How might this shape Black political behavior?

All of the chapters included in this volume tackle some aspect related to these questions.

The first section of the volume deals with the history of African-American political psychology. This section provides the antecedents for understanding the contemporary study of Black political psychology by illustrating how scholars have thus far examined the first half of the model presented in Figure 1. Chapter One traces the intersection of political science, psychology, and Black politics by conducting a content analysis of three major journals in these disciplines. As has been noted elsewhere, this chapter will illustrate that the relationship between political science and psychology is largely one-sided—political science borrows from psychology much more than psychology borrows from political science. This chapter also demonstrates, however, that the relationship becomes more reciprocal when it comes to the study of African Americans. The goal of Chapter Two is to determine the current state of affairs in African-American political psychology by identifying which themes are most prevalent in the literature. Two major research veins have appeared in the study of African-American politics—a race-relations literature, which focuses on African Americans' place in American political culture vis-à-vis Whites, and an African-American politics literature whose emphasis is more on political empowerment and cultural distinctiveness. By employing a multimethod approach which includes a literature review of the early scholarship on African-American politics, case studies of pioneering works, and content analysis of articles in major research journals, this chapter finds that the race relations frame is availed much more often than the Black politics frame, due mainly to the influence of early works in the field that exclusively employed this paradigm.

Part 2 of this volume—*Contemporary Issues in the Psychology of Black Identity*—explores the contours of Black identity by delving into the dynamics of the third step in our model. African-American racial identity is political in and of itself. To be sure, Black identity is born out of the politics surrounding the United States' race relations (Dawson 1994; Gurin et al. 1989). This section explores how, when, and to what extent African-American racial group identity shapes Black political preferences and evaluations. Further, the chapters in this section examine the boundaries of racial identity as well as how Black identity compares and competes with alternative identities. Part 2 begins with Chapter 3, which investigates the nature of Black and White American's various levels of identity. Analyzing data from 216 prospective jurors, the authors test whether there exist racial differences in personal world views, racial group experiences, and experiences as American citizens. The authors reveal significant differences at the racial group level but few racial differences at the personal world and national group levels. Chapter 4 attempts to understand the political consequences of racial group identity by examining group-based differences in emotional responses to political events. Analyzing data from a number of national surveys and from an original lab experiment, the authors demonstrate that an individual's emotional response to political events are conditioned by the whether the event is perceived to disproportionally benefit or harm members of that individual's racial in-group. As its title suggests, Chapter 5, explores whether Black identity can be primed or whether it is chronically salient. This chapter argues that psychological theories that focus on the activation of racial attitudes among White Americans are insufficient to explain how racial messages influence the opinions of Black Americans. In two separate laboratory experiments, the author tests the effects of explicitly racial, implicitly racial, and verbal cues on both Black and White Americans' assessments of an ostensibly non-racial political issue. The author finds that attitude activation works differently for African Americans than for Whites. Only frames that provide oblique references to race successfully activated racial out-group resentment for Whites. Among Blacks, explicit references to race most reliably elicited racial thinking by activating racial in-group identification. Chapter 6 complicates the idea of Black identity by arguing that the role of race and gender in electoral politics must be examined simultaneously because of their mutually reinforcing relationship. Using precinct-level data, experimental data, and national exit poll data from two congressional election years, the authors demonstrate that Black women are the strongest supporters of Black female candidates but that Black female candidates with significant experience in politics can attract both Black and White voters, regardless of gender. Chapter 7 also argues that racial identity is an important ingredient in candidate support among African Americans. Here the author examines measures of racial group identification and the *Implicit Association Test* to investigate if an implicit positive preference exists among African-American voters for African-American candidates.

Given the nature of Black identity explored in Section 2, Section 3—*Contemporary Issues in the Psychology of Black Political Attitudes and Behavior*—features a number of works which look at how Black identity influences African-American political attitudes and behavior. Here, we present chapters that explore how the last part of our model works. The major theme that runs through these chapters is that the same unique experiences that have shaped Black identity cause group-based considerations to interact with and contort other political orientations, thereby affecting subsequent engagement in the political arena. The first three chapters in this section investigate different facets of the racial divide. In Chapter Eight, we see where race and religion intersect. Attempting to understand why conservative religious appeals are often ineffective among Blacks, the author makes the case that Blacks' religious interpretation significantly differs from that of Whites' and thus leads to different interpretations of politics. Using survey data, this chapter explores support for a number of issues and political orientations, including party identification and support for gender, racial, and sexual equality. Chapter Nine offers a dynamic framework for explaining racial differences in political interest. The author argues that macrolevel shifts, over time, in America's racial tolerance are an important component to understanding changes in Black political interest. The author tests this expectation using data from the American National Election Studies. Chapter 10 examines whether partisan appeals to race can influence the racial divide in Black and White American's opinions. Using an experiment embedded in a random-sample survey, this study finds that when racial cues were present, the racial divide in political perceptions increased substantially, at times rivaling the effects of partisan identification. The final two chapters illustrate how Blacks have been able to transform negative situations into political capital. Chapter 11 seeks to clarify the relationship between racism and empowerment among African Americans by incorporating qualitative data of 18 African-American activists interviewed in various northeastern United States locations. This study argues that many Black activists, in response to the pervasive threat to psychological and physical well-being that racism poses, generate a sense of empowerment that fuels their activism. Finally, Chapter 12 examines spatial variation in African-American voter turnout. This chapter posits that majority African-American precincts located in majority-Anglo congressional districts will have lower average turnout rates and ballot roll-off because they do not find their local races salient. Using aggregate data, the author argues that instead of expending resources in electoral races in which the outcome will likely yield a winner who will not be descriptively representative, Blacks located in predominately White congressional districts will transfer their political capital to activities that will likely result in group-related benefits.

The chapters in this volume by no means constitute the full realm of possible topics related to Black political psychology. To be sure, many of these studies are preliminary in nature. Rather, this volume is meant to be a catalyst for the future study of the psychology that underlies Black political identity, attitudes, and behavior. It is our hope that the questions, hypotheses, and analyses generated in this volume will inspire future research on this topic.

PART 1

THE HISTORY OF AFRICAN-AMERICAN POLITICAL PSYCHOLOGY RESEARCH IN TWO DISCIPLINES

A Meeting of the Minds: Exploring the Intersection of Psychology, Political Science, and Black Politics

Tasha S. Philpot, Kyle Endres, and John Iadarola

Using a variety of measures, scholars (for example Krosnick 2002) have noted the asymmetry in the relationship between political science and psychology. Whether it is student participation in the Summer Institute in Political Psychology, the number of psychologists hired as faculty in political science departments versus political scientists hired in psychology departments, or the relative number of articles published in each other's flagship journals, "political science and political scientists have placed much more value on political psychology than have psychologists" (Krosnick 2002, 192). But is this universally true? Are there areas in political science where psychologists are more likely to reciprocate the relationship? Our answer is yes. We believe that it is within Black psychology that one finds a heavier reliance on political science than found elsewhere. We argue that the mere existence of a Black psychology is political. Therefore, while mainstream psychology only rarely delves into the political, Black psychology and political science are more intimately intertwined. Further, we contend that Black politics serves as a nexus between political science and psychology. In what follows, we give a brief history of the fields of Black politics, Black psychology, and political psychology. Lastly, we present an analysis of three academic journals in political science and psychology to demonstrate our point.

A BRIEF OVERVIEW OF THREE FIELDS OF STUDY

The idea that Black politics, Black psychology, and political psychology are all connected is easy to conceive given that each of these is a hybrid subfield. As the name suggests, political psychology is primarily a combination of political science and psychology. "As a field of study, political psychology arose from the applied practice of trying to relate psychological phenomena to political reality" (Perez 2001, 348). As it has progressed, political psychology has drawn from a variety of subfields within psychology, including social, developmental and psychoanalytical (Sears 1989) and has incorporated aspects of political science, history, psychiatry, sociology, and legal studies (Iyengar 1993).

The nature of political psychology has evolved over time. Horowitz (1979) identifies three paradigm shifts this field of study has undergone. The first phase, occurring during the first half of the twentieth century, was dominated by personality psychology. This phase is best exemplified by the pioneering work of Harold Lasswell (see Lasswell 1930, 1948). Research during this period incorporated Freudian philosophy into explanations of mass and elite political behavior (McGuire 1993). Psychobiographies, such as Freud's (1910) *Leonardo da Vinci and a Memory of His Childhood* also fit into this category of research (Runyan 1993). During the 1950s and 1960s, political psychology became heavily influenced by sociology and the focus of research shifted from the individual to society. As Horowitz explains, "The rhetoric was not all that different, but the flow was different. Instead of the individual having an outflow to the social system, the social system determined the nature of the personality system" (Horowitz 1979, 101). In the final phase, we see the emergence of a more political, science-oriented version of political psychology. It is during this phase that you find political scientists using a psychological framework to develop new theories to explain political behavior, such as in Campbell et al.'s (1960) *The American Voter*. Out of this phase came the rise of survey research (McGuire 1993). To this, McGuire (1993) adds the political cognition and decision era of the 1980s and 1990s, which focuses on "the content and operations of cognitive systems and choice behavior" (30). Much of this work is conducted through laboratory experiments and includes debates, such as whether political evaluations are impression-driven or memory-based (see Lodge et al. 1989 for instance). Currently, political psychology is an amalgamation of all of the phases, with perhaps the greatest emphasis on the social and cognitive psychological mechanisms related to political attitudes and behavior.

While Black politics is generally found couched within political science departments, it is innately interdisciplinary. There is no other way to accurately account for the complex nature of Blacks' political standing in America. Certainly, one of the most enduring and deep-rooted cleavages in the United States falls along racial lines (Kinder and Sanders 1996; Hutchings and Valentino 2004). Even the structure of many of the United States' governing institutions (e.g., the Electoral College, Congress, the two-party system) is a direct result of arguments surrounding U.S. race relations (Walton and Smith 2003; Philpot 2007; Hutchings and Valentino 2004). As early as the 1800s, the tension between wanting to adhere to America's creed of equality for all and perpetuating the institution of slavery and later Jim Crow racism has been well-documented as the most glaring contradictions in the United States' political culture (Myrdal 1944; Tocqueville 1835). Hence, to fully understand Black politics, the subfield must encompass the broad range of institutional, sociopolitical, economic, historical, psychological, and environmental factors that affect Black political incorporation, both within the Black community and outside of it.

Although mainstream political science has not always valued the contribution of this line of research (McClerking and Philpot 2008), Black political scientists have always pursued questions of power and conflict within the Black community and between the Black community and other groups in society (McClain and Garcia 1993; Walton et al. 1995; Walton et al. 1989). Nevertheless, the integration of Blacks, and, consequently, the incorporation of Black politics into mainstream political science have been slow-moving. By the time Jewel L. Prestage received her PhD in political science in 1954 (the first Black woman ever to do so), only 21 other Blacks had received their doctorate in the discipline. Shortly thereafter, however, this number would triple (Woodard and Preston 1985). The study of Black politics gained prominence during the 1960s and 1970s, partly because the activities surrounding the Civil Rights Movement made the topic more interesting and partly because formal barriers to Blacks entering doctoral programs began to lift (Wilson 1985; McClerking and Philpot 2008). It was during this time that the number of Blacks entering doctoral programs reached an all-time high (Woodard and Preston 1985). Also during that time, Black politics became a formal institution with the establishment of the National Conference of Black Political Scientists in 1969.

Since the 1970s, approximately 2,000 African Americans have received doctorates in political science and public administration (WebCASPAR). Though not all of them study Black politics, this growth in Black political scientists has yielded a rich diversity of theoretical and methodological approaches. Of particular relevance to this chapter is the increase in the number of empirical studies of Black cognition, ideology, and identity, which draw directly from psychology. Examples of such studies are presented in this volume.

The evolution of Black psychology, as a subfield, in many ways parallels that of Black politics. The historical development of a Black psychology has been hindered at times for a variety of scientific and social reasons. Various threads of psychological theory have thwarted attempts to objectively study and speak on Black psychology. While these differ in content and duration, what ties them together is their strong political nature. Overt racism is perhaps the most obvious historic example, but the influence of social Darwinism gave "scientific" backing to one thread of argument that would continue on into modern times: that racial difference in human condition and achievement are caused not by environment, but by innate characteristics (see The JBHE Foundation 1996). The historical nature of the Black family structure, differential patterns of employment, and racial differences in crime rates were seen not as symptoms of environment and political differences between the races, but as evidence of a "tangle of pathology," which convinced many that there is something inherently different about Black Americans (Guthrie 1980). Thus, from its beginnings, the psychological study of Black Americans has been colored in ways that have both sociopolitical causes and longstanding, widespread political ramifications.

Arguably, Black psychology became formalized with the creation of the Association of Black Psychologists (ABPsi). Like many of the Black professional organizations, both inside and outside of the academy, ABPsi was born out of dissatisfaction with the status quo. Specifically, the founding members of ABPsi believed that the American Psychological Association was taking "nonsupportive, if not racist, positions regarding ethnic minority concerns" (Belgrave and Allison 2006, 16). As a result, Black psychologists formed a separate organization in 1968, which is still in existence. One of the goals of this new organization was to "address themselves to significant social problems affecting the Black community and other segments of the population whose needs society has not fulfilled" (Association of Black Psychologists). Thus, built into its mission from the onset was a sense that its membership was obliged to address the social, political, and economic inequalities Blacks face in American society. Six years later, in 1974, the organization began publishing the *Journal of Black Psychology*. Dedicated to publishing "scholarly research and theory on the behavior of Black and other populations from Black or Afrocentric perspectives" (Association of Black Psychologists 2010), the journal further institutionalized the study of Black psychology. It is here where we expect to find psychology and political science connected by Black politics.

NOT QUITE TALKING ABOUT A 50/50 LOVE

Political science has been referred to as a "borrowing discipline," in so far as it has, since its beginning as a field in its own right, borrowed both substantively and methodologically from sociology, anthropology, and perhaps most significantly, economics (Sears 1989). In each of these examples, a strong case can be made for the existence of a mutually beneficial cross fertilization of the disciplines. Just as political science has borrowed statistical and mathematical methods from economics and qualitative techniques from sociology, so have these disciplines sampled from and contributed to the study of politics in return. Nevertheless, there exists "what is, in some respects, a 'theoretical trade deficit' between disciplines in which political scientists tend to import more theoretical ideas than export" (Rahn et al. 2002, 167).

This asymmetric relationship is equally, if not more, pronounced with respect to psychology (although see Iyengar 1993). When measured by distribution of graduate students, article publication, or location of graduate departments and concentrations (see Sears and Funk 1991), political science appears more interested in the psychological that psychology is in the political. Certainly there are exceptions, as a brief look through past editions of *Political Psychology* can attest, but the driving force behind the productivity of the subfield has historically come from political scientists focused on behavior (McGuire 1993).[1]

Why did a mainly unidirectional relationship between political science and psychology develop? In its beginnings, before the term "political psychology" had become widespread, students of political behavior began to move the focus of political science away from its traditional emphasis on the bureaucratic, legal aspects of politics. In what has been referred to as the "continuation of political realism by other means," work by such scholars as Merriam, Gosnell, and Lasswell introduced and refined new methodologies and topical foci that blurred the line between political science, sociology, economics, and psychology (Simon 1985). Although these contributions were in some cases not initially greeted enthusiastically by the discipline, over time work on such diverse topics as the use of symbols, political socialization, and small group behavior began to prove useful in explaining a wide range of political behaviors in a variety of democratic settings (Knutson 1973).

As political science advanced as a field and the study of political behavior grew, so too did its need for suitable tools with which to conduct its research. While surveys contributed to the development of large, fruitful datasets, the tools and methods of traditional psychology filled a particular academic niche for political science at a time when those tools were truly needed (Hyman 1959; Sears 1989). Psychology, perhaps because of its longer history and previously established relationship with the field of sociology, did not have that same need. Thus, by the 1970s, when political psychology was at last a recognizable and fairly autonomous area of study, much of the research and literature of the subfield had almost necessarily been conducted by political scientists. Led by these same scientists, courses on political psychology were overwhelmingly organized and taught under the banner of political science. By the same process, where codified subfields in political psychology exist, they do so almost universally within political science departments (Sears and Funk 1991).

With this in mind, we paraphrase the question posed in our opening paragraph: Does Black psychology serve as equilibrium for the relationship between political science and psychology? As stated earlier, we believe it does. But such is an empirical question, to which we turn to now.

DATA AND METHODS

Our goal is to uncover the overlap between political science, psychology, and Black politics. In particular, we are interested in whether Black politics permeates Black psychology at a greater rate than mainstream political science permeates psychology. To this end, a content analysis was conducted using online databases; JSTOR was used for the *American Political Science Review* (APSR), PsychARTICLES (EBSCO) was used for the *Journal of Personality and Social Psychology* (JPSP) and Sage Journals Online was used for the *Journal of Black Psychology* (JBP). These three journals were chosen because of their prominence in their respective fields. APSR has been published by the American Political Science Association since 1906 and is the flagship journal in political science. As stated earlier, JBP began publication in 1974 and is the official journal of the Association of Black Psychologists. Published by the American Psychological Association, JPSP has been in circulation since 1965. Its focus is on attitudes and social cognition, interpersonal relations and group processes, and personality processes and individual differences (American Psychological Association 2010). In all cases, book reviews and non-article content were excluded. All APSR article were examined for psychological content by searching for the key words, "psychology" or "psychological" in the text. Similarly, all JPSP and JBP articles were inspected for political content by searching the text for the terms, "politics" or "political."

RESULTS

Almost from its inception, the APSR has published articles that reference psychology in some way, although with relative scarcity in the first few decades (see Figure 1.1). One of the earliest pieces published in this journal which references psychology is James Bryce's presidential address at the Fifth Annual Meeting of the American Political Science Association in 1908, held jointly with the American Historical Association. In it, he argues that in order for science to become influential, scholars must make their work attractive to audiences. As a remedy to this end, he prescribes taking lessons from "Ethics and Psychology" on the "general and permanent tendencies of men in communities" (Bryce 1909, 6). By the 1920s, articles referencing psychology appear more frequently. Roughly 25 percent of articles in the *American Political Science Review* mention psychology during this decade. This rate remained relatively stable until the 1950s, when just over a half of all articles mentioned

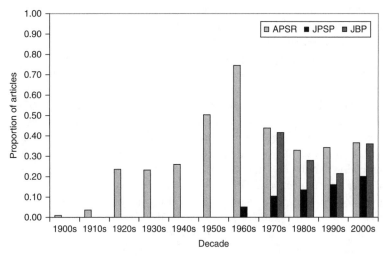

Figure 1.1   A comparison of discipline crossover.

psychology. The percentage of articles peaked at 75 percent during the 1960s, which is essentially the beginning of the behavioral revolution. Because of the prominence of seminal voting studies of U.S. elections written during this period (e.g. Campbell et al. 1960), we have come to associate the behavioral revolution with American politics. However, many of the articles published in the APSR in the 1960s that reference psychology were actually written by scholars in the field of international relations who sought to explain the psychology behind the power struggle between international actors (for example Singer 1963). Following this zenith, the percentage of articles decreased to 44 percent in the 1970s and has fluctuated between 33 and 37 percent in the three most recent decades. In the contemporary period, articles range in topic from information processing and decision making of voters (Valentino et al. 2002) to understanding suicide terrorism (Pape 2003).

As expected the *Journal of Personality and Social Psychology* has yet to reference politics as frequently as the APSR refers to psychology. Interestingly, the first article to discuss politics in this journal appears in 1965. Entitled, "Race and Belief as Determinants of Behavioral Intentions," this article examined whether Whites' attitudes towards Blacks correlated with their support for civil rights legislation (Triandis and Davis 1965). This lends support to our argument that the study of racial politics can steer more psychologists toward political psychology. The number of articles involving politics in the *Journal of Personality and Social Psychology* has increased each decade since its initial publication, from 5 percent of articles during the 1960s to 20 percent of articles during the 2000s. Many of the more recent articles related to politics also involve the study of race as well (Kay et al. 2009; Son Hing et al. 2008; Eibach and Keegan 2006).

Looking at the percentage of articles that reference politics in JBP, we find strong evidence to support our argument. In general, the *Journal of Black Psychology* publishes as much as three times more articles related to politics than JPSP in some years. Its high point is during the 1970s, the tail end of the Black freedom struggle. Here we find a few articles on racial group identity, including a review of William Cross's work, which will be discussed in greater detail in the next chapter (Cross 1978). In the following two decades, the number of articles declined to 28 percent and 21 percent, respectively. The 2000s marked an increase to 36 percent, many of which explore the psychological impact of various public policies. Note also that the *Journal of Black Psychology*'s reference to politics is fairly comparable to the *American Political Science Review*'s reference to psychology from the 1970s to the present, with the exception of the 1990s, when the two publications differed by about 13 percentage points. From this standpoint, the relationship between psychology and political science is about even.

CONCLUSION

In sum, we find strong support for our expectation that the study of race is inherently political. In this chapter, our content analysis reveals strong support for the idea that although mainstream psychology has paid little attention to the study of politics, scholars interested in the psychology of African Americans see the interaction of race and politics as an essential part of understanding Black psychology. Indeed, given the political reasons behind the development of the study of Black psychology, many of these researchers believe it difficult if not impossible to separate the study of African Americans from the study of politics. In the next chapter, McClerking and Walton further discuss the evolution of the intersection of Black politics and Black psychology.

CHAPTER 2

THE POLITICAL SCIENCE IMAGE OF THE BLACK MIND: POLITICS IN THE PSYCHOLOGY OF AFRICAN AMERICANS

HARWOOD K. MCCLERKING AND HANES WALTON, JR.

IN 1955, LONG BEFORE THE PREEMINENCE OF THE POLITICAL SCIENCE subfield of political psychology, with its intrapsychic concepts and sundry measurement techniques and procedures, African-American historian Elsie Lewis published a pioneering work entitled "The Political Mind of the Negro, 1865–1900." This study tried to map out the psychological contours of the collective minds of several leading African-American spokespersons, such as "Frederick Douglass and the Reverend J. Stella Martin of New York, George T. Downing of Rhode Island, Peter H. Clark and John M. Langston of Ohio, and Martin R. Delaney, and Robert Purvis of Pennsylvania" (Lewis 1955, 189). Using the speeches, convention addresses, lectures, newspaper articles and editorials as well as pamphlets and books of these leaders, Professor Lewis crafted a bold and penetrating portrait of the collected mentalities of these selected leaders from the Civil War, Reconstruction, and post-Reconstruction periods. This was an innovative and pioneering work in African-American political psychology.

When the political behavioral revolution began its dominance in political science in the 1960s, the psychoanalytical study of political leaders that had been evolving since the 1930s (for the pioneering study on this topic, see Lasswell 1930, 1948) eventually focused its attention upon an African-American leader Malcolm X in 1981 and tried to map out the psychological contours of his political mind (Wolfenstein 1967, 1981). Thus, in a period of 26 years the disciplines of history and political science had moved from a collective to an individual study of African-American political psychology. Yet, these two case studies did not crossfertilize each other, and the subfield of political psychology was still embedded within the broad area known as political behavioralism. Despite this fledging beginning, there was at this moment in time quite a scholarly journey to be made.

Therefore, the focus of this chapter is on the nature, scope, and significance of the knowledge about the African-American political mind and behavior. As we proceed, we address several questions. First, does such knowledge even exist? Secondly, if it exists, is such knowledge collective, individualistic, or some combination of both? Thirdly, is this extant knowledge disparate, cumulative, and reliable? And finally, what are the other strengths and weaknesses of this knowledge? Put differently, at this moment in time, what is the current state of affairs in the study of African-American political psychology?

DATA AND METHODOLOGY

To determine the state of affairs in African-American political psychology, this sociology of knowledge chapter will employ a threefold data-gathering and analysis strategy (for a near comprehensive and systematic coverage of this literature, see Walton 1973; Walton et al. 1989; Walton 1985, 1989; Walton et al. 2001). First, it will undertake a literature review of the scholarly works on African-American politics and behavior to estimate the amount of work on the topic. This strategy will identify the relevant data. But to get beyond the broad overview, this chapter will undertake several case studies of pioneering works. These case studies will focus upon the early works and the transitional studies that brought the concepts of political psychology to the area of African-American politics. Such works will give us a sense of the theoretical patterns emerging from the groundwork and foundational knowledge shaping the study of Black political psychology.

At this point, we will need to know what has appeared about the African-American political mind since the emergence of political science. We will undertake an empirical content-analysis based review of numerous political science journals, including such major journals as *American Political Science Review*, *Journal of Politics*, and *Political Science Quarterly*, to see how much knowledge these academic journals have produced about the political mind of African Americans. This approach will provide this chapter with a comprehensive and systematic coverage of the field.

But we want to go beyond the mere coverage of the field. How do we test, assess, and evaluate this body of knowledge? To undertake this task, we will be guided by our theoretical framework drawn from the work on the race and politics literature developed by Professors Cheryl Miller, Joseph P. McCormick II, and Hanes Walton, Jr., which demonstrated that the entire body of race and politics literature falls neatly into two major categories: (1) a race relations politics literature; and (2) an African-American [Black] politics literature (Walton et al. 1995). Each literature has an underlying perspective and outlook. The race relations literature emphasizes and prioritizes cooperation over conflict. This literature asserts that racial peace as defined by Whites takes priority over racial justice, demands for racial equality, and the right to vote. Movements toward civil rights and voting rights by African Americans cannot afford to antagonize, anger, or push Whites into going any faster than they want to go. Hence, Whites must lead and be given the time to provide African Americans their constitutional rights. Embedded in this literature are specific ideas and notions about the African-American political mind. Scholars in political psychology with this perspective have used the field to justify and serve this tradition. Such is not neutral scholarship.

The African-American politics literature argues that justice, morality, and constitutional rights take precedence over White racial sensibilities. Racial peace is not *the* highest and dominant priority. This literature supports political empowerment and parity. In this literature, African Americans seek to eradicate White dominance and to find various ways to empower themselves and correct the numerous deficiencies inherent in their communities due to the social and political systems known as slavery, segregation, and desegregation. The focus of this literature is on intragroup dynamics, rather than intergroup relations. Therefore, one finds in this literature specific ideas and notions about the African-American political mind (Walton et al. 1995). Have scholars with this perspective emerged in political psychology? What is the nature of their work?

Collectively, these two perspectives form the theory used in this chapter and it will enable us to structure and organize the literature found in the sundry journals. Once categorized, further assessments and evaluations will be made by using concepts and theories about African-American political psychology developed by psychologists from the African-American political experiences in America. The case study data will highlight the two outstanding works in this area and will contrast and compare their concepts with those concepts developed in the field and then applied uncritically to African Americans. Armed with such insights, our analysis will be able to suggest (project) conceptualizations and theories that are flawed and those that fit best with the African-American data. Herein lies our key to assessing the state of the area of African-American political psychology.

After having collected our three data sources: (1) identification data; (2) case study data; and the (3) journal data, this chapter will use descriptive statistics to discern trends, patterns, and potential relationships. This empirical methodology will enable us to describe, characterize, and illuminate each segment of the literature. It will help us categorize and structure the data and then see how and if it is linked and related. Next, this methodology will enable this study to uncover important testable propositions about the emergence, evolution, and usefulness of concepts dealing with African-American political behavior. And such an approach will allow some degree of synthesis and projections for the future about African-American political psychology.

THE PIONEERING LITERATURE ON AFRICAN-AMERICAN POLITICAL PSYCHOLOGY: BEFORE ELISE LEWIS

The application of psychological theory to political behavior has distant origins for political scientists. For example, Nancy Maveety's pathbreaking volume on the academic pioneers of the study of judicial behavior demonstrates three different types of academic approaches in this area: those with the attitudinal models, those with strategic models, and those with historical-institutionalist models (Maveety 2003). This is just in one area of political science. While it was Professor Harold Lasswell who suggested that psychoanalytical concepts be applied to politics and political behavior (Lasswell 1948, 1930), most pioneers brought it into political science via political biographies of different types of political leaders (see Greenstein 1969; Lerner 1971). Simply because of the diversity of political leaders—in the early years of political psychology (as part of political behavior)—no systematic approach prevailed. Instead, what evolved were scattered approaches and scattered findings.

Simultaneous with the rising political psychology approach was the sociological approach. In the 1930s, sociologists discovered African Americans' leaders and began the process of studying them with their concepts and theories (Johnson 1937; Burgess 1962; Walters and Smith 1999). In fact, their studies came to dominate if not gain hegemony over the field. However, at the University of Chicago, one of Professor Lasswell's colleagues, Professor Harold Gosnell heeded his advice and applied some of Lasswell's psychological ideas to his pioneering work on the African-American political leaders in the city of Chicago. Although this work didn't rely solely upon psychological insights, Gosnell did have some interesting observations (Gosnell 1935).

Despite these interesting observations and his sidestepping of sociological concepts for psychological ones, the trend of a sociological approach to the study of African-American political and protest leaders continued unabated despite Gosnell's book. And the first synthesis and consensus didn't occur until the appearance of Gunnar Myrdal's (1944) *An American Dilemma*. Making no use of the memorandum study on African-American leadership prepared for his volume by African-American political scientist Ralph Bunche, Myrdal concluded that both the African-American leadership elites and masses were pathological (Walton and Smith 2000). To attain such a question-able scholarly and academic posture, Myrdal pushed aside not only Bunche's work but also the scattered work in political psychology by men like Gosnell and the huge body of work developed by sociologists. And given the large number of accolades that Myrdal's volume received from every segment of American society, it should come as no surprise that by the time the political behavioral revolution came in the discipline in the 1960s, the hegemonic theory and understanding about the African-American political mind was its pathological nature. Here is where most of the political behavioralists (political psychologists) began their intrapsychic studies and analyses, Professor Lewis notwithstanding.

THE AFRICAN-AMERICAN POLITICAL MIND: FOUR CASE STUDIES

Before we get to the presentation of the four case studies, we discuss an important trendsetter for the cases. That trendsetter is the first of the prominent Myrdalian theorists on Black political behavior to appear in the discipline of political science: James Q. Wilson with his *Negro Politics: The Search for Leadership* and a series of articles on the topic. Both the book and the articles declared that there was no African-American leadership due to their pathological minds (Walton et al. 1992). Nor could this community generate such leaders given their sorry psychological state; thus, Wilson took it upon himself to assist those who claimed to be leading the community. His works became the preeminent how-to manuals as he counseled his so-called leaders to accept segregation and make the best of it. And as that social system collapsed, he counseled going slow—gradualism for the sake of pluralism in America. Wilson's book arrived just prior to the political behavioral revolution and, therefore, didn't carry any of the major trappings of that revolution like empiricism, but it did influence several of the major studies following its publication. We now move on to the four case studies.

In 1966, Professors Donald Matthews and James Prothro published the initial full-political behavior study of African Americans entitled *Negroes and the New Southern Politics*. In this work, they not only quote and constantly rely upon the Wilson book (Matthews and Prothro 1966, 12n, 8, 176n, 335–6, 9, 63), but even after their empirical work demonstrates otherwise, they conclude that "in order to increase the amount of Negro participation in southern politics, Negro attitudes and cognitions must be altered. This is a far more difficult and time-consuming task than altering the formal political system or social structure ... [C]hange in the Negroes' objective status may not quickly change the psychological characteristics instilled by decades of subordination" (Matthews and Prothro 1966, 312). They continue with their conclusion: "Segregation's greatest triumph has been its impact on Negro minds. For some the scars are permanent; nothing short of death will eliminate their crippled psyches from the political scene. For the others the scars will respond but slowly to the salve of objective equality" (Matthews and Prothro 1966, 312). This is Wilson and Myrdal at their intellectual best. With this work, their pathological portrait of the African-American political mind had received strong empirical support.

Three years after the appearance of the Matthews and Prothro book, in 1969, another Myrdalian theorist's work appeared. Professor Harry Holloway wrote *The Politics of the Southern Negro: From Exclusion to Big City Organization*. Unlike the Matthews and Prothro book, which relied upon a region-wide survey of both Southern Blacks and Whites supplemented by several community studies that employed face-to-face interviews and census and voting data, Professor Holloway used face-to-face interviews in six of the eleven states of the old Confederacy. And in this data approach, Holloway used both rural and urban places for comparisons and contrasts. Said methodological approach harkened back to the prebehavioral revolution period, but Holloway borrowed heavily from several of the major political behavioral studies of his time, especially the conceptual schema used in the widely acclaimed, *The Civic Culture* (Holloway 1969). Ignoring the fact that this work was a survey based study of comparative politics that looked at Great Britain, Mexico, United States, Germany, and Italy and didn't make any use of the African Americans in the survey (Almond and Verba 1980), Holloway applied uncritically the concept of a political culture and the idea of a traditional society with apathetic nonparticipants to describe African-American political psychology.

He wrote: "as for the Negro personality, conditions tended to produce the accommodating individual expected by white supremacists ... the Negro man lived in a world in which the whites not only dominated but made the Negro aware of it" (Holloway 1969, 23). At this point in his analysis, Holloway declared without qualification that "the white man's domination and insistence on deference ultimately reached into the Negro mind and created a sense of inferiority. The Negro saw himself, in a sense, as the white man saw him and accepted the view that he was deserving of an inferior place in society. Several consequences followed. One ... was (political) apathy and lack of ambition" (Holloway 1969, 22). With these behavioral observations, Holloway had incorporated Myrdal, Wilson, Matthews and Prothro as well as the leading research findings up to this point in time.

Despite the fact that there were at least two fatal flaws in Holloway's conceptualization and interpretive analysis, he persisted in advancing his inaccurate conclusions. In the Matthews and Prothro book, which immediately preceded his, they demonstrated that the main concepts, civic competence and political culture, as developed in *The Civic Culture* had no meaning or applicability to southern Negro political psychology (Matthews and Prothro 1966). Nor could an empirical relationship be established with this variable. But they didn't stop there. Of the concept of political culture and its attendant idea of different political subcultures in the eleven states of the South, Matthews and Prothro showed that this concept had no explanatory powers. Here is how they put it: "southern political subcultures ... contribute little to explaining Negro participation beyond what we can say on the basis of socioeconomic factors." They continued: "This makes political culture a most convenient residual variable—to it are attributed all differences that cannot otherwise be explained. We need not resort to such mysticism" (Matthews and Prothro 1966, 173). Thus, at best, this concept of political culture or the broader civic culture was only functional as a descriptive reality.

Either Holloway didn't read their book; read the book but ignored their empirical findings on this matter; or simply ignored both the book and its findings. Whatever his strategy, he did not qualify, modify, or critically assess the conceptualization in *The Civic Culture* book. He simply moved the concept directly into his book.

The second major fatal flaw with his book was what Professor Chris Achen called the crosslevel inference problem. Holloway relied upon aggregate voter registration and election returns data for his empirical analyses. Yet to explain African-American political psychology and political mind, he used findings generated at the individual level from surveys and polls to interpret findings generated by political units, such as counties and precincts. This cannot be done without the use of some highly specialized statistical techniques (Achen and Shively 1995). And since Holloway didn't make use of any such techniques, his interpretations themselves became mysticism. Few in the academic community bothered to publicly embarrass Holloway for his slight-of-hand epistemological maneuver. In fact, many followed directly in Holloway's intellectual footsteps as the Voting Rights Act of 1965 led to more and more political participation and activity in the African-American community.

Collectively, these two case studies set the tone and established paradigms for the study of African-American political psychology as the political behavioral movement swept through the 1960s and beyond. As mentioned earlier, even though African Americans continued to contradict these theories, frameworks, and conceptualizations as the Voting Rights Act assisted in their empowerment, the assertions of Myrdal, Wilson, Matthews and Prothro, and Holloway were not denied nor jettisoned. Rather, the work was used selectively to explain African Americans' heightened electoral and political participation. Basically, these ideas never really went away.

But it was not just the political activity of African Americans themselves that called into question the behavioral image of their political mind and political psychology as described by the discipline. In the areas of psychology and political psychology, there arose contending and challenging images of the African-American political mind, which the field of political science neglected, and failed to put the needed and obvious correctives into place.

The third case study and the first of the psychological studies of African-American identity to rethink the self-hatred work of Myrdal, Wilson, Matthews and Prothro, and Holloway appeared in 1991 by William E. Cross, Jr., entitled, *Shades of Black: Diversity in African-American Identity*. This work took on the studies of African-American psychology that used "primitive modes of analysis" as well as those, that used "oversimplification." Professor Cross's work analyzed all of the "social scientific literature on Negro identity written between 1936 and 1967 [which] reported that self-hatred and group rejection were typical of Black psychological functioning" (Cross 1991, ix). The reexaminations of these works led the author to see that "perhaps pathology was not typical of a 'Negro identity,' nor was mental health the province of 'Blackness.' (And) given the possibility that the dimensions of the Negro identity were more often normal than pathological, perhaps not everything about the Negro identity *required* change" (Cross 1991, xii). From these findings and understandings, Professor Cross developed an entirely new theory of African-American psychology, which he saw as rooted in the biculturalism demanded by the unique African-American experiences in America. Scholar-activist W.E.B. DuBois recognized it early on but had not grounded it in the new discipline of psychology. Professor Cross remedied this defect and called his new theory Nigrescence. This concept that grew out of the African-American experiences in America noted that African Americans were based simultaneously in two different and distinct cultures and worked out their psychology and resultant political psychology from this dualistic reference point (Cross 1991). Only a very small segment of the students in race and politics paid this new development much concern or rethought the prevailing paradigms. Thus, the theory of Myrdal, Wilson, Matthews and Prothro, and Holloway marched on and on.

Our fourth and final case study subjected Professor Cross' new theory to rigorous empirical testing and analysis in 2001. Richard L. Allen's book, *The Concept of Self: A Study of Black Identity and Self-Esteem*, set forth these interesting results. First, Prof. Allen says this about the uniqueness of his empirical study. "Unlike most past studies, I used two national studies, one cross-sectional and the other longitudinal. Thus, I was better able to more faithfully explore the dynamic of self-esteem and its generalizability" (Allen 2001, 84). Then, of the value of Professor Cross's theory to his own empirical study, Allen notes: "exploring the studies that used measures of both personal identity and of black identity from 1939 to 1987 ... Cross reported that there was little evidence supporting the conclusion that African Americans had a negative self-conception" (Allen 2001, 60). Therefore, as Professor Allen saw it, "given the major flaws and prominent omissions in the self-hatred literature, and the neglected areas in the study of the black self-concept, there is a great deal of theoretical and empirical work which remains undone" (Ibid). For Allen, Cross' work had literally exploded all of the old myths which had for decades masqueraded as important and hegemonic empirical work and launched the need for reexamination. This is what Allen sought to achieve in his pioneering case study.

To provide the theoretical underpinnings for his study, Allen relied upon DuBois' concept of "double consciousness," which Cross had rechristened as "biculturalism" at the theoretical level in the field of psychology. Talking about this DuBoisan idea, Allen writes: "after emancipation, Africans not only fought against other forms of physical imposition (e.g., sharecropping and later the 'Black Codes'), but also against all attempts to control their perception of the world and their self-image" (Allen 2001, 29). Hence, as Allen sees it, this struggle is what DuBois referred to as "double consciousness."

This led Allen in developing the conceptualization for his empirical study to understand that "one of the important elements of the double consciousness construct and how it was developed by DuBois is that it encapsulates the psychological and sociohistorical realities of oppression and points to the strength of the African American culture. ... Further, DuBois's conceptualization suggests that although the culture and the people are under constant attack; the culture provides the people the wherewithal to develop a positive sense of self or the means to 'resolve the tension between pride and shame in self'" (Allen 2001, 29). Thus, with the help of both DuBois and Cross, Allen fine-tuned his theoretical framework. Prior to the book, Allen revealed in a pioneering article in the *American Political Science Review* how this theoretical framework works in African-American political psychology and their political mind. This work appeared in 1989, a full decade before the book (Dawson et al. 1990). This innovative work challenged the longstanding hegemonic theory of Myrdal and his many disciples.

In the book, Allen concludes after an exhaustive empirical analysis that "although past and present impediments and unwholesome characterizations of Africans still exist, these besieged people have managed to remain without a broken spirit or a shattered self. The theory ... explain[ed] ... an African self that more actively defines itself out of its own history, culture and desired future" (Allen 2001, 178). Here are the empirical foundations for a new perspective on the African-American political mind and the groundwork for an African-American political psychology.

Together, the case studies of Cross and Allen confront, challenge, and deny the image of the Black political mind generated by Myrdal, Wilson, Matthews and Protho, and Holloway, which has been so warmly embraced by the political behavioral revolution in political science. The question now is how has the recently emergent subfield of political psychology, having now fully separated itself from political behavior, embraced the extraordinary work in political psychology and made the transition to it theoretical framework? Has the new field continued on with the old image or taken to the new image? To attain this answer, we now turn to an analysis of the academic journal articles on the subject and later back to our four case studies to help with the assessment and evaluations.

EXTENDING THE ANALYSES OF THE AFRICAN-AMERICAN POLITICAL MIND: THE JOURNALS

We examined the political psychology and political mind of Blacks in a major source of political science discourse: books. Using four main books as exemplars, we note the early theories that construct the sense of why Blacks act the way they do and the empirical work that attempts to test these assorted theories. Using the four books, we theorized that these works discuss Blacks through the dynamic of the race relations vs. African-American (Black) politics frame. The first two older works lean toward the logic of race relations, while the second set of newer work expresses the Black politics frame.

Now we seek to understand how this paradigm, the race relations vs. Black politics frame, plays out in the journals of political science. We use political science journals from the late nineteenth century to early twenty-first century to examine African Americans and political psychology. Our method is a computer-driven content analysis of political science journals stored on an electronic database (JSTOR), which is our data source. There are 34 political science journals referenced in this database, covering from approximately 1885 to the present day.

Our search strategy is to limit our computer word search to these terms "Political Psychology" in association with "African Americans" (and other cognates for "African American[s]": "Black[s]", "Negro[es]", and even "Colored[s]", due to the extreme time span covered). Using this particular strategy, we find that political science journals used both terms "political psychology" and "African American" or its synonyms 219 times in articles. The first documented usage is in an 1898 article, ironically named "The Study and Teaching of Sociology." These search terms were never used in an article title (also, no articles included "Psychology" plus "African American" or synonyms in the title either, for that matter).

So, how exactly are African Americans discussed in the journals of political science over this time period? More explicitly, how does the dominant race relation vs. Black politics frame shape journal discussions of the political psychology of African Americans? To establish this we have to examine the content of the aforementioned 219 journal articles. Using further content analyses, we discern that only 37 of the 219 articles directly address the political psychology of African Americans as major topics of discussion within the article. So, we categorize these 37 articles in terms of race relations and Black politics (see Figure 2.1). Surprisingly, even though our search was from the late nineteenth century, the first articles that are classifiable do not show up until the 1970s. This suggests that the development of political psychology's examinations of Blacks began to show up in print after the height of the Civil Rights Movement. The pattern also shows that these discussions accelerate during the 1990s, where 28 of the 37 articles are found. And what of the frames found in these 37 articles? It seems that the race-relations frame is more dominant.

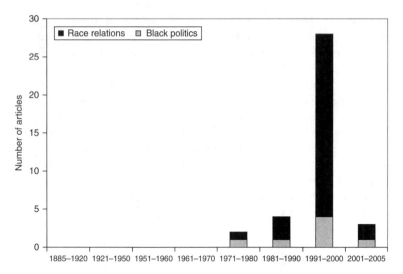

Figure 2.1   Political science journals' discussion of African Americans in terms of race relations vs. Black politics, 1885–2005.

The race-relations frame shows up once in the 1970s, 3 times in the 1980s, 24 times in the 1990s, and twice in the truncated twenty-first century search. Thus, race relations is the dominant frame in 30 out of the 37 classifiable articles (approximately 81 percent). This definitely seems to be the frame of choice in political science!

CONCLUSION

In this chapter, we reviewed some of the history of political psychology of Blacks as seen in the published works of the political science discipline. We examined the history of the political psychology of Blacks in political science discourse. We employed analyses of both major sources of this discourse: books and journal articles.

Walton, Miller, and McCormick (1995) note that the academic disciplines mirror the nonacademic world's sensibilities, including those regarding race. They argue that political science addresses Blacks through the same lens of America: race relations vs. Black politics. The definition of race-relations politics tradition concerns "themes about the fundamental differences between whites and blacks [emphasizing White superiority]" or "beliefs about the necessary dependence of blacks on the white majority's willingness to accommodate black concerns." And the African-American [Black] politics tradition is a frame that "supports parity and empowerment. Here, blacks would seek to eradicate white dominance, to empower themselves."

Building on Walton, Miller, and McCormick (1995), we theorize that these works address Blacks through the lens of the insider/outsider dynamic of the race relations vs. Black politics frame. Using four main books as structural and theoretical exemplars, we note the theories that construct the sense of why Blacks act the way they do and the empirical work that attempts to bolster these assorted theories.

We then use a content analysis of political science journals from the late nineteenth century to early twenty-first century to examine the connection between African Americans and political psychology. We note that the journals tend to use the African-American experience along the race relations vs. Black politics paradigm, with the race relations frame being availed of much more often than the Black politics frame. Thus, we see consistency over the discipline as both the major books and the mainstream journals tend to emphasize the logic of race relations at the expense of a pro-Black politics framework. Some observers may be disappointed by our findings suggesting the dominance of the race-relations frame. Maybe time will restructure this, but the past efforts of political science do highlight race relations as the way to understand the political psychology of African Americans.

PART 2

CONTEMPORARY ISSUES IN THE PSYCHOLOGY OF BLACK IDENTITY

Beliefs in Black and White: How Race Influences Americans' Perceptions of Themselves, Their Racial Group, and Their National Group

Roy J. Eidelson and Mikhail Lyubansky

Over the past century, African Americans have made significant progress on a broad range of fronts, including life expectancy, employment and income, education, and political representation (e.g., Sears et al. 2000; Thernstrom and Thernstrom 1999). Moreover, the rapidly growing multicultural movement (e.g., Fowers and Richardson 1996) has signaled a new *zeitgeist* in terms of racial and ethnic relations. For arguably the first time in U.S. history, there is widespread recognition that none of the nation's many racial and ethnic groups are inherently or culturally superior to any other (National Opinion Research Center 2002a). Furthermore, the multicultural movement has successfully transplanted into the mainstream the previously radical notion that cultural diversity ought to be not merely tolerated but rather encouraged and celebrated.

Nevertheless, multiculturalism has hardly been a panacea. Despite the mainstreaming of egalitarian ideology, Blacks[1] continue to lag behind Whites on most important measures associated with life quality in the United States. For example, a significantly lower percentage of Blacks

(48 percent) than Whites (72 percent) own their own home (U.S. Census Bureau 2002a), and similar discrepancies are evident in health insurance coverage (Bennefield 1998), education (U.S. Census Bureau 2003), job income (U.S. Census Bureau 2002b), and job satisfaction (Riley 2000; Tuch and Martin 1991). The cause of this pervasive inequality cannot be reduced to a single factor. However, it seems self-evident that racial inequality will persist until racism and race-based discrimination are fully eliminated (see Glick and Fiske 2001, for a recent theoretical formulation of modern prejudice) and Whites no longer derive benefits from their racial status (e.g., McIntosh 1998).

Not surprisingly, Black and White Americans continue to have vastly different perceptions regarding the realities of racial inequality. For example, according to national surveys conducted by the National Opinion Research Center (NORC), 66 percent of Blacks but only 34 percent of Whites thought that racial inequality in jobs, income, and housing was primarily the result of discrimination (Schuman et al. 1997). Without doubt, the different life experiences on the two sides of the color line contribute heavily to this discrepancy. However, it is also significant that Whites tend to locate racism in color-consciousness (and therefore see "color-blindness" as the solution),[2] whereas Blacks are more likely to see racism as a system of power and privilege and to consider the affirmation of racial difference (i.e., racial identity) as a core element of their historical and present experience (Hughes and Tuch 2000; Omi and Wynant 1994).

THREE LEVELS OF IDENTITY

One potentially fruitful avenue for illuminating the underpinnings of this apparent perceptual divide between the races is to incorporate psychological approaches that recognize the *multiple* identities through which Blacks and Whites filter their experiences. Of particular value may be the critical distinction made by social identity theorists (e.g., Tajfel 1982; Tajfel and Turner 1986) between personal identity and social identity. Personal identity refers to the individual's sense of self derived from his or her personal characteristics and interpersonal relationships. At this level, each African American or White American is viewed as a distinct individual, without consideration for characteristics that members of the same group might hold in common.

In contrast to personal identity, social identity refers to an individual's sense of self derived from his or her membership in one or more groups. Most people have multiple social identities, reflecting their identification with more than one group (e.g., Roccas and Brewer 2002). In this chapter, we are interested in two specific social identities: one based on racial group and the other based on national group identification. The former quite clearly represents the primary separation between Blacks and Whites and the predominant focus of much research on race relations. On the other hand, the latter represents an important shared or "superordinate" identity for Blacks and Whites—as Americans.

An individual's racial and national identities can vary in the extent to which they are comfortably aligned or, alternatively, in conflict. In this regard, for African Americans the concept of "double consciousness" is long-standing, and it refers in part to the challenges posed by the need to negotiate their Black and American identities in a social context that sometimes pits one against the other (Du Bois 1903; Lyubansky and Eidelson 2005). Less attention has been given to a possible parallel dilemma for White Americans, because they are generally less likely to see themselves in racial terms and therefore to be relatively unaware of their own racial socialization and privilege (McIntosh 1998). However, recent work investigating the rise of "White nationalism" in the United States (e.g., Swain 2002) suggests that race is already an important distinct source of identity for some members of the majority group. Perhaps more importantly, Winant's (1997) analysis of the "new politicization of Whiteness" suggests that White identity may be becoming increasingly more salient for all Whites, even as the identity itself has become confused and contradictory, holding both the legacy of White supremacy and the multicultural ideal of recognizing and valuing difference.

In this chapter, we are interested in examining the extent to which each of these three separate levels of identity—personal identity, racial group identity, and national group identity—contribute to perceptual differences in the ways that Blacks and Whites understand the world. This question is of much more than mere academic interest. A better understanding of where the divergences and convergences in perceptions lie may help to determine how best to bridge and repair the racial divide.

FIVE BELIEF DOMAINS

As targets for our three-level exploration of Black-White differences in perception, we selected the five key belief domains that Eidelson and Eidelson (2003) have identified as spanning the personal and group contexts, because they are simultaneously fundamental to the daily and existential pursuits of individuals and pivotal to the central concerns and shared narratives of groups. These five domains revolve around issues of *vulnerability, injustice, distrust, superiority,* and *helplessness.* Each belief has been described in detail elsewhere (Eidelson and Eidelson 2003), so here we offer only a brief description of its particular relevance for Blacks and Whites in the United States today.

The vulnerability belief, whether applied to one's personal world or to the circumstances of one's group, is characterized by the conviction that the world is a dangerous and risky place, where safety and security are difficult to obtain and catastrophic loss lurks on the horizon (e.g., Beck, Emery, and Greenberg 1985). Vulnerability-related concerns have been a centerpiece of the post-9/11 environment in the United States, finding expression in heightened perceptions of both personal and national threat (e.g., Eidelson and Plummer 2005; Huddy et al. 2002). At the same time, threat percep-tions continue to play a key role in the context of racial group competition between Blacks and Whites (e.g., Bobo and Hutchings 1996). From a dif-ferent vulnerability perspective, worries about assimilation and the loss of group distinctiveness (e.g., Brewer 1991) also appear as important features of the contemporary African-American narrative.

The injustice belief is based on the individual's perceptions of being personally victimized and mistreated by others or the view that in-group members receive undeserved, substandard, and unjust outcomes, perhaps due to a biased or rigged system created by a more powerful out-group (e.g., Horowitz 1985). This injustice mindset is also frequently linked to a historical perspective that emphasizes past episodes or periods of abuse and exploitation at the hands of others, which certainly characterizes the history of slavery in the United States. Experiences and perceptions of mistreatment persist for many African Americans, particularly in relation to discrimination in key areas, such as housing (e.g., Massey and Denton 1993). At the same time, grievances are common among Whites who object to policies such as affirmative action designed to promote racial equality (e.g., Bobo and Kluegel 1993).

The distrust belief focuses on the presumed hostility and malicious intent of other individuals or groups. In reference to the personal world, this mindset may range from a predisposition toward suspicion and anticipated deceit to, in the extreme, outright paranoia. At the group level, the conviction that outsiders harbor malevolent designs toward the in-group is sufficiently widespread that "dishonest" and "untrustworthy" are considered to be central elements in the universal stereotype of out-groups (Campbell 1967; LeVine and Campbell 1972). In the United States, heightened suspicion of non-Americans has characterized the immediate post-9/11 environment, while interpersonal distrust between Blacks and Whites represents a long-standing feature of race relations in this country. Similarly, many African Americans also view mainstream institutions with suspicion, including law enforcement and the judicial system (Schuman et al. 1997).

The superiority belief revolves around the conviction that the individual or the in-group is morally superior, chosen, entitled, or destined for greatness—and the corresponding view that others are contemptible, immoral, and inferior (LeVine and Campbell 1972). This belief has been used to explain, legitimize, and ruthlessly enforce in-group status advantages (Sidanius 1993), often via political entrepreneurs' selective recounting of the in-group's history and embellished narratives of accomplishments (Brown 1997). For the United States, the 9/11 terrorist attacks brought to the fore a national narrative describing a battle of "good versus evil" (Eidelson and Plummer 2005). At the racial level, this belief domain was central to the historical institution of slavery, built in part upon assumptions of White superiority and Black inferiority. More recent decades have witnessed movements by both races to elevate and protect their unique cultures. "Black is beautiful" emerged as a slogan to promote pride in African Americans and to overcome still-prevalent negative stereotypes, even as many "non-prejudiced" whites continue to endorse the belief that poverty and other forms of racial inequity exist in large part due to Blacks' cultural inferiority (Kluegel 1990).

Finally, the helplessness belief (Abramson, Seligman, and Teasdale 1978; Buchanan and Seligman 1995) refers to the conviction that the individual or the in-group is unable to favorably influence or control events and outcomes. This belief plays a prominent role in different types of group mobilization. Since an effective social movement is inherently risky and depends upon the promise of some reasonable likelihood of success (e.g., Brewer and Brown 1998; Gamson 1992; Homer-Dixon 1999), organized political mobilization is severely hampered—while extremist activity may be simultaneously facilitated—when group members perceive their in-group as helpless to improve circumstances by working within the system. The nation's retaliatory military action in Afghanistan in response to the 9/11 attacks was viewed in part as a demonstration that the United States was not and would never be a helpless target (Eidelson and Plummer 2005). At the same time, helplessness may indeed be salient at the racial level for many Blacks, given that efforts to achieve racial equality have faced significant obstacles, particularly in regard to education and income (U.S. Census Bureau 2002b; 2003), as well as in the criminal justice system (Wagner 2005).

THE CURRENT STUDY

In the exploratory study reported here, we surveyed Black and White Americans to determine whether their beliefs in these five domains converged or diverged at each of the three different levels of identity. We posed four interrelated research questions:

1. *Personal Identity: Do Blacks and Whites differ in the extent to which they see their own individual lives as characterized by personal vulnerability, injustice, distrust, superiority, and helplessness?* We expected that group differences based on personal identity, if any, would be smaller than those based on racial group identity. In particular, differences might be muted if Black and White respondents evaluated their circumstances primarily in comparison to their own fellow in-group members, as suggested by research on social comparison and the person-group discrepancy effect (Festinger 1954; Postmes et al. 1999).

2. *Racial Group Identity: Do Blacks and Whites differ in the degree to which they hold these five beliefs about their respective racial groups?* Here we expected significant race group differences because beliefs about vulnerability, injustice, distrust, and helplessness all capture important components of the Black experience as a disadvantaged minority in the United States. In the case of superiority, it also seemed likely that Blacks would express greater racial pride, both in light of their presumed stronger racial identity and the greater stigma associated with Whites expressing beliefs about racial group superiority.

3. *National Group Identity: Do Blacks and Whites differ in how strongly they hold these five beliefs in regard to their national group identity as Americans?* We expected that group differences based on national group identity, if any, would be smaller than those based on racial group identity, precisely because this identity is shared by both racial groups. At the same time, to the extent that beliefs about one's racial group influence beliefs about one's national group, some differences between Blacks and Whites might indeed appear.

4. *Are beliefs in these five domains linked to other important individual difference variables?* We recognized that beliefs at all three identity levels might be related to other individual characteristics for one or both racial groups (see National Opinion Research Center 2002b; 2002c). Therefore, we also examined the significance of age, gender, level of formal education, family income, political orientation, religiosity, and strength of group identification in relation to the five belief domains.

DATA AND METHODOLOGY

Surveys were completed in April 2002 by prospective jurors waiting possible empanelling at a municipal courthouse in Philadelphia,

Pennsylvania. On four occasions over the course of a month, volunteers were recruited in a large courthouse waiting room and were invited to anonymously fill out a 20-minute survey for which each respondent received a candy bar as a token of appreciation for his or her participation. Approximately one-half of those present each day agreed to participate. Only those respondents who identified their racial/ethnic group as "African American/Black" or "Caucasian/White" and their national group as "American" were included in the data analyses (15 respondents did not meet these criteria; another 16 were excluded because they did not complete the survey). This resulted in an overall sample size of 216, comprising of 100 self-identified Black Americans[3] and 116 self-identified White Americans.[4]

The Individual-Group Belief Inventory (IGBI; Eidelson 2002; 2009) was used to measure respondents' personal beliefs about their personal worlds, their racial group, and their national group in regard to issues of vulnerability, injustice, distrust, superiority, and helplessness. The complete IGBI is designed to measure each of these five belief domains at three levels of analysis: (1) beliefs about the personal world (e.g., "Other people are often unfair to me"); (2) beliefs about the in-group (e.g., "I believe other groups are often unfair to my group"); and (3) perceptions of the in-group's collective worldviews (e.g., "My group believes that other groups are often unfair to it"). At each level, each belief is measured by three-items endorsed on a 5-point, Likert-type scale ranging from *Strongly Disagree (1)* to *Strongly Agree (5)*. The respondent's score for each belief scale is the arithmetic sum of the three items measuring that belief.

In this study, we did not include the third-level items (i.e., perceptions of collective worldviews). In addition to the personal world items, we included two versions of the personal beliefs about the in-group items (one set for the racial group and one set for the national group). Sample items from each three-item IGBI scale measuring respondent beliefs about the personal world are: "My safety and security are uncertain" (Vulnerability); "Other people criticize me more than they should" (Injustice); "Other people will try to deceive me if given the chance" (Distrust); "I am superior to other people in many ways" (Superiority); and "I have very little control over my future" (Helplessness). Parallel IGBI items measuring beliefs about the racial group and the national group are: "I believe my (racial/ethnic or national) group's safety and security are uncertain" (Vulnerability); "I believe my (racial/ethnic or national) group is criticized by other groups more than it should be" (Injustice); "I believe that other groups will try to deceive my (racial/ethnic or national) group if given the chance" (Distrust); "I believe that my (racial/ethnic or national) group is superior to other groups in many ways" (Superiority); and "I believe that my (racial/ethnic or national) group has very little control over its future" (Helplessness).

Group identification was measured using six items (with five-point, Likert-type scales ranging from *Strongly Disagree* to *Strongly Agree*) adapted from Brown et al. (1986). For the racial group identification scale, these items read: "I identify with other members of my racial/ethnic group," "My racial/ethnic group is important to my identity," "I think of myself as a member of my racial/ethnic group," "I feel close to other members of my racial/ethnic group," "When someone criticizes my racial/ethnic group, it feels like a personal insult," and "When I talk about members of my racial/ethnic group, I usually say 'we' rather than 'they.'" For the national group identification scale, the phrase "racial/ethnic group" was replaced by "national group" in each item.

The administered questionnaire also included a series of demographic questions. Single-item questions asked the respondents about their age, gender, level of formal education (on a six-point scale from "no formal education" to "graduate work/advanced degree"), family income (on an eight-point scale from "less than $10,000" to "$100,000 or more"), level of religiosity (on a seven-point scale ranging from "Not at all religious" to "Very religious"), and their political orientation (on a seven-point scale ranging from "Liberal" to "Conservative").

The survey measures used in this study were structured into four sections in the following way. In the first section, the respondents answered the 15 IGBI items that measure beliefs about the personal world. For the second section, the respondents first identified their racial group and indicated their level of identification with that group. They then completed 15 IGBI items measuring their beliefs about this racial group. The third section of the survey paralleled the second section but instead focused the participants on their American national group (in contrast to their racial group). The final section of the survey instrument included the demographic questions.

RESULTS

To explore potential differences between the Black and White respondents in the strengths of their beliefs (Research Questions 1 through 3), a series of tests (one for each belief domain) were conducted at each of the three levels of analysis. Two variations of these analysis sets were conducted. In one approach, the between-group differences were assessed while using age, gender, education, family income, religiosity, political orientation, strength of racial group identification, and strength of national group identification as covariates. In the other approach, the Black-White differences were measured without controlling for these individual difference variables. For each IGBI belief scale, the magnitude of the difference between the two samples was comparable for both approaches. Therefore, for simplicity, the *t*-test results from the second approach (i.e., without covariates) are presented here. Table 3.1 displays these unadjusted means

Table 3.1   Personal, racial-level, and national-level IGBI measures by racial group

	Blacks	**Whites**	**Difference**
Personal World			
Vulnerability	8.81	8.27	.54
	(2.61)	(2.44)	
Injustice	7.30	6.92	.38
	(2.58)	(2.11)	
Distrust	8.29	7.53	.76*
	(2.57)	(2.10)	
Superiority	7.49	7.64	.15
	(2.45)	(2.17)	
Helplessness	5.56	5.80	.24
	(1.98)	(1.95)	
Racial Group			
Vulnerability	10.42	7.72	2.70*
	(2.59)	(2.56)	
Injustice	11.72	8.13	3.59*
	(2.39)	(2.66)	
Distrust	9.48	6.89	2.59*
	(2.29)	(2.14)	
Superiority	8.92	6.82	2.10*
	(2.49)	(2.48)	
Helplessness	8.01	6.31	1.70*
	(2.82)	(2.35)	
National Group			
Vulnerability	11.11	10.89	.22
	(2.61)	(2.59)	
Injustice	9.46	9.74	.28
	(2.89)	(2.90)	
Distrust	10.18	9.76	.42
	(2.57)	(2.55)	
Superiority	9.35	9.63	.28
	(2.84)	(2.88)	
Helplessness	7.30	6.38	.92*
	(2.50)	(2.04)	
N	100	116	

Note: Values are unadjusted means. Standard Deviations appear in parentheses below means. Starred differences are significant at the p < .05 level.

and standard deviations. Following these exploratory tests of mean group differences, to answer Research Question 4, separate analyses were conducted to determine whether any of the demographic or other individual differences measures were related to the belief scales, either across both samples or differentially in one group versus the other (using standard z-tests for comparing correlations in independent samples).

RESEARCH QUESTION 1: DO BLACKS AND WHITES DIFFER IN THEIR BELIEFS ABOUT THEIR PERSONAL WORLDS?

At the level of the respondents' personal beliefs about their personal worlds (distinct from their social group identities), the only significant difference was in the distrust domain where Blacks on average scored. 76 points higher than their White counterparts. That is, in their personal lives, Black respondents considered a distrustful posture toward others to be more appropriate than did White respondents. None of the other domains revealed significant differences.

RESEARCH QUESTION 2: DO BLACKS AND WHITES DIFFER IN THEIR BELIEFS ABOUT THEIR DIFFERENT RACIAL GROUPS?

As hypothesized, in sharp contrast to the similarities in the personal world beliefs of Blacks and Whites, there were large differences between the two samples in beliefs about their respective racial groups. Blacks scored significantly higher than Whites in all five domains. The differences between the two groups are as follows: vulnerability (2.70), injustice (3.59), distrust (2.59), superiority (2.10), and helplessness (1.70). A follow-up analysis was conducted for each belief domain in which the Black-White difference in racial group beliefs was tested controlling for the respondents' parallel personal world beliefs. For each domain the magnitude of the difference between samples was not substantially changed.

RESEARCH QUESTION 3: DO BLACKS AND WHITES DIFFER IN THEIR BELIEFS ABOUT THEIR SHARED NATIONAL GROUP?

At the national group level, the White and Black respondents revealed more similarities than differences in their beliefs. Helplessness was the only belief domain on which the two groups differed significantly, with Blacks scoring .92 higher than Whites. There were no significant racial group differences on beliefs about national group vulnerability, injustice, distrust, or superiority. The size of the differences ranged from .22 to .42, with none of them reaching traditional levels of significance. As with racial group beliefs, the magnitudes of these differences between samples in beliefs about their American national group were not substantially changed when the parallel personal world beliefs were controlled for.

RESEARCH QUESTION 4: HOW ARE INDIVIDUAL DIFFERENCE VARIABLES LINKED TO BELIEFS FOR BLACKS AND WHITES?

For both Blacks and Whites there were significant and largely comparable relationships between strength of identification with a group (racial or national) and strength of beliefs about that group. This was especially true in regard to the American national group, where convictions about vulnerability, injustice, distrust, and superiority (but not helplessness) were all significantly correlated (at the $p < .05$ level) with stronger national group identification. The correlation coefficients for each of these measures were: .32, .44, .22, and .38 respectively for the Black sample and .48, .55, .51, and .54 respectively for the White sample. The pattern was similar but substantially weaker for strength of racial group identification and beliefs about the racial group: in the Black sample, the correlations were .22, .23, .17, .15, and .28 for vulnerability, injustice, distrust, helplessness, and superiority respectively, with helplessness and distrust not reaching statistical significance. The White sample parallel correlations were .14, .19, .10, .11, and .32, with vulnerability, distrust, and helplessness not being significantly correlated.

Level of formal education was the demographic variable with the most pervasive pattern of relationships with the respondents' beliefs and it produced consistent differences between the Black and White samples. For the White sample, education was in general significantly negatively correlated with strength of beliefs at the personal world, racial group, and national group levels; in contrast, education tended to be uncorrelated with belief strength in the Black sample at all three levels. At the personal world level, with correlation coefficients of –.33, –.32, –.29, and –.43 respectively, the more educated Whites felt less vulnerable, less mistreated, less distrustful, and less helpless than their less educated White counterparts. The exception was superiority, which had a correlation of .25, making more educated Whites higher on personal superiority than less educated Whites.

Similarly, in regard to beliefs about one's racial group, education was uncorrelated with belief strength in the Black sample but in the White sample it was significantly negatively linked to vulnerability (–.29), injustice (–.39), distrust (–.25), and helplessness (–.36); beliefs about racial group superiority were unrelated to education in both groups.

The same pattern emerged for beliefs about the American national group, with more education (for Whites only) associated with less vulnerability (–.24), less injustice (–.32), less distrust (–.24), and less helplessness (–.34), with superiority again not significant.

Individual differences in religiosity had divergent relationships with some beliefs in the Black and White samples. This was most apparent in the vulnerability domain. Blacks who were more religious described themselves (i.e., at the personal world level) and their racial and national groups as *less* vulnerable, while more religious Whites tended to see themselves and their groups as *more* at risk. The correlations were significantly different between the two samples at all three levels: for the personal world, the correlations were –.25 and .10 for Blacks and Whites respectively; for beliefs about their racial group, the correlations were –.28 and .19 respectively; and for beliefs about their shared American national group, the correlations were –.09 and .19 respectively. The same general pattern was also found in regard to three other beliefs about the racial group: for injustice, the correlations were –.21 and .07 for Blacks and Whites respectively; for distrust, the correlations were –.20 and .08 respectively; and for helplessness, they were –.24 and .11 respectively.

Political orientation as reflected in liberal versus conservative leanings also proved to be differentially linked to certain beliefs for Blacks and Whites. For Blacks, beliefs about racial group vulnerability and injustice (both with correlation coefficients of .23) were significantly stronger among the more liberal respondents, whereas these two beliefs tended to be associated with greater conservatism (nonsignificant correlations of .07 and .09 respectively) among the White respondents. At the national group level of analysis, White conservatives held stronger beliefs than White liberals about group vulnerability (.24) and distrust (.28). For Blacks, the correlation for group vulnerability (–.12) and distrust (–.01) were nonsignificant but in the opposite direction. For both groups, conservatives tended to hold stronger beliefs about national group injustice (i.e., mistreatment at the hands of other groups) than did liberals: for Whites the correlation was .37; for Blacks it was .19.

Overall, age proved to be a relatively unimportant variable in regard to its relationships with the respondents' beliefs. However, there was a tendency for younger participants in both samples to view themselves as personally superior, although this correlation (–.24) was significant only in the White sample but not in the Black sample (–.14). In addition, there was a significant difference between Blacks and Whites in the relationship between age and beliefs about racial group vulnerability. For Blacks, these two variables were negatively correlated (–.18) whereas for Whites they were positively associated (.27). That is, younger Blacks and older Whites were the respondents who tended to see their respective racial groups as in jeopardy.

DISCUSSION

In this chapter, we were interested in examining similarities and differences in the beliefs of Black and White Americans from the perspectives of their personal identities, their racial group identities, and their national group identities. We focused on the five belief domains—vulnerability, injustice, distrust, superiority, and helplessness—that Eidelson and Eidelson (2003) have identified as spanning the realms of personal and group experience, and as bearing directly on issues of distress and conflict.

When these five beliefs were compared at the level of personal identity, distinct from any explicit focus on group membership, the Black and White samples were quite similar in almost all domains. Distrust was the only one of the five domains in which a significant difference emerged, with Blacks reporting greater interpersonal suspicion than Whites. This difference is consistent with other studies of trust (e.g., Shavers-Hornaday et al. 1997) as well as with a post-9/11 national phone survey, which found that 46 percent of Whites but only 15 percent of Blacks believed that "people are trustworthy" (National Opinion Research Center 2002b).

In regard to beliefs about one's racial group (i.e., through the explicit lens of one's racial group identity), we expected and found very large differences between Blacks and Whites, with the former reporting stronger beliefs across all five domains. Beliefs about collective vulnerability, injustice, distrust, and helplessness all reflect important challenges facing a group. It, therefore, is not surprising that the Black respondents held beliefs more consonant with seeing their racial group in a tenuous and potentially adversarial position than did their White counterparts. It is interesting that the largest discrepancy between the racial groups was found in the injustice domain, which perhaps best characterizes the centuries-old contrast between Black and White experiences in America. The stronger race-group superiority beliefs reported by the Black sample in comparison to the White sample may reflect two complementary factors—the commonplace salience of "racial pride" within minority communities that have struggled to embrace their difference and the probable discomfort of many White Americans with the explicitly racist ideology associated with claims of White supremacy.

When we turn to beliefs about the American national group (i.e., through the explicit lens of one's national group identity), Blacks and Whites seemingly put aside their contrasting beliefs about their respective racial groups and tended to see their shared American group in much the same way. Helplessness was the only domain in which the two groups differed significantly, with Blacks seeing the national group as more helpless than Whites; this difference is also consistent with national public opinion surveys (National Opinion Research Center 2002b; 2002c).

It is important to consider the implications of the similarities and differences we found between the beliefs of Blacks and Whites at the personal, racial group, and national group levels of analysis. The similar personal identity beliefs stand in sharp contrast to the divergence in the respondents' beliefs about their respective racial groups. One possible explanation for why Blacks and Whites tended to see their personal worlds in comparable ways involves the nature of social comparison processes. Assessments of personal experiences—such as mistreatment by others—are typically made within the boundaries of one's in-group (e.g., Festinger 1954; Buckingham and Alicke 2002). Thus, Blacks may use other Blacks as their standard of comparison, while Whites use other Whites as their benchmark—leading to similar averages in belief strengths between the two groups. In contrast, when assessing the experiences of one's racial group, the standard of comparison becomes the other racial group, which in the case of Blacks and Whites would naturally lead to assessments that differ substantially from each other. This use of different standards of comparison is also consistent with the literature on the person-group discrepancy effect (for example, Kessler, Mummendey, and Leisse 2000; Postmes et al. 1999), which has also shown, for instance, that respondents tend to identify discrimination as a greater problem for their group than for themselves personally (Crosby 1984; Moghaddam, Stolkin, and Hutcheson 1997).

However, an additional plausible explanation for our findings is that the contrasting similarities and differences in beliefs between Blacks and Whites about their personal worlds and racial groups respectively reflect the differing pace of progressive changes in individual versus structural racism in the United States. As noted earlier, there has been a significant moral shift within the White community regarding the acceptability of racism. However, most Whites (in contrast to most Blacks) still define racism as an individualistic phenomenon, characterized by color consciousness and prejudicial thoughts or behavior on the part of one person towards another (Bonilla-Silva 2003). In this regard, much of the progress that has taken place in race relations has occurred on the personal level (e.g., a reduction in personal attacks, racial slurs, and openly disrespectful behavior), while progress at the structural level (e.g., in the areas of employment, education, and criminal justice) has been both slower and more tenuous. But it is also important to note that it is unclear whether Blacks and Whites would expect members of the other racial group to report similar personal level beliefs (as reported in our study) and whether they would accept these assessments as reasonable and reliable. As one example, discovering that members of the other racial group see themselves as equally vulnerable at the personal level could serve as either a source of positive connection between groups or, to the contrary, as evidence of the out-group's alienating and invalidating world-view.

In this context, the convergence of beliefs at the national group level is also noteworthy. To a large extent, it appears that divergent beliefs about racial group circumstances did not find expression in different beliefs about the American national group for the Black and White respondents. That is, this superordinate identity as Americans produced highly consensual views across the racial divide in regard to the nation's current circumstances (with the previously noted exception of the helplessness domain). This consensus may, in part, be attributed to the greater sense of national unity produced by the 9/11 terrorist attacks seven months prior to the collection of our data. For example, it is clear that, at least for a few months, concerns regarding national security were atypically prominent and salient for most Americans (Black and White). The events of 9/11, therefore, are an important part of the context for our study and should be viewed as such—rather than as a source of "noise" or "nuisance." Examining national group beliefs in the context of conflict is informative and, in at least some ways, more relevant to understanding group relations than when national security is unthreatened and national identity is not particularly salient.

The similarities and differences between the two samples in their beliefs as reported through the lenses of their personal, racial group, and national group identities were not meaningfully changed by statistically controlling for a broad range of individual difference variables—strength of group identification (racial and national), age, gender, education, family income, religiosity, and political orientation. This indicates that the large differences between the two samples in racial group beliefs in all likelihood reflect truly divergent experiences and perceptions that emerge from being Black versus White in America today. From the set we considered, level of formal education proved to be the variable most consistently linked to individual differences in the belief strengths of the respondents. At all three levels of identity, the same difference appeared in the way that education was related to beliefs for Blacks versus Whites. For the Black respondents, education was uncorrelated with the strength of their beliefs at the personal, racial group, and national group levels. In sharp contrast, for the White respondents, greater education was significantly correlated with weaker beliefs about vulnerability, injustice, distrust, and helplessness across all three levels.

Speculatively, this pattern suggests that the beliefs of Blacks and Whites may emerge in different ways and may be susceptible to differing influences. For Whites, education seems to moderate how they see themselves and their racial and national groups (e.g., as in jeopardy, as mistreated, etc.); the more educated hold less extreme mindsets than their less educated counterparts. But why not the same pattern for the Black respondents? Perhaps because for many Blacks, these key beliefs emerge more directly from their actual experiences as a disadvantaged minority, and/or because education for many Blacks does not as substantially alter the reality they face. Also, due to the slower pace of structural race-related changes in the United States, Blacks may not perceive the relationship between education and opportunity to be particularly strong, creating more suspicion and less susceptibility to the messages propounded by higher education. At the same time, the absence of a relationship between education and beliefs in the Black sample raises the question of what other variables, unmeasured in our study, might be linked to individual differences in beliefs among Blacks (and perhaps among Whites as well).

Limitations of our study should be highlighted, beginning with the general caveat that much of our analysis was exploratory in nature. This was a conscious decision, based on the view that raising questions, even speculatively, could facilitate further research. That said, without additional studies including more broadly representative samples, our findings must be viewed tentatively. Our samples were not large, and while we believe that the participants were reasonably representative of those who both met the legal requirements and accepted the summons to report for jury duty in Philadelphia, these selection criteria alone demonstrate that the respondents were not necessarily representative of the broader populations of Blacks and Whites throughout the United States, including other geographical regions and especially nonurban settings. The underrepresentation of Black men (29%) relative to Black women (71%) is particularly evident. However, since our statistical analyses failed to yield any significant effects linked to gender, the impact of this particular sample bias is likely minimal.

Also noteworthy are the substantial intercorrelations among the IGBI belief domain measures. We considered combining several of these measures into broader composite scales, but we felt that the constructs of interest (i.e., vulnerability, injustice, distrust, superiority, and helplessness) were theoretically distinct in regard to our focus and we, therefore, deemed it preferable to examine each belief separately. Moreover, confirmatory factor analyses using the IGBI in prior research with a U.S. sample documented that a five-factor model produced a better fit to the data than did alternative models with fewer factors (Eidelson 2002).

Methodologically, it should also be noted that the IGBI items were presented to all participants in the same order (i.e., without any counter-balancing). This represents a potential confound, but the first author has tested for IGBI order effects in another study and found no significant differences in the relative strength of beliefs linked to whether personal-world or group-level items are presented first (Eidelson 2005).

In conclusion, we focused on the beliefs of Black and White Americans in the five domains of vulnerability, injustice, distrust, superiority, and helplessness because of their salience as triggers or constraints on inter-personal and intergroup conflict and distress (Eidelson and Eidelson 2003). The present study revealed relatively small group differences in beliefs at the personal and national group levels, combined with quite large differences in beliefs at the racial group level. What picture do these findings paint of race relations and racial equality in this country today? No simple answer emerges. The large differences between Blacks and Whites at the racial group belief level make it clear that there is still much work to be done to narrow the gap between these two groups, at least in the way they perceive their racial group circumstances. The lack of comparable discrepancies at the personal world level is in some ways encouraging but, at the same time, may also represent a potential source of inertia in addressing the larger societal divides. Our findings may be indicative of relative progress in race relations at the personal level and a welcome reminder that the efforts of countless individuals to fight racism in the United States are not in vain. They may also suggest that the efforts to create structural changes in this arena remain both important and achievable. That is, these findings may reflect a historical trajectory that takes into consideration where we are as well as where we have been.

CHAPTER 4

FEELING DIFFERENT: RACIAL GROUP-BASED EMOTIONAL RESPONSE TO POLITICAL EVENTS

TASHA S. PHILPOT, ISMAIL K. WHITE, KRISTIN WYLIE, AND ERNEST B. MCGOWEN

THE RACIAL DIVIDE IN AMERICAN POLITICS is a large and enduring one. To be sure, attitudes about race can determine which policies, parties, and candidates get supported by American voters. Why do these racial divisions persist? Previous research on the racial divide has identified material interests, sympathy and resentment toward social groups, political principles and audience as sources of the racial divide (Kinder and Sanders 1996; Kinder and Winter 2001). But how do these factors get actualized? What are the causal mechanisms that link things like social group and self-interests to political evaluations? We attempt to address these questions in the current project by illustrating how emotions moderate the connection between race and politics.

The activation and expression of emotions in our everyday lives is unavoidable. Activities ranging from the mundane to the extraordinary can elicit emotional response. Whether we are stubbing our toes or casting ballots on Election Day, our behavioral and cognitive responses to phenomena are often accompanied by an affective reaction as well (see Breckler 1984). In fact, scholars argue that emotions are the most primary and basic response to social stimuli (e.g. Zajonc 1980) and can occur even in the absence of cognition (Breckler 1984; Moreland and Zajonc 1977).

Consequently, emotions can influence our behavior, memory, judgment, and decisions (Fiske and Taylor 1991).

Already, there has been quite a bit of research on emotions and politics that demonstrates how important emotions are to understanding the determinants of political preferences. For instance, Abelson et al. (1982) found that affective evaluations of candidates were a stronger predictor of candidate preference than personality judgments of the candidates. Similarly, Ragsdale (1991) found that emotions were a stronger predictor of presidential evaluations than rational constructs, such as personal finances and the economy. Emotional response to economic conditions, even independent of cognition, predicts political evaluations (Conover and Feldman 1986).

At the same time, while scholars have examined the link between emotions and political evaluations, the role of racial group–relevant considerations has yet to be fully delineated. Psychologists have examined the link between emotional response to racial/ethnic groups and racial attitudes (Stangor et al. 1991; Mann 1959; Woodmansee and Cook 1967). Still, we do not know how different political events can elicit divergent racial group–based emotions and how these emotional responses affect political evaluations and behavior.

We begin to fill this void by determining the predictors of racial differences in emotional response to political events. We argue that political events that highlight and exacerbate racial group differences will yield divergent emotional responses. In what follows, we discuss the extant literature in psychology on group-based emotional response to stimuli. Based on this research, we develop a theoretical framework for understanding how racial groups in particular respond to political stimuli. We argue that divergent, racial group–based emotional response to a political event is a function of whether the perceived benefits or penalties resulting from that event permeate group boundaries. Specifically, negative emotions arise when members of an in-group believe they will be disproportionately harmed relative to an out-group. Likewise, members of a group will exhibit positive emotions if they perceive their group to benefit as a consequence of the political event.

This study adds to our understanding of politics, emotional response, and race relations in a number of respects. First, scholars have shown how racial considerations influence support for policies and candidates (Dawson 1994; Tate 1993; Kinder and Sanders 1996). In this chapter, we first expand our knowledge of the relationship between race and politics by demonstrating how racial considerations resonate on a more visceral level. Already, research has explored how racial cues can resonate subconsciously (Mendelberg 2001; Valentino, Hutchings, and White 2002). We extend this line of work by further illustrating another way in which race influences politics in a less cognitive manner. Second, the discussion of emotions and politics has largely been confined to the electoral arena (Brader 2006). Here, we demonstrate how the racial divide can be widened by events that occur outside of the campaign environment. Finally, we not only focus on *when* racial group–based emotional response will occur, but *why* different political events result in divergent response. In doing so, we go beyond extant research by providing the precise causal mechanisms behind emotional response as well as demonstrating how emotions, independent of other factors, affect political evaluations.

GROUP CUES AND CONDITIONED EMOTIONAL RESPONSE

In general, scholars have found that emotional response is conditioned on whether the individual perceives an act or event as being relevant (either negatively or positively) to his or her interests (Roseman 1984; Smith and Ellsworth 1985; Frijda 1986; Scherer 1988; Conover and Feldman 1986; Damasio 2000). Frijda argues that "emotions are elicited. ... They appear to act through their significance, their meaning, their rewarding or aversive nature" (Frijda 1986, 4). Consequently, the expression of emotions of anger and contempt are associated with experiences that had negative consequences for an individual. Likewise, happiness is brought about by encounters that are perceived to be pleasant and enjoyable by the individual (Smith and Ellsworth 1985).

Emotional response, however, is very context-specific (Sherif and Sherif 1966). Roseman argues that "*it is interpretations of events rather than events per se that determine which emotion will be felt*" (1984, 14; italics in original). On a daily basis, we encounter objects and events that can be perceived subjectively, e.g., a glass being half full or half empty. The more "unstructured" of these objects and events lend themselves to multiple interpretations (Sherif and Sherif 1966). From this perspective:

> Two individuals with significantly differing perceptions of the same event (or a single individual with differing interpretations at different times) would respond with different emotions. Likewise, two individuals with similar perceptions of the same (or different) events would experience the same emotion.
>
> Roseman 1984, 15

Among factors guiding reactions to events are individuals' past experiences and/or perceptions of intentionality (Scherer 1988). For instance, you might respond more readily with anger after having a baseball thrown through your front window if the person did it on purpose or has done so accidentally multiple times. Thus, "if we know how a person sees his or her environment, we are better able to identify that person's emotional state; conversely, if we know what the person is feeling, we can deduce much about how that person is interpreting his or her circumstances" (Smith and Ellsworth 1985, 831).

The expression of emotions can be a social as well as an individual phenomenon. That is to say, people are capable of experiencing emotional responses to stimuli on behalf of a social group with which they identify. A social group is "two or more persons who are in some way socially or psychologically interdependent" (Turner 1982, 15). A sense of connectedness can be a function of ascribed attributes such as sex, race, and age or can result from shared values and attitudes. Individuals can possess several memberships to various social groups. As Tajfel explains, "some of these memberships are more salient than others; and some vary in salience in time and as a function of a variety of social situations" (1982, 2–3). Nevertheless,

> once individuals' common social identification of themselves is "switched on," they tend to perceive themselves and others in terms of that category membership. ... The cognitive output of a functioning social identification is, in a nutshell, stereotypic perception. This regulates social behaviour in two main ways. Firstly, assigning oneself criterial attributes such as emotions, motives and norms can instigate and control behaviour directly. Secondly, the way we perceive others will influence indirectly how we act towards them.
>
> Turner 1982, 29

As a result, group members are able to emotionally empathize with other members of the group, even absent personal acquaintance with those members (Turner 1982; Cialdini et al. 1976). Once they do so, "people can experience affect on behalf of the group and be moved to act toward group goals" (Smith 1993, 302).

When understanding inter-group relations, emotions play a particularly important role. Hamilton and Mackie (1993) contend that the "history of intergroup relations is rich in evidence of intense emotional, even passionate forces guiding thoughts, feelings, perceptions, and behaviors of group members" (3). Much of what guides in-group emotional response is how that group fairs in relation to another in either a real or perceived competition. Further, the spoils of the competition need not be material; groups may see themselves competing over nontangible things such as values, standards, or even bragging rights (see Brewer 1979). Mackie and colleagues (2000) argue that "when social group identity is salient, group members' appraisals of the strength or weakness of the in-group relative to the out-group ... dictate whether they felt anger toward the other group and in turn whether their behavioral intentions toward the other group were offensive" (Mackie et al. 2000, 603).

By manipulating the salience of group identity, Mackie et al. found that individuals expressed higher levels of anger and contempt toward a group that appeared to be in conflict with their value system. Although this study only focused on those groups defined by support or opposition for a particular issue, it helps illustrate how readily in-group members respond emotionally to those outside of the group's boundaries when the group's interests are at risk (see also Stephan and Stephan 1996).

With respect to race, there is reason to believe that making racial group interests salient can educe a similar response. In a study of the Dutch, Dijker (1987) found that negative emotions such as anxiety, concern and irritation about Turkish/Moroccan immigrants and Surinamers increased as respondents' self-reported prior contact with these ethnic groups also increased. Moreover, negative feelings intensified when respondents saw a greater distance between the other ethnic groups and themselves. In a similar study, Vanman and Miller (1993) asked college students in Southern California to list the emotions they would feel if they were to have a casual conversation with someone from a different race. In response, "the most frequently chosen emotions were irritation (54.9%), dislike (46.9%), apprehension (45.5%), and anxiety (41.3%)" (221). In contrast, more than 80 percent of respondents reported experiencing happiness and enjoyment when asked to imagine an intraracial conversation. Hence, not only are people able to express emotions in terms of their in-groups, but also toward out-groups as well.

RACIAL GROUP-BASED RESPONSE TO POLITICAL EVENTS

Beyond emotions, the tendency for individuals to exhibit biased evaluations and actions based on group membership is well-documented. People have a tendency to favor their own group over one to which they do not belong, even when group distinctions are arbitrary (Billig and Tajfel 1973; Rabbie and Horowitz 1969; Doise et al. 1972; Tajfel 1970). When it comes to race, in-group–out-group bias becomes more pronounced. Previous research has found that group relevance can play a powerful role in shaping how people interpret politics. For example, White Americans' attitudes about racial outgroups prove to be a powerful predictor of their opinions on racial policy (Kinder and Sears 1981; Kinder and Sanders 1996; McConahay 1982). For African Americans, it is the perception of psychological connectedness or closeness to Blacks as a group (i.e., group identification) that has been found to be essential in accounting for their largely liberal views of policies, such as affirmative action (Conover 1984; Gurin et al. 1989; Dawson 1994; Tate 1993). This research has also been extended to examining the effect of political discourse on opinion formation. Studies on racial priming, for example, have shown that racially stereotypical out-group cues have the effect of boosting the impact of out-group attitudes on the opinions of White Americans (Gilens 1999; Valentino 1999; Valentino et al. 2002; Mendelberg 2001). Likewise, recent research on the effects of racial priming on African Americans has demonstrated the power of in-group cues to prime Black racial group identification (White 2007).

Despite the scope of research on the effects of in-group and out-group stimuli on opinion formation, the connection between these stimuli and emotionality remain unclear. From previous research, we know that there is a link between group attitudes and emotional response. Under what circumstances this link gets activated is still largely a mystery. Recent work by Brader and colleagues has begun to bridge this gap in the literature. Examining the effects of conditioned emotional responses, Brader et al. (2006) found that cueing a stigmatized out-group (Latino immigrants) increased anxiety, which in turn mediated changes in both opinion and action. While this work has informed our understanding of the mediating role that emotions play in defining the relationship between out-group cues and opinion formation, we still know very little about the catalysts of race-based emotional responses to both in-groups and out-groups.

How then do political events elicit divergent racial group–based emotional response? It is understood that not all events induce the same response. Indeed, many factors determine whether someone will respond emotionally to political phenomena. For instance, Marcus and MacKuen (1993) find that some political campaigns garner enthusiasm while others raise anxiety among voters. Further, Brader finds that different music and images induce varying emotional responses to political ads. Given the importance of group-based considerations to politics (Berelson et al. 1954; Campbell et al. 1960; Gurin et al. 1989; Tate 1993; Dawson 1994; Green et al. 2002; Hutchings 2003; Philpot 2004), we argue that we should also see divergent emotional responses to political stimuli perceived to be particularly relevant to their racial group. This not only includes emotions relative to one's in-group but also emotional response to those events perceived to affect one's out-group as well.

MODEL OF RACIAL GROUP-BASED EMOTIONAL RESPONSE

When citizens encounter a political event, it elicits an emotional response. According to Frijda,

> Emotions result from match or mismatch between events and concerns. Positive emotions can be said to result from events that represent match: actual or signaled concern satisfaction. Negative emotions result from

events that represent mismatch: actual or signaled interference with concern satisfaction

Frijda 1986, 278

In other words, positive emotions arise when people's expectations about an event are actualized. As Conover (1988) notes, political thinking is dominated by "the desire to know who is getting what and whether they deserve it" (57). Therefore, individuals will express negative emotions when their expectations about an event have not been met and a benefit or penalty has been received without warrant. Subsequently, their emotions affect their political evaluations, whether it is the decision regarding for whom to vote or the decision to vote at all. This is the relationship outlined by previous scholars.

Our contribution to the understanding of this process is the addition of group membership as a moderating variable. From this standpoint, the extent to which a political event is relevant to a group determines the intensity of emotional responses. As Mackie, Devos, and Smith (2000) argue, "if group membership becomes part of the self, events that harm or favor an in-group by definition harm or favor the self, and the self might thus experience affect and emotion on behalf of the in-group" (603). Therefore, we posit that members of a group will experience positive emotions, such as pride and happiness when a political event has yielded a positive outcome for the group. Likewise, group members will exhibit negative emotions like sadness and anger in response to a political event that is interpreted as having an adverse effect on the group, especially relative to another group. Support for this argument can be found in a study conducted by Valentino, Hutchings, Philpot, and White (2006), which showed that Blacks' emotions intensified when they read an article about a candidate that threatened their interests. As a result, we hypothesize that when the rewards and penalties that result from a political event spread across group boundaries, there should be no divergent response. Conversely, we will see differentiated emotional responses when one group interprets the event as helping or harming group members at the expense of another group.

Specifically, our hypotheses are as follows:

H1: A political event will result in a positive emotional response when a racial in-group has been advantaged disproportionately

H2: A political event will result in a negative emotional response when a racial in-group has been disadvantaged disproportionately

H3: A political event will result in a negative emotional response when a racial out-group has been advantaged disproportionately

H4: A political event will result in a positive emotional response when a racial out-group has been disadvantaged disproportionately

METHOD

In order to test the hypotheses outlined above, we utilize both survey and experimental data. While the former offers a first glance at differences across racialized and nonracialized events, the latter provides greater confidence in the causal factors at work. First, we probe the emotional responses to five significant events in American society—September 11th, the Columbia space shuttle explosion, the O. J. Simpson case, Hurricane Katrina, and the 2008 election of President Barack Obama. These events provide variation in the degree of racialization, with the September 11th attacks and the Columbia space shuttle explosion being nonracial (at least in terms of black and white) and the other three events being significantly racialized. To measure these responses, we employ national random sample surveys of American adults conducted in the days immediately following each event. To gauge emotional response to the terrorist attacks on September 11th, 2001, we used the *Pew Research Center for the People & the Press: Post-Terrorist Attack, September 19, 2001*, which was conducted via telephone from September 13–17, 2001 and had 1,200 respondents. We used three Gallup/CNN/USA Today polls to assess emotional reactions to the space shuttle crash, the O. J. Simpson verdict, and Hurricane Katrina.[1] All three of these polls were based on telephone interviews. The *Space Shuttle Columbia Crash Reaction* poll was conducted on February 2, 2003, and had a sample size of 462. The *O. J. Simpson Verdict* poll was conducted on October 3, 1995 (n=639), and the *Hurricane Katrina and New Orleans/Race* poll, conducted September 8–11, 2005, had a total sample size of 1,267 (national adult sample of 1,005 plus an oversample of 262 Blacks). Finally, we use the 2008 American National Election Study (ANES) to examine emotional reactions to the election of President Obama (ANES 2009). Through face-to-face interviews conducted in preelection (September 2-November 3, 2008) and postelection (November 5-December 30, 2008) waves, the 2008 ANES featured 2,323 respondents, including 577 African Americans and 512 Latinos.

The experiment employs a 2x2 cell design. The goal of the experiment is to expose subjects to scenarios involving group competition. Each scenario varies by the outcome of the competition. The experiment was administered via an online interface. Subjects were first asked a battery of questions related to their issue positions and ideological ideals. Following these questions, they were then instructed to read an article that served as our experimental manipulations. After they had finished reading the article, subjects were asked to self-report their emotional responses to the article they just read. Finally, subjects answered a number of questions about groups and people in the news as well as their demographic information.

For this experiment, we used undergraduate students as subjects. Approximately one-third of the students were recruited from summer courses and offered extra credit in exchange for their participation. Students were e-mailed the link to the survey, which they could take at any time. The remaining students were recruited from a campus dormitory. These subjects completed the survey on laptops provided to them by the authors. In exchange for their participation, they received $5 in cash. The survey took approximately 15–20 minutes to complete. Regardless of recruiting method, subjects were randomly assigned to the experimental conditions.

As stated above, the experimental manipulation was delivered in the form of a contrived article. The article's headline read, "Debate Continues over the Creation of Independent School District." The body of the article contained the following information: (1) members of the East Baton Rouge Parish School Board will be considering a proposal from the "Central City Residents for Better Schools" that would lead to the creation of an independent school district within the Parish; (2) the separation will transfer property taxes from the East Baton Rouge School System and give it to the Central City independent school system; (3) In recent years, other areas of the city have also attempted to gain control of local schools from the Baton Rouge Parish School Board; (4) Sam Mitchell, a School Board member from Central, believes that the district can best run its own schools; and (5) Backers of the new school district have to round up a two-thirds vote of the East Baton Rouge Parish School Board and a majority support from the voters of East Baton Rouge Parish.

Subjects either read that that East Baton Rouge Parish was predominately Black and Central City was predominately White or that East Baton Rouge Parish was predominately White and Central City was predominately Black.

In the analyses of both the survey and the experimental data, we measure emotions using self-reported emotional response. In the survey results, emotional responses to each event are measured by dichotomous variables where respondents indicated whether they did or did not experience a particular emotion. For the experiment, we ask respondents whether anything they read in the article made them feel angry, sad, happy, or proud. Each potential emotional response was coded on a four-point Likert scale ranging from one (not at all) to four (very).

RESULTS

The survey data provide suggestive evidence for our model of racial group–based emotional response. Below, we briefly discuss the details of each event and then explore the emotional responses to each of them by racial group.

On September 11, 2001, the United States endured a tragic terrorist attack, suffering some 3,000 deaths and the absolute destruction of the twin towers of the World Trade Center in New York. According to the *9/11 Commission Report*, conducted by the National Commission on Terrorist Attacks Upon the United States, nineteen young Arabs acted in coordination with al-Qaeda to hijack four commercial airliners, intending to strike the twin towers, the Pentagon, and either the U.S. Congress or the White House. While the fourth airliner was brought down prior to reaching its target, and the damage inflicted upon the Pentagon was contained, the havoc wrought upon Lower Manhattan was severe. However, beyond the structural damage and the loss of life was the tremendous impact on the psyche of the American people. While the attacks raised anti-Arab and anti-Muslim sentiment, the event was not racialized in the traditional Black/White sense. Not surprisingly then, respondents indicated feeling emotions of depression, sadness, and fear, regardless of race. As we see in Table 4.1, although White respondents were significantly more likely than were African-American respondents to report sadness, there were no statistically significant differences by race for feelings of depression and fear. Further, the vast majority of both groups were saddened by this event.

Space shuttle Columbia was launched on January 16, 2003, from the Kennedy Space Center in Florida with the mission to complete space, life- and physical sciences–related research. Upon returning from the 16-day mission, the shuttle exploded over the plains of East Texas and immediately raised questions about safety operations in the nation's space agency (McDanels et al. 2006). Resurfacing painful memories of the space shuttle Challenger crash in 1986, Congress, the media, and the American public spent the next few weeks in anticipation of the conclusions from the accident investigation. In the end, it was determined that a piece of falling debris had damaged a section of the wing, which caused the heat shield to malfunction during reentry. While questions were ultimately raised about the organizational culture at NASA, some say the agency's handling of the information and acceptance of blame saved NASA from threats of abolition and restored public confidence in ongoing missions like the International Space Station (Kauffman 2005). Table 4.1 presents emotional responses to this event. Again, race was not an issue in the debate surrounding the space shuttle crash. Consequently, public opinion data demonstrate that, regardless of race, respondents reported extremely high levels of sadness following the crash.

After a high-profile, low speed chase through the streets of Los Angeles, former NFL running back O. J. Simpson began one of the most sensational criminal trials in recent memory. Accused of murdering his

Table 4.1   Emotional response to political events, by race

	Blacks	Whites	Difference
	September 11, 2001 Terrorist Attacks		
Depression	71.8%	71.9%	.1
Sadness	85.9%	95.4%	9.5*
Fear	76.9%	79.1%	2.2
	Space Shuttle Columbia Crash		
Sadness	94.9%	96.3%	1.4
	O.J. Simpson Verdict		
Outrage	12.9%	31.2%	18.3*
Surprise	40.0%	53.8%	13.8*
Sadness	28.6%	51.3%	22.7*
Pleasure	78.6%	16.8%	61.8*
Disgust	7.1%	50.9%	43.7*
	Hurricane Katrina and Aftermath		
Anger	76.3%	60.0%	16.3*
Shock	80.1%	77.4%	2.8
Sadness	99.2%	97.5%	1.7
	Barack Obama Winning the 2008 Presidential Election		
Anger	.7%	11.8%	11.1*
Disappointment	.7%	39.2%	38.5*
Fear	7.2%	23.9%	16.7*
Happiness	97.9%	48.7%	49.2*
Hope	96.4%	64.6%	31.8*
Pride	95.0%	48.7%	46.3*

Note: Values are weighted means. Starred differences are statistically significant at the p < .05 level.
Source: Pew Research Center for the People & the Press: Post-Terrorist Attack, September 19, 2001; Gallup/CNN/USA Today Poll: Space Shuttle Columbia Crash Reaction, February 2, 2003; Gallup/CNN/USA Today Poll: O.J. Simpson Verdict, October 3, 1995; Gallup/CNN/USA Today Poll: Hurricane Katrina and New Orleans/Race, September 8-11, 2005; American National Election Study 2008 Time Series Study.

wife Nicole Brown-Simpson and her companion Ronald Goldman, the trial exposed a racial divide in public opinion as racially charged epithets and corruption on the part of the Los Angeles Police Department became the centerpieces of Simpson's defense. While Whites viewed the case as a criminal matter, Blacks tended to place more of the blame on biases in the criminal justice system. Following an acquittal by a majority-Black jury in the criminal case and a guilty finding by a majority-White jury in the civil case, both reporters and academics began studying this racial divide, finding anecdotal and empirical evidence for differences in perception (Enomoto 1999). Unlike emotional responses to the non-racialized events reported above, public opinion data demonstrate that responses to the O. J. Simpson verdict were extremely divided by race. While over 50 percent of White respondents indicated feelings of disgust, only 7.1 percent of Black respondents expressed this emotion. On the contrary, some 78.6 percent of Black respondents reported feelings of pleasure, compared to only 16.8 percent of White respondents. In fact, all five emotions probed here demonstrate statistically significant differences across respondent race.

In late August 2005, the United States was hit by one of the most costly and deadly tropical storms the country had ever experienced. Classified as a Category 5 hurricane, Hurricane Katrina caused approximately $75 billion in damages to the United States' Gulf of Mexico coast. Hurricane Katrina hit New Orleans, Louisiana especially hard, leaving approximately 80 percent of the city flooded in up to 20 feet of water (Knabb, Rhome, and Brown 2005). The vast amount of property damage, injury, and loss of life left residents in Louisiana, Mississippi, and Alabama devastated. Survey data presented in Table 4.1 depict heightened levels of sadness and shock among respondents throughout the nation. However, African-American respondents reported feeling angry at significantly higher rates than did White respondents. In an earlier study (White et al. 2007), we explored the root of this difference and discovered that levels of perceived racialization of Katrina and its aftermath differed by race, finding shockingly substantial differences. Whereas over 76 percent of Black respondents agreed that the disaster revealed our nation's remaining problems of racial inequality, only 36.78 percent of White respondents concurred. For the most part, African-American respondents attributed the misery of Katrina's primarily Black victims to race-based governmental neglect, with most White respondents suggesting that race was irrelevant. This demonstrates the potential for immense racial differences in the perceived racialization of events.

On November 4, 2008, the United States elected its first African-American president, Barack H. Obama. The election was hotly contested, with unprecedented participation by youth and Black voters and an overall voter turnout of over 56 percent of the voting age population and more than 74 percent of registered voters.[2] According to the Pew Research Center, "The electorate in last year's presidential election was the most racially and ethnically diverse in U.S. history, with nearly one-in-four votes cast by non-whites" (Lopez and Taylor 2009, i). From the primary to the general election, the campaign context was highly racialized. The campaigns of Obama's principal opponents in the race (Hillary Clinton in the primary and John McCain in the general) worked to prime rural White voters' fears of a non-White leader, pundits warned of an inevitable "Bradley Effect," and the world brimmed over with enthusiasm about the possibility of a minority occupying the heretofore exclusively White White House. As was the case with the two aforementioned racialized events, survey data presented in Table 4.1 reveal significant differences in the emotional responses reported by White and Black respondents. African Americans reported much higher levels of hope, pride, and happiness than did White respondents, who instead indicated feelings of anger, disappointment, and fear at rates significantly higher than did Black respondents.

The above table reveals the statistically significant differences across racial groups in their emotional responses to racialized events. Particularly striking are the differences in respondents' perceptions of the role of race in the fallout surrounding Hurricane Katrina. These findings demonstrate the relevance of race and perception in determining individuals' emotional responses, and are bolstered by the absence of these racial differences in respondents' reactions to nonracialized events, such as the September 11th terrorist attacks and the Columbia crash. Building on the work of Roseman (1984) and others, we argue that these differences across the two racial groups' emotional responses emerge from their disparate perceptions of the racialized events. However, while this variation in racialization of political events allows us to make tentative suggestions regarding the role of group membership for emotional response, causal hypotheses are most rigorously tested in experimental settings. Therefore, we next present the findings from an experiment that enables us to manipulate relevant factors.

The experimental results provide additional support for our argument regarding emotional response. In Table 4.2, we see that Blacks are angrier when they lose than when they win. Further, they are most angry when both groups lose. White subjects, in contrast, indicated very similar levels of anger within each of the conditions. This difference in anger across racial categories may be best explained by the deleterious implications for primarily Black inner-city schools of decades of White flight and its associated explosion of White independent school districts in distinct geographic areas. The African-American subjects may have been more likely than Whites to appreciate the negative consequences of establishing race-based school districts, and as such, more prone to identify with and express anger in light of their racial in-group's plight.

Both African-American and White subjects indicated greater sadness when the creation of the independent school district benefited their racial out-group at the expense of their racial in-group. Similar to anger, Blacks expressed the greatest sadness when both groups lost. As we hypothesized, they were least sad when their group won and the out-group lost. Strangely, Whites were saddest when all groups won, and they were equally as sad when their group won and the out-group lost as they were when their group lost and the out-group won.

Table 4.2   Racial differences in emotion, by experimental condition

	Black	**White**
	Anger	
Blacks win/whites lose	2.25	2.92
	(1.26)	(1.00)
	4	*12*
Whites win/blacks lose	2.38	2.93
	(0.52)	(1.00)
	8	*14*
All win racial	3.00	3.44
	(1.00)	(0.73)
	3	*9*
All lose racial	3.29	3.11
	(0.76)	(1.12)
	7	*9*
	Sadness	
Blacks win/whites lose	2.50	2.92
	(1.29)	(1.24)
	4	*12*
Whites win/blacks lose	2.75	2.79
	(0.71)	(1.19)
	8	*14*
All win racial	2.67	3.56
	(0.58)	(0.73)
	3	*9*
All lose racial	2.86	2.56
	(1.07)	(0.88)
	7	*9*
	Happiness	
Blacks win/whites lose	3.25	3.08
	(0.96)	(0.51)
	4	*12*
Whites win/blacks lose	3.13	3.36
	(0.35)	(0.84)
	8	*14*
All win racial	3.67	3.33
	(0.58)	(0.87)
	3	*9*
All lose racial	4.00	2.89
	(0.00)	(0.93)
	7	*9*
	Pride	
Blacks win/whites lose	3.75	3.25
	(0.50)	(0.62)
	4	*12*
Whites win/blacks lose	3.25	3.64
	(0.46)	(0.50)
	8	*14*

(continued)

Table 4.2   continued

	Black	**White**
All win racial	2.67	3.33
	(1.15)	(0.87)
	3	*9*
All lose racial	3.86	3.56
	(0.38)	(0.53)
	7	*9*

Note: Means are derived from responses based on a four-point Likert scale ranging from one (not at all) to four (very), with standard deviations in parentheses, and N's italicized.

We also observe noticeable racial differences in happiness and pride in response to the various racial group competition manipulations. Blacks show the least amount of happiness when they lose and Whites win. Blacks show a considerable amount of happiness when they win, regardless of whether or not Whites lose. White respondents are least happy when everyone loses and most happy when they win and Blacks lose.

Similarly, the outcome of the competition depicted in the experimental manipulations elicits divergent response with respect to pride. Blacks are more proud when they win and Whites lose than when the opposite occurs. Whites are also more proud when they win and Blacks lose. They are equally as proud when both groups win. Here, Whites are least proud when all groups lose.

These results are in line with our expectations and show that racial group politics can not only influence negative emotion but also positive ones as well. Although the limited number of respondents within each experimental condition and racial group caution against firm conclusions, these results do provide suggestive evidence for our argument regarding racialization, identification, and perception. When political events are racialized, individual emotional responses are triggered in distinct and racially group-conscious ways.

CONCLUSION

We have demonstrated that different political events can elicit divergent racial group-based emotions. Whereas nonracial events foster emotional responses that are similar across racial groups, political events that emphasize and exacerbate racial group differences stimulate racial group-conscious behavior. These findings carry implications for our understanding of how emotions interact with race in American political life. The relevance of the social construct of race derives from one's relationship with the other—it is not merely an individual's identification with his racial in-group that induces group-conscious behavior, but also the perceived competition with his racial out-group. Although we have suggested that such perceptions may determine political evaluations and behavior, future work should explore this relationship further, giving more attention to the conditions under which individuals perceive an event to be racialized and precisely how individuals' perceptions of racial group competition are activated.

By utilizing both survey and experimental data, this chapter offers an individual-level approach for understanding the relevance of race for emotional response, as well as an examination of the causal processes through which race and emotion interact. We would like to note that while many of these differences are statically insignificant, their pattern and consistency allow us to feel confident in these results. In future tests, we hope to expand the number of subjects and the population from which our sample is drawn, thereby enhancing the external validity of and confidence in our findings. Notwithstanding these limitations, we are confident in the findings reached here and in prior work (White et al. 2007), which both point to the distinct realities experienced by White and Black citizens and the importance of this racial divide for understanding divergent emotional responses and the political evaluations and behavior these emotions evoke. These findings discredit the recurrent myth of a colorblind society and challenge us as a nation to acknowledge the resilient persistence of the racial divide so we may confront the disparate perceptions and emotions such divisions perpetuate.

Acknowledgment: This work was supported by the National Science Foundation [SES-0840550, SES-0610267].

CHAPTER 5

WHEN RACE MATTERS AND WHEN IT DOESN'T: RACIAL GROUP DIFFERENCES IN RESPONSE TO RACIAL CUES

ISMAIL K. WHITE

WHEN GEORGE W. BUSH WENT PUBLIC IN 2005 TO CONVINCE AMERICANS that his administration had the right plan for Social Security reform, he played what the NAACP called "the race card": he appealed to Blacks' racial group interest in Social Security reform. The President called the current system "inherently unfair" to African Americans because of their lower life expectancies, implying that his plan would fix the resultant racial discrepancy in benefits.[1] This attempt to generate support for an ostensibly nonracial policy among Black Americans through appeals to racial group interest, while not an uncommon political strategy, is not the sort of "race card" that scholars have attempted to study systematically. Rather, the focus has been on how the media and political elites can racialize ostensibly nonracial political issues by priming White Americans' racial attitudes, most effectively through the use of "implicit" racial cues, such as images of racial minorities or racial "code words" (Mendelberg 1997; 2001; Gilliam and Iyengar 2000; Valentino, Hutchings and White 2002), and how such racialization of political issues can result in significant reductions in White Americans' support for these policies (Gilens 1999; Bobo and Kluguel 1997).

Despite advances in our understanding of how racialized messages affect the opinions of White Americans, noticing this "other race card" in American political discourse points to a number of important unanswered questions about the effects of racial messages on the American public. Most glaring is that of how racialized portrayals of ostensibly nonracial political issues affect Black opinion. Not only do most studies of racial priming not include analysis of Black opinion (but see Gilliam and Iyengar 2000 and Bobo and Johnson 2004), but most studies of Black public opinion do not consider the possibility of the manipulability of the attachment of race to political issues for Blacks. Is Blacks' racial thinking about politics at all responsive to racial cues? And if it is, are there distinctions between the effects of "explicit" and "implicit" racial cues on Black opinion? Could politicians accomplish the same effect on Black opinion without making explicit appeals to group interest? And finally, are there different implications for White opinion from explicit racial cues that merely mention Black group interest in an issue, rather than the explicitly pejorative cues on which the existing literature has focused?

The purpose of this article is to forward our understanding of the consequences of racial appeals in American politics by answering the above questions. To do so, I pull from the literatures on racial priming and Black politics to develop, and then test, a theoretically grounded account of the effect of racial cues on Black Americans, and to clarify expectations about White Americans' responses to the explicit group-centric racial cues commonly invoked in appeals to Blacks. This account delineates the type of racial cues that should be accepted or rejected by each racial group. It challenges conventional wisdom that the role of racial attitudes in Black political decision-making is chronic, arguing instead that the racial meaning of ostensibly nonracial issues among African Americans is malleable and dependent upon appropriate racial cues to encourage racial interpretations. Moreover, by accounting for the effects of racial cues on both Black and White Americans, this study contributes to a more complete picture of how race is—and is not—used in American politics.

THEORIES OF RACIAL PRIMING

Generally speaking, work on racial priming in political science suggests that by associating race with certain political issues or candidates, the media and other political elites have the power to alter White Americans' views about politics, by making their views of Blacks important in shaping their political judgments.[2] Mendelberg (2001) arguably offers the most comprehensive theoretical framework for understanding the effects of racial priming on the opinions of White Americans. Briefly stated, Mendelberg argues that racial priming works because the racial cues present in these messages make racial schema (in this case Whites' attitudes about African Americans) more accessible in memory. Those schema are then used automatically in subsequent evaluations of candidates or policy issues. What makes Mendelberg's theory of racial priming unique, however, is her contention that racial priming *must* function at an implicit level in order to have any impact on opinion. At work, Mendelberg argues, is a conflict for White Americans between their belief in the norm of equality on one hand and their resentment toward Blacks on the other. Awareness of the racial nature of a message, she argues, will lead most Whites to reject that message, because they would not want to violate the equality norm. Thus, only those racial messages that implicitly elicit racial thinking will effectively prime racial thinking on political issues for White Americans.

While Mendelberg's work concentrates on the effects of implicit racial visual cues, others have argued that some verbal cues also can be implicitly racial (Valentino, Hutchings, and White 2002; Hurwitz and Peffley 2005). Valentino et al. (2002) argue that those ostensibly nonracial issues that have already been "coded" as racial offer implicitly racial rhetoric. That is, previous connections between Blacks as a group and issues such as crime and social welfare provided through media portrayals and other political communication (e.g., Gilens 1999; Gilliam and Iyengar 2000) render implicit racial meaning to these ostensibly nonracial issues. References to these issues, in turn, function as verbal implicit racial cues. As Valentino et al. (2002) note, an apt example of this type of implicit racialization can be found in Bob Dole's 1996 campaign, where he "criticized Bill Clinton for sponsoring several 'wasteful spending proposals' such as 'midnight basketball' or 'alpine slides in Puerto Rico'" (76). Such an ad, without making any visual or explicit verbal references to race, works to attach racial attitudes to Americans' evaluations of Clinton through references to policies linked to minority communities. Hurwitz and Peffley (2005) find that invoking even a single racially coded phrase—"inner city"—can work to attach Whites' racial attitudes to their preferences on ostensibly nonracial policies. Thus, while explicit racial verbal cues fail to prime racial thinking among White Americans, implicit verbal cues have been shown to be effective.

Despite the usefulness of Mendelberg's theoretical paradigm and its elaboration by Valentino et al. (2002) and Hurwitz and Peffley (2005) in explaining the workings of racial messages for White Americans, the ability of this theoretical perspective to account for how racial messages might shape the opinions of Black Americans is not clear. Most notably, the theoretical justification for the ineffectiveness of explicit racial cues among Whites does not extend to African Americans. The norms of racial equality and tolerance that lead Whites to reject explicitly racial messages are not necessarily in tension with Blacks' racial group identification as they are with Whites' racial resentment. Hence, racial attitude activation among African Americans may not necessitate an automatic priming process dependent upon a lack of awareness of the racial content of a message. The explicit appeals to Black racial group interest and the needs of the black community commonly offered by Black political leaders may be rejected by Whites anxious not to appear intolerant, but if Black racial group interest is about overcoming discrimination and inequality, such explicit racial appeals would contain no such grounds for rejection among Blacks.

THEORIES OF BLACK PUBLIC OPINION

Although little is known about the effects of racial cues on African Americans' political attitudes, previous research examining the origins of Black political opinions may offer some insight about how Blacks might respond to racialized political messages. The perception of psychological connectedness or closeness to Blacks as a group (i.e., group identification) has been found to be essential in accounting for the largely liberal views that Black Americans hold on a range of important political matters from affirmative action, to guaranteed jobs for the unemployed (Dawson 1994), to increased spending on food stamps (Tate 1993). Due to the power of racial considerations in explaining such a wide array of political attitudes, racial group identification has come to be regarded by some as the central organizing construct through which African Americans come to understand politics—surpassing other explanations of opinion formation in both statistical significance and substantive importance. Dawson, for instance, points out the centrality of racial identification in his comparison of the importance of individual self-interest and racial group interest in explaining Black political behavior. Citing the enormous disparities between the social positions of Black and White Americans, Dawson argues that "as long as African-Americans' life chances are powerfully shaped by race, it is efficient for individual African Americans to use their perceptions of the interest of African Americans as a group as a proxy for their own interest" (1994, 61). Indeed, Dawson and others find that racial considerations matter more to Black political opinion formulations than more widely held beliefs such as party identification and liberal/conservative ideology (Allen, Dawson, and Brown 1989; Tate 1993; Kinder and Sanders 1996).

The attention given to understanding the effects of racial group identification on Black opinion, however, has not produced conceptual clarity about the conditions under which racial group identification should or should not matter in explaining Black opinion. Do African Americans see all political issues through a racial lens, or is it necessary for issues to be defined as racial in order for African Americans to think of them as such? Some have suggested that racial group identification should be chronically accessible for Black Americans because of its repeated activation in Black institutions and politics (e.g., Dawson 1994; Lau 1989). That is, because Black Americans experience repeated political appeals to their racial identities, those identities should be more available, generally speaking, as Blacks construct their political opinions. Yet, chronic accessibility would only imply higher activation potential for Blacks' racial attitudes (Higgins 1996; Price and Tewksbury 1997), not necessarily answering the question of what makes Blacks realize that potential in some situations and not in others. Answering that question seems imperative given that scholars have observed variation in the attachment of racial group identification to political issues. While racial group identification explains Blacks' opinions about issues that are explicitly racial, such as affirmative action (Tate 1993; Dawson 1994), and reparations for slavery (Dawson and Popoff 2004), there is less evidence that racial group identification consistently matters in forming Blacks' opinions on ostensibly nonracial issues. For example, while Tate (1993), using the 1984 National Black Election Study, finds a relationship between racial group closeness and Blacks' support of social welfare programs that might have implicit racial meaning, such as food stamps and guaranteed jobs, Kinder and Winter (2001) find little evidence of a relationship between in-group closeness and opinions on social welfare policies in the 1992 National Election Study. Tate (1993) also finds no relationship between racial group identification and Blacks' opinions on other ostensibly nonracial issues, including matters of foreign policy, funding for public schools, and universalistic programs like Medicare.

There is another set of observations that arise from the literature on Black politics that should inform our understanding of when and how racial cues may matter in the formation of Black political opinion—Blacks' recognition and opinions of diversity within the Black community. More than a century ago, W. E. B. DuBois (1903) implored White Americans to recognize the promise of "the talented tenth" of Black America for engendering uplift of the race. He also documented intraracial politics driven by concern over how some segments of the Black population, particularly those of the "criminal class," reflected poorly on the race (DuBois 1899). Scholars since DuBois have documented the way factors such as social class, age, and gender cause real divisions in Black politics (Gilliam and Whitby 1989; Wilson 1978). More recently, scholars have begun to hone in on the specific question of the conditions under which an issue is deemed a "Black issue"—one that warrants Blacks' attention on the grounds of group interest. Most notably, Cohen (1999) argues that the interests of marginal groups within the Black community are commonly shunned from the "Black politics" agenda. Her argument, in particular, implies that linked fate politics are qualified by which segment of the Black population is perceived to be affected by the issue. In sum, this line of research suggests that the effect of racial cues among Blacks may depend on what representations of Blackness the cues invoke.

ACTIVATING BLACK RACIAL GROUP IDENTIFICATION

The preceding discussions highlight the need for a conceptual framework for understanding how racial messages influence Black opinions that accounts for when and how Blacks' racial attitudes are activated. Despite the powerful influence Black racial identification has on Blacks' political judgments, its attachment to ostensibly non-racial issues cannot be assumed as automatic. Further, an account of racial attitude activation for Blacks must deviate from explanations of racial priming developed in reference to White Americans in its treatment of the work of explicit and implicit racial cues.

I argue that, in the realm of ostensibly non-racial issues, racial cues within most forms of political communication serve to activate racial attitudes for Black Americans. In response to a racial cue, Black Americans should not only engage the non-racial considerations—such as partisanship or liberal/conservative ideology—suggested by the content or framing of the issue, but should also increase their reliance on racial considerations. On the other hand, when racial cues are not present, African Americans—like White Americans—have no reason to attach their racial beliefs to an ostensibly non-racial issue. Absent a racial cue, Blacks should see the policy in much the same way as Whites, using non-racial predispositions such as partisanship and ideology. There are, however, two important distinctions to be made between racial attitude activation for Blacks and Whites.

First, because Blacks, themselves, are the objects of racial cues, we should not expect these cues to elicit out-group attitudes as they do for Whites. Instead, racial cues that associate African Americans with a particular policy should activate Black in-group attachment or racial group identification. This point is rather straightforward and reflects one of the essential differences in Black and White Americans' understandings of racial policies (Dawson 1994; Gurin, Hatchett, and Jackson 1989; Kinder and Sanders 1996).

Second, and more important, there should be differences in the types of racial cues that activate racial thinking among Black and White Americans. Existing theories of racial priming imply that Whites' racial attitudes should be activated only by implicit racial messages; explicit racial cues draw attention to a violation of norms of racial equality and tolerance, causing Whites to reject the racial message. Such norms, however, are not necessarily in tension with Blacks' racial group identification, as they are with Whites' racial resentment. Thus, the reason for Whites' rejection of explicitly racial messages should not apply for Blacks. Explicit racial cues should activate Blacks' racial attitudes *because* they define a racial group interest in the issue.

Implicit racial cues, however, may not be as effective in activating racial thinking among Blacks on ostensibly nonracial issues. The work of implicit cues depends on a connection between the actual construct identified by the cue—inner city residents, for example—and racial meaning. Previous work on how implicit racial verbal cues, or "code words," function among White Americans posits that the racial meaning comes from repeated association of the code words with "blacks": welfare recipients are repeatedly (and disproportionately) portrayed as black (Gilens 1996; 1999), as are violent criminals (Gilliam and Iyengar 2000). Such coding is, of course, stereotype-consistent among Whites, conforming to negative views of Blacks. Such negative meaning, however, may be grounds for the cues' rejection among Blacks. To the extent that implicit racial cues are those that invoke "marginal" elements of the Black community, their racial meaning among Blacks may be interpreted as not in the interest of the race. Without explicit appeals to race, Blacks may find it easier to reject linked fate politics for these "marginal" segments of the Black community.

METHODS AND PROCEDURES

Experiments have become an important tool within the study of political communication and media effects to isolate the causal impact of communication on political attitudes and behavior (e.g., Iyengar and Kinder 1987; Nelson, Clawson, and Oxley 1997; Miller and Krosnick 2000). By manipulating media content, and randomly assigning subjects to treatment and control conditions, researchers have been able to isolate the essential components of a message that alter citizens' attitudes. Exactly because of their ability to isolate the causal effect of political communications, experiments seem the ideal tool for examining the effect of implicit and explicit racial cues in political discourse on African-American and White public opinion.

I employ two experiments to test my hypotheses about the effect of racial cues on ostensibly nonracial issues. Both studies manipulate exposure to racial cues about the issue through construction of news articles that offer different issue frames. Similar to Druckman (2004), I define issue frames as messages that emphasize "a subset of potentially relevant considerations [which] leads individuals to focus on these considerations when constructing their opinions" (672). How the issue frames enable the creation of implicit and explicit racial cues will be discussed in the details of each experiment. The first experiment centers on an emerging political issue with no obvious connection to race: the (then pending) Iraq War. The Iraq experiment allows me to test whether explicit group-centric and implicit racial cues can attach racial attitudes to a nonracial issue. In the second experiment, I turn to an ostensibly nonracial issue that others have suggested should already have implicit racial meaning: social welfare programs. The welfare experiment, then, allows me to test the effectiveness of explicit and implicit racial cues in changing the importance of racial attitudes to preferences on an issue that may already be loaded with racial meaning.

THE IRAQ EXPERIMENT

The issue of the (then pending) 2003 Iraq War provided an ideal opportunity to examine the effects of explicit and implicit racial verbal cues by employing variations of the oppositional frames actually used in elite political debate. That is, from the debate over pending military action in Iraq, I was able to isolate nonracial, implicitly racial, and explicitly racial rhetoric against the war, which I used to create three frames for the argument against military action in Iraq for use in the experiment. Each of these frames provided different justifications for opposing the use of military force in Iraq and each of the frames had varying degrees of racial emphasis. The issue frame, then, provided the cue about the racial meaning of the war, invoking either an implicit or explicit verbal racial cue, or excluding any language that might be thought to have inherent racial meaning.

The explicitly racial frame, termed the *Minority/Black Soldiers Frame*, drew on arguments that Black political elites had begun to articulate expressing a conflict between racial group interest and the war. Opposition to the war was linked to concern for the disproportionate number of poor and minority soldiers in the enlisted ranks of the United States armed forces that would be put in harm's way.

The implicitly racial frame, labeled the *Domestic Issues Frame*, was also drawn from the rhetoric of Black political leaders, although other Democratic politicians made similar appeals. Without making any explicit reference to race, this frame emphasized the potential cost of war for domestic social programs, particularly those for the poor and underprivileged. This frame employed an implicit racial cue, similar to those that have previously been found to prime racial thinking among Whites, although it seems that the use of such frames by Black leaders was in an attempt to use issues that rest at the foundation of their support—social welfare programs—to mobilize opposition to the use of military action in Iraq.

Within the mainstream partisan debate, arguments in opposition to a war in Iraq centered on the fact that the United States lacked the support of the United Nations and stressed that the use of military force in Iraq would not be justified without that support. This rhetoric supplied the nonracial opposition frame, labeled the *UN Support Frame*, which focused only on the lack of support for military action from allies and international institutions.

Each of these three oppositional frames was employed in the experiment as a separate manipulation, which consisted of a news magazine article detailing a fictitious debate between two Ohio congressmen—one Democrat and one Republican—on the proposed war in Iraq. All of the experimental conditions presented two-sided messages about the war: the Republican expressed a consistent statement in support of using force to remove Saddam Hussein from power, and the Democrat voiced opposition. What changed across the conditions were the terms in which the Democrat articulated his argument against the war. Table 5.1 summarizes the key verbal cues in each of the conditions.

Table 5.1   Verbal cues in Iraq War frames

Explicitly racial minority/ Black soldiers frame	Implicitly racial domestic issues frame	Nonracial UN support frame
Representative Brown began by stating that he is currently opposed to military action in Iraq stressing his concern that a war in Iraq would result in considerable U.S. casualties, particularly among racial minorities. Brown observed, "the great majority of the soldiers in the United States Army who will be put in harm's way are from poor, Black and Hispanic families— not the children of millionaires and members of Congress."	Representative Brown stated that he is opposed to military action in Iraq, stressing his concern that there are more pressing domestic issues to which the nation's leaders should be attending. "The war that my constituents want us to wage is a war on poverty, a war on layoffs, a war on inadequate healthcare and a war on the lack of affordable housing," said Brown.	Representative Brown stated that he is opposed to military action in Iraq, stressing his concern that military action could only be justified by working through the United Nations and with the support of European allies. "We must decide in concert with our allies how to deal with Iraq. International political support is necessary in order to justify any military action," said Brown.

The experiment was carried out in computer labs at three separate locations: the University of Michigan in Ann Arbor, Michigan; Southern University in Baton Rouge, Louisiana; and Louisiana State University in Baton Rouge, Louisiana. Both student and nonstudent adult subjects were recruited to participate in the study from the areas surrounding each university and were told that they would receive $10 cash for their participation. One hundred and thirty three self-identified African-American subjects and 101 self identified White subjects participated in the experiment.[3] The experiment was conducted from February 17, 2003, to March 3, 2003, just prior to the start of the 2003 invasion of Iraq.

As participants entered the lab, they were randomly assigned to one of three experimental conditions or a control condition. Participants in the control group did not read any article about Iraq, but instead read a nonpolitical article.[4] After reading the articles, respondents answered an extensive battery of posttest questions that included questions about their support for the war in Iraq, issue importance ratings, and racial and political attitudes. Upon completion of the posttest questionnaire subjects were debriefed, paid, and dismissed.

The sample does not differ dramatically from that of the nation as a whole on most political dimensions, although there are some marked differences, of course, in other demographics. On the important dimensions of partisanship and racial group identification, Black subjects were very similar to the national population. For Whites, the experimental sample is slightly more Democratic and somewhat more racially liberal than the population as a whole. Although 30 percent of the participants were nonstudents, in terms of age and education the sample still differs from the national population for both Blacks and Whites. The median age of experimental participants is twenty-two years and the average participant is college educated. Analysis of variance, however, indicated that neither these sociodemographic variables nor the partisan and attitudinal variables differed across conditions, so we can be reasonably confident that the results observed are, in fact, the result of exposure to the various conditions.

FINDING RACIAL INTEREST IN THE PROSPECTS FOR WAR IN IRAQ

Turning to the data from the Iraq experiment provides opportunity to test the distinct effects of explicit and implicit racial cues on the opinions of Black and White Americans. Again, consistent with previous research on racial priming, the expectation is that for Whites, only the frame that obliquely cues race—through reference to racially "coded" welfare programs—will encourage racialized thinking about the use of military force Iraq. For Blacks, the explicit racial frame (*Minority/Black Soldiers Frame*) should cue racialized interpretations of the pending war in Iraq via its clear connection between racial group interest and opposition to the war. Although only oblique references to race are made in the implicit racial frame (*Domestic Issues Frame*), given the traditional focus of Black leaders on social welfare issues, I expect that African Americans will recognize the relevance of antipoverty programs to African-American racial group interest, and thus use their racial considerations to evaluate the use of military force in Iraq.

To evaluate these expectations, I model subjects' level of support for the use of military force in Iraq as a function of the three sets of considerations most relevant to the frame cues: racial, ideological, and dove/hawk predispositions. Support for military action in Iraq is captured by a scale of three questions; each referenced the pending conflict with Iraq in slightly different terms, but answers to all three are significantly related. Racial considerations are captured by measures of both in-group identification and out-group resentment. In-group attitudes are assessed by a measure of racial group–linked fate, gauging the degree to which Black and White respondents' believe their own welfare is related to that of their own racial group. As do Kinder and Winter (2001), I measure out-group resentment using the reverse coding of the out-group feeling thermometer (Black/White). Ideology is measured with the standard seven-point scale, with higher values indicating a more conservative ideology. The dove/hawk measure taps subjects' general attitudes about the appropriateness of military force versus diplomacy in foreign conflicts. All measures are scaled to range from 0 to 1(See Appendix A for question wording and scale construction). Each attitude is interacted with each condition in order to test for the activation of each attitude following subjects' exposure to the explicit racial, implicit racial, and nonracial cues.[5] The model is estimated separately for Black and White subjects using OLS regression.

The results of the models of Black and White subjects' support for military action in Iraq are presented in Tables 5.2 and 5.3, respectively. Interactions between each experimental condition and the explanatory political attitudes highlight the differences in the ingredients of subjects' evaluations of the Iraq War depending on exposure to explicit racial, implicit racial, and nonracial frames of the argument against the war. For ease of interpretation, the tables present the baseline effects of each variable in the control condition in the first column, and the total effect of each variable within each condition (i.e., baseline plus interaction coefficient) in the following three columns. Bolded cells indicate that

Table 5.2   Predictors of Black support for the use of military force in Iraq by experimental condition

	Control	Minority/Black soldiers frame	Domestic issues frame	UN frame
In-group identification	–.07	**–.46***	–.03	.17
	(.17)	**(.12)**	(.09)	(.11)
Out-group resentment	–.01	.01	–.14	.13
	(.17)	(.18)	(.13)	(.23)
Ideology	–.21	–.31*	–.05	.01
	(.15)	(.11)	(.12)	(.18)
Dove/Hawk	–.17*	–.16*	–.01	–.13
	(.07)	(.08)	(.08)	(.08)
N	34	33	39	27

Note: Entries are OLS coefficients from a single model that also includes controls for being a student. First column entries are baseline coefficients; other columns display linear combinations of baseline and attitude by condition interaction coefficients. Bolded results indicate a statically significant (p<.05, one-tailed t-test) slope change from the control condition. *Denotes p<.05 for one-tailed t-test of the relationship between that variable and support for the war in Iraq within that condition.

Table 5.3   Predictors of White support for the use of military force in Iraq by experimental condition

	Control	Minority/Black soldiers frame	Domestic issues frame	UN frame
In-group identification	–.04	–.07	.05	.15
	(.14)	(.15)	(.16)	(.13)
Out-group resentment	–.20	–.35*	**.80***	–.24
	(.22)	(.17)	**(.22)**	(.17)
Ideology	.10	.21	.40*	.13
	(.16)	(.19)	(.19)	(.17)
Dove/Hawk	–.31*	–.39*	**–.01**	–.27*
	(.11)	(.13)	**(.10)**	(.09)
N	24	21	24	32

Note: Entries are OLS coefficients from a single model that also includes controls for being a student. First column entries are baseline coefficients; other columns display linear combinations of baseline and attitude by condition interaction coefficients. Bolded results indicate a statically significant (p<.05, one-tailed t-test) slope change from the control condition. *Denotes p<.05 for one-tailed t-test of the relationship between that variable and support for the war in Iraq within that condition.

the attitude by condition interaction was statistically significant (p<.05). Given the oppositional stance of the manipulated frame, the predictions are unidirectional. Specifically, the expectation is that in-group identification should be a more significant predictor of opposition to the war among Blacks in the *Minority/Black Soldiers Frame* and the *Domestics Issues Frame* conditions. Among Whites, out-group resentment should become a stronger predictor of support for the Iraq War, but only in the implicitly racial *Domestic Issues Frame* condition.

As expected, race was a relevant consideration in evaluating the Iraq issue for those Blacks who were exposed to the explicitly racial *Minority/ Black Soldiers Frame*. In this condition, where subjects read references to the consequences of the war for Blacks and other minorities, in-group identification became an important predictor of significantly less favorable opinions about the use of military force in Iraq among Blacks. The model predicts, in fact, that support for the war among highly racially identified Blacks would be nearly half of that among Blacks with no sense of group identification. In addition, as expected given that Blacks are the objects of the racial frames in this condition, Black subjects' attitudes about Whites (out-group attitudes) did not appear to be related to their support for military action. Moreover, increased reliance on racial group identification in evaluating the issue of war in Iraq was the only significant change caused by the message containing the explicit racial cue.

Whites exhibited a very different pattern in the explicitly racial frame condition. Consistent with previous research, Whites' racial attitudes were unrelated to their attitudes about the use of military action in Iraq when the racial consequences of an issue were explicitly discussed. Neither in-group identification nor out-group resentment became predictors of White subjects' support for a war in Iraq in the *Minority/Black Soldiers Frame* condition.

Turning to the implicit racial cue offered by the *Domestic Issues Frame* condition, the results indicate that, also just as previous research would suggest, when Whites were exposed to a frame of the war in Iraq that associates the issue with obliquely racial issues, a strong connection was created between Whites' support for the use of military action in Iraq and their racial attitudes. The statistically significant effect of Whites' racial attitudes comes, as expected, from their out-group resentment. More racially resentful White subjects in this condition reacted to the implicitly racial arguments against a war in Iraq by becoming far more likely to support a war in Iraq. The implicit racialization of the Iraq issue also dislodges the effect of general predispositions about the use of force in international affairs. A statistically significant positive coefficient on the interaction between the *Domestic Issues Frame* condition and the dove/hawk measure added to the negative baseline dove/hawk coefficient implies a zero effect of these attitudes in this condition. Implicit racial cues, then, can work so effectively that race can trump other considerations among Whites.

While implicit racial verbal cues significantly altered the ingredients of Whites' assessments of the Iraq issue, African-American subjects' opinions were not significantly affected by the implicit racial issue frame in any way. Most important, there is little evidence to support the expectation that implicit racial cues elicit racial thinking among African Americans. The effect of Black in-group identification is statistically indistinguishable from zero. There is also no discernable relationship between out-group resentment and support for military action in Iraq in this condition. The results of this manipulation indicate that there may, in fact, not be a direct connection—at least in the minds of African Americans—between racial considerations and domestic issues that disproportionately affect African Americans as a group. What is an implicit racial cue for Whites may not, in fact, hold significant racial meaning for Blacks. It is also possible, however, that the references to social welfare issues, despite their regular appearance in Black political discourse, activated Blacks' concerns about "marginal" segments of the Black community, causing them to reject the implicit racial appeal. While I am unable to test these propositions in this experiment, I will return to them in the welfare experiment.

Finally, exposing subjects to the nonracial *UN Support Frame* condition, as expected, did not increase the importance of racial considerations in shaping opinions about the conflict in Iraq among Blacks or Whites. In the absence of any racial cue to connect Black or White group interest— or attitudes about Blacks or Whites—to the use of military force in Iraq, racial considerations played little or no role in shaping subjects opinions about this particular ostensibly nonracial policy. In fact, neither Whites' nor Blacks' opinions were significantly shaped in any discernable way by the condition: none of the attitude-by-condition-interaction coefficients was statistically discernable from zero.

Although the results for Whites in this experiment and the existing results on the priming of race on ostensibly nonracial issues that focus primarily on White Americans demonstrate that implicitly racial cues do the work of racializing issues for White Americans, the results of this experiment for Blacks underscore the need for race-specific understandings of racial priming. The results of this study point to important racial differences in the effectiveness of *explicit* and *implicit* racial cues in activating racial thinking about a previously nonracial issue. The results of the experiment are also clearly supportive of the argument that African Americans do not see all political issues through a racial lens; instead, racial thinking about politics among African Americans is something that is strongly shaped by how public policies are discussed. When exposed to a message that lacked *explicit* racial content, Blacks used other issue-relevant considerations to formulate their opinions about politics. When race was brought front and center in the discussion of the war in Iraq, Blacks' in-group identification, as measured by Black-linked fate, mattered most. When race was merely cued implicitly, however, Blacks did not connect their group identification with the ostensibly nonracial issue of war. Inconsistent with theories of racial priming based on White Americans, then, implicit cues are not *the* driving force behind activating racialized thinking in the American public. Yet, questions remain about why implicit racial cues fail to elicit racial thinking among Blacks and whether the attachment of race to an ostensibly non-racial issue is still malleable when the issue may already contain implicit racial meaning.

The Welfare Experiment

The welfare experiment was designed both to test whether the key results about the effectiveness of explicit and implicit racial cues in the Iraq experiment extended to other issue domains, and to increase leverage specifically on the question of why Blacks are unresponsive to implicit racial cues. I employed the same logic and general design as in the Iraq experiment, using verbal cues embedded in a fictitious news story about a debate between two Ohio congressmen, one Republican and one Democrat. This time the debate is over proposed federal spending cuts on social welfare programs, with food stamps and Medicaid mentioned specifically. The key difference in the design is that there are now four experimental conditions: one with explicit racial cues, one without racial cues (other than the issue, itself), and two conditions that offered different types of implicit racial cues. The differences in the implicit racial cues were designed to help unpack whether the effectiveness of implicit racial cues depends upon the representation of the Black community that they suggest.

Across all of the experimental conditions the news story offered the same account of a Republican proposal for federal social welfare spending cuts, and of the opposition of the Democratic Party to those cuts. Manipulation of the racial cues across conditions was even more precise than in the Iraq experiment, as it was accomplished simply by replacing the description of the group the Democratic congressman claimed would be particularly affected by the spending cuts as he voiced his opposition. Table 5.4 presents the passages that changed across conditions to provide the cues. The explicit racial condition included references to Black and African-American families, while the nonracial condition replaced those references with "working" American families. One of the implicit racial conditions used the term "inner city" to describe the families affected by the cuts. Given the effect of this term in Hurwitz and Peffley's (2005) study

Table 5.4 Verbal cues in food stamps frames

Explicitly racial African Americans	Implicitly racial inner-city Americans	Implicitly racial poor Americans	Non-racial working Americans
House Democrats stirred debate today on a proposal that would lead to a major restructuring of the nation's welfare system, with claims that the Republican plan would disproportionately hurt black and Hispanic families.	House Democrats stirred debate today on a proposal that would lead to a major restructuring of the nation's welfare system, with claims that the Republican plan would disproportionately hurt inner-city families.	House Democrats stirred debate today on a proposal that would lead to a major restructuring of the nation's welfare system, with claims that the Republican plan would disproportionately hurt poor families.	House Democrats stirred debate today on a proposal that would lead to a major restructuring of the nation's welfare system, with claims that the Republican plan would hurt working American families.
"[P]rograms like food stamps and Medicaid represent important safety-nets for many African-American families, keeping them from falling deeper into poverty."	"[P]rograms like food stamps and Medicaid represent important safety-nets for many inner-city families, keeping them from falling deeper into poverty."	"[P]rograms like food stamps and Medicaid represent important safety-nets for many poor families, keeping them from falling deeper into poverty."	"[P]rograms like food stamps and Medicaid represent important safety-nets for many American families, keeping them from falling deeper into poverty."
"[T]his recent round of budget cuts would have a disastrous impact on black Americans," Brown argued. "Thousands of African-American families could lose food stamp benefits and many more would be left without adequate access to affordable health care."	"[T]his recent round of budget cuts would have a disastrous impact on those who live in inner-cities," Brown argued. "Thousands of inner-city families could lose food stamp benefits and many more would be left without adequate access to affordable health care."	"[T]his recent round of budget cuts would have a disastrous impact on poor Americans," Brown argued. "Thousands of low income families could lose food stamp benefits and many more would be left without adequate access to affordable health care."	"[T]his recent round of budget cuts would have a disastrous impact on American families," Brown argued. "Thousands of working American families could lose food stamp benefits and many more would be left without adequate access to affordable health care."

of White opinion, I expect this implicit cue to be associated particularly with negative depictions of Black ghettos and urban crime scripts (Gilliam and Iyengar 2000). The second implicit racial condition refers to the families most vulnerable to the cuts simply as poor Americans. Given the traditional concern about disproportionate rates of poverty among African Americans and the concentration of Black leaders on antipoverty and social welfare programs, I expect that the label "poor Americans" should carry an implicit connection to race among Blacks. Given the degree to which others have found antipoverty and welfare programs inherently racially coded among White Americans, the reminder of the programs' concentration on "the poor" may also function as an implicit racial cue among Whites.

This experiment was carried out both in computer labs at the University of Texas in Austin, Texas and Southern University in Baton Rouge, Louisiana, and at various locations in both cities through the use of laptop computers, from February 28 to March 23, 2006. The sample is comprised of adult subjects—half students and half nonstudents—who were recruited to participate in the study from the areas surrounding each university. Nonstudent subjects were told that they would receive $10 cash for their participation. Onehundred and sixty self-identified African-American subjects and 181 self-identified White subjects participated in the experiment. Participants were much younger than the national population; the median age is approximately 26 years. The participants were also more educated than the national population, with most subjects indicating that they had some college education. Analysis of variance, however, indicates that neither sociodemographic variables nor relevant partisan and attitudinal variables differed across conditions.

As participants entered the lab (or equivalent facility), they were randomly assigned to one of the four racial cue conditions or a control condition. Subjects in the control group did not read any article about welfare issues, but instead read a nonpolitical article about the accidental shattering of an antique vase in a London museum. After reading the articles, subjects answered an extensive battery of posttest questions, which included questions about their support for increased spending on food stamps, issue importance ratings, and racial and political attitudes. Upon completion of the posttest questionnaire subjects were debriefed, paid, and dismissed.

WELFARE IN BLACK AND WHITE

I begin the evaluation of the racial cues in the welfare experiment by modeling subjects' level of support for increased spending on the central welfare program discussed in the manipulated articles—food stamps—as a function of the most relevant considerations that might be used forming an opinion on the issue. Thus, in addition to racial attitudes, the model includes measures of ideology, individualism, egalitarianism, and general feelings about the poor. In-group racial identification is again gauged by a measure of racial in-group linked fate, while the measure for out-group resentment is captured by out-group stereotyping. Ideology is measured with the standard seven-point scale, with higher values indicating a more conservative ideology. Individualism is measured with a scale comprised of questions that capture the subjects' perception of link between hard work and success. Egalitarianism is measured by a scale that captures peoples' beliefs about equality. Feelings about the poor are gauged by a 101-point feeling thermometer assessing the subjects' feelings of warmth or coolness toward poor people (See Appendix A for question wording and scale construction). All measures are again scaled to range from 0 to 1, and each attitude is interacted with each condition to test for its activation by each cue type. The model is estimated separately for Blacks and Whites using OLS regression.

Results of the models of Blacks' and Whites' support for increased spending on food stamps are presented in Tables 5.5 and 5.6, respectively. As in the Iraq experiment, the tables present the baseline effects of each attitude in the control condition in the first column and the total effect of each variable within each condition in the following columns, with bolded cells indicating a statistically significant attitude by condition interaction. The predictions are unidirectional: effective racial cues should make racial group identification a significantly stronger predictor of support for increased spending among Black subjects, while they should make racial out-group resentment a significantly stronger predictor of opposition to increased spending among Whites. Only the implicit racial cues are expected to activate racial attitudes among Whites. Explicit racial cues are again expected to be effective among Blacks, but the expected effectiveness of the implicit cues among Blacks is conditioned by type. If Blacks are rejecting connections between racial group interest and the interests of particularly "marginal" elements of the Black community, then the negatively loaded "inner-city" cue should be ineffective among Blacks, while the "poor" cue should be more likely to activate racial thinking about the food stamps issue.

The results for Whites generally conform to expectations, with the exception that the "poor Americans" cue did not work to attach racial attitudes to support for food stamps spending. Although the coefficient on the interaction between the poor Americans condition and out-group resentment is in the hypothesized negative direction, it fails to reach traditional levels of statistical significance. There are, in fact, no significant

Table 5.5 Predictors of Black support for increased spending on food stamps by experimental condition

	Control	African Americans	Inner-city Americans	Poor Americans	Working Americans
In-group identification	−.30 (.19)	**.40*** **(.16)**	−.27 (.20)	**.15** **(.18)**	−.01 (.19)
Out-group resentment	.29 (.23)	.01 (.16)	.34 (.27)	.17 (.26)	−.01 (.20)
Ideology	−.34 (.26)	**.44*** **(.21)**	−.40 (.22)	.05 (.24)	−.27 (.20)
Individualism	−.16 (.21)	−.31 (.19)	.14 (.21)	.07 (.17)	−.19 (.25)
Egalitarianism	−.04 (.24)	−.42 (.43)	−.33 (.41)	**.80*** **(.28)**	.08 (.26)
Feelings toward the poor	.42* (.24)	−.16 (.24)	.31 (.25)	**−.24** **(.26)**	.09 (.26)
N	32	33	30	34	31

Note: Entries are OLS coefficients from a single model that also includes controls for being a student, income, party identification, and gender. First column entries are baseline coefficients; other columns display linear combinations of baseline and attitude by condition interaction coefficients. Bolded results indicate a statically significant (p<.05, one-tailed t-test) slope change from the control condition. *Denotes p<.05 for one-tailed t-test of the relationship between that variable and support for spending on food stamps within that condition.

changes in the ingredients of Whites' opinions about spending on food stamps across any of the conditions except for in the implicitly racial "inner city" condition. As expected, in response to the "inner city" cue, Whites' out-group resentment becomes an important factor in shaping their level of support for increased spending, with the most resentful Whites being less than half as supportive as the least resentful, all else constant. It is also worth noting that despite previous work on the extant racial coding of welfare programs, among this particular group of Whites there was no discernable relationship between their racial attitudes and their opinions on this particular welfare issue in the control condition.

Blacks also exhibit a pattern of results that generally adheres to expectations. As in the Iraq experiment, while racial attitudes were apparently not related to Blacks' evaluations of the issue in the control condition, exposure to the explicit racial cues readily attaches racial group interest to Blacks' expressions of support for increased spending on food stamps. Unlike the Iraq experiment, the results for the implicit cue conditions lend some insight into whether and how implicit racial cues can activate racial thinking on an ostensibly nonracial issue among Blacks. The more precise implicit racial cues used in this experiment suggest a difference in Blacks' responses to different cue types. The inner city cue—the implicit cue

Table 5.6   Predictors of White support for increased spending on food stamps by experimental condition

	Control	African Americans	Inner-city Americans	Poor Americans	Working Americans
In-group identification	−.01	−.12	.01	−.04	−.04
	(.11)	(.17)	(.18)	(.12)	(.13)
Out-group resentment	.28	.34	**−.54***	−.13	.08
	(.17)	(.22)	**(.21)**	(.21)	(.23)
Ideology	.01	−.16	.39	−.36*	.21
	(.18)	(.20)	(.26)	(.18)	(.20)
Individualism	−.19	−.20	−.32*	−.26*	−.27
	(.14)	(.17)	(.18)	(.13)	(.18)
Egalitarianism	.20	.29*	.62*	.02	.12
	(.22)	(.16)	(.22)	(.21)	(.23)
Feelings toward the poor	.29	.19	−.01	.20	.59*
	(.22)	(.26)	(.39)	(.34)	(.22)
N	38	35	34	39	35

Note: Entries are OLS coefficients from a single model that also includes controls for being a student, income, party identification, and gender. First column entries are baseline coefficients; other columns display linear combinations of baseline and attitude by condition interaction coefficients. Bolded results indicate a statically significant (p<.05, one-tailed t-test) slope change from the control condition. *Denotes p<.05 for one-tailed t-test of the relationship between that variable and support for spending on food stamps within that condition.

expected to be most closely associated with negative representations and/or "marginal" elements of the Black community—produced no change in Blacks' use of racial attitudes in constructing their opinions about the issue of food stamps. There is some evidence, however, that the less negatively loaded poor cue was effective in activating racial thinking about the issue. A positive, statistically significant coefficient on the interaction of the poor Americans condition and racial group identification suggests that Blacks in this condition were more likely to use their racial attitudes in deciding their level of support for spending on food stamps. The predicted effect of racial group identification, however, while positive as expected, is quite small. Not only is the predicted effect of racial group identification on support for increased welfare spending less than half of that in the explicit racial cue condition, but the results also indicate that the general principle of egalitarianism became far more important than racial group identification in shaping Blacks' opinions in the poor Americans condition. In sum, while there is some evidence that the right sort of implicit racial cue might be effective in activating racial thinking about an ostensibly nonracial issue among Blacks, that evidence is far from overwhelming.

To more directly test the hypothesis that it is the connection of the implicit racial cue to negative representations of Blacks that causes the rejection of a link between racial group interest and the issue being discussed, I turn next to a set of analyses that consider whether such negative representations are activated by the implicit cue conditions. If so, I examine whether this moderates the effect of the implicit racial cue on the connection between racial group interest and the relevant issue position. Given that previous work in Black politics, beginning with that of DuBois, has pointed to sharp intraracial politics around the issue of crime, and given the complete ineffectiveness in the welfare experiment of the implicit racial cue assumed to be tied more to crime—rather than just poverty—"criminal" seems a likely negative representation of Blacks to moderate the effect of implicit racial cues (see Mendelberg 1997 and Valentino 1999 for further discussion of the connection between welfare and crime). That is, what DuBois termed the "criminal class" may be the element of the Black community that the implicit racial cues, particularly the inner city cue, are bringing to mind. Deeming this element of the Black community's interests outside of the interests of the race would cause Blacks to reject the cue's suggested connection between racial group interest and the issue being discussed. I, therefore, turn to a measure that gauges subjects' concern about crime. The measure captures whether subjects listed crime among the three most important issues facing the country. I look first at the distribution of this measure across the experiment's conditions to see if concern about crime was, in fact, more common in the implicit cue conditions. I then examine the power of concern about crime to moderate the effect of racial group interest on opinions on food stamps across the conditions.

The percentages of respondents in each condition who listed crime among the top three problems facing the United States are presented in Table 5.7, with the results for White and Black subjects listed in separate columns. For the sake of comparison, the table also includes the percentages of subjects who mentioned two other issues relevant to the social welfare concentration of the experiment, poverty and race, as well as the percentages for the other two most commonly mentioned issues, education and war. Among Black subjects, only one condition produced a significant change in the importance of any issue. Consistent with expectations about the negative coding of the inner city cue, Blacks in the inner city condition were almost twice as likely to mention crime as an important issue (37% did so) as those in the control group (19%). Thus, in the only condition meant to activate racial thinking about the food stamps program that completely failed to do so among Blacks, there is some evidence to suggest that Black subjects were more likely to be thinking about negative, criminal representations of their racial

Table 5.7   Issue importance by experimental condition

	Crime		Race		Poverty		Education		War	
	Black	White	Black	White	Black	White	Black	White	Black	White
African Americans	21	**20**	44	17	56	31	26	**29**	24	23
Inner-city Americans	**37**	**24**	27	9	37	**35**	20	24	23	32
Poor Americans	15	3	24	18	44	26	15	15	21	26
Working Americans	23	3	29	11	52	29	19	23	35	43
Control	19	2	31	13	41	18	16	13	38	32

Note: Cell entries are the percentage of subjects in that condition who mentioned the issue as one of the three most important issues facing the country today. Bolded results indicate a statically significant ($p < .05$, one-tailed t-test) difference from the control condition.

group. In comparison, Whites also worried significantly more about crime when exposed to the implicitly racial inner city cue (24%) than in the control condition (2%). This is consistent with the increased role of negative attitudes about Blacks in the formation of Whites' opinions about food stamp spending in the inner city condition. Whites were also more likely to say that crime was an important issue in the explicit racial cue condition (20%).

While the importance ratings are suggestive of a role for the activation of negative or marginal representations of Blacks in moderating the effect of the inner city cue's ability to activate racial thinking about food stamps, they do not directly test the hypothesis. It is also unclear from the importance ratings that such a moderating effect can explain why the implicit cues in the poor Americans condition were less effective than the explicit cues in linking racial group interest to increased support for spending on food stamps. Crime, after all, was not more likely to be mentioned by Blacks in the poor Americans condition. In order to test the moderating hypothesis, I model support for increased spending on food stamps among Blacks as a function of their racial group identification and their ratings of the importance of crime, including the interactions of those two attitudes across each condition. That is, the model includes the three-way interactions between racial group identification, crime importance, and condition. I estimate the model using OLS regression. The moderating hypothesis predicts that the coefficients on the three-way interactions for the two implicit racial conditions should be negative and significant; Blacks who become more concerned about crime in response to the implicit cues should be rejecting the cues' attempts to link racial group identification with support for social welfare programs, including food stamps.

Indeed, the results are consistent with the moderating hypothesis. As shown in Table 5.8, the only conditions in which the three-way interaction coefficients are statistically significant are the two implicit cue conditions. These negative interaction coefficients indicate that when Blacks became more concerned about crime in response to the implicit cues, the connection between higher levels of group identification and increased support for spending on food stamps was attenuated.

To ease interpretation of the implications of the moderating effect, Figure 5.1 graphically displays mean levels of support for increased spending on food stamps among Blacks across the experimental conditions, with subjects broken into groups defined by high and low levels of racial group identification and levels of concern about crime. The top left cell of the figure demonstrates that within the explicit race cue condition, blacks with higher levels of group identification expressed more support for increased spending on food stamps than those with low levels, regardless of their concerns about crime. This simple pattern, expected if subjects are using the cue of group interest in the food stamps program consistently to attach their racial group identification to their opinions about the program, is not replicated in any of the other cells. Blacks in the nonracial working Americans condition—displayed in the bottom-right cell of the figure—which should not have activated concerns about crime nor group identification, behave accordingly by exhibiting no significant differences in the mean support for food stamps spending.[6]

The graphs of Blacks' support for food stamp spending in the two implicit racial conditions tell the more complicated story of the moderating effects of activated concerns about crime. In the top-right cell, the graph illustrates that among Blacks exposed to the inner city cue, those with higher levels of group identification who were concerned about crime seemed particularly likely to distance themselves from the concerns of inner city families; they expressed lower levels of support for food stamp spending than all the other subjects in the condition. The bottom-left cell of Figure 5.1 highlights that for those in the poor Americans condition; concerns about crime also changed the relationship between group identification and support for spending on food stamps. Among those unconcerned about crime, Blacks more highly identified with the racial group were, as in the explicit racial cue condition, more supportive of the program. For those who felt crime was an especially important issue, however, stronger group identifiers were less supportive. Implicit racial cues, it seems, can do the same work on Black opinion as explicit racial cues, but only to the extent that they do not simultaneously

Table 5.8 The effect of crime importance and Black in-group identification on Black support for increased spending on food stamps

Experimental conditions	
African Americans	−.37*
	(.18)
Inner-city Americans	−.38*
	(.21)
Poor Americans	−.42*
	(.18)
Working Americans	−.03
	(.22)
Attitudes	
In-group identification	−.18
	(.16)
Importance of crime	−.39
	(.29)
In-group closeness x importance of crime	.55
	(.51)
Interactions	
African Americans condition X	
In-group identification	.58*
	(.23)
Importance of crime	.38
	(.37)
In-group closeness x importance of crime	−.53
	(.59)
Inner-city Americans Condition X	
In-group identification	.42
	(.27)
Importance of crime	.96*
	(.44)
In-group closeness x importance of crime	−1.44*
	(.65)
Poor Americans Condition X	
In-group identification	.50*
	(.23)
Importance of crime	1.35*
	(.76)
In-group closeness x importance of crime	−1.70*
	(.95)
Working Americans Condition X	
In-group identification	.07
	(.28)
Importance of crime	−.03
	(.41)
In-group closeness x importance of crime	.11
	(.64)

(*Continued*)

Table 5.8   continued

Constant	1.01*
	(.18)
N	161
Adj-R²	.09

Note: *p<.05 one-tailed test of significance. Entries are OLS regression coefficients and standard errors. Each model also includes controls for being a student, income, party identification, and gender.

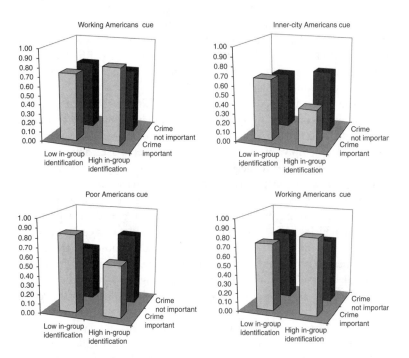

Figure 5.1   Black support for food stamps by in-group identification and crime importance by condition.

activate Blacks' concerns about negative representations or marginal elements of the Black community.

CONCLUSION

This study has sought to clarify the role of race in shaping American public opinion by detailing and testing a theoretical account of when and how Blacks' racial attitudes become attached to ostensibly nonracial issues. Contrary to accounts that would suggest racial group identification is the consistent central organizing principle of Black political opinion, the results of the study suggest that the attachment of Blacks' racial predispositions to ostensibly nonracial issues is malleable, and that racialized context can play an important role in defining the racial implications of politics for Black Americans. Additionally, the results support the argument that implicit and explicit racial messages play different roles in activating Blacks' racial group identification and Whites' racial group resentment. While racial cues are only effective in activating Whites' racial attitudes on ostensibly nonracial issues when they are implicit, the same is not true for Blacks. Explicit racial cues successfully activated Blacks' in-group identification across two very different ostensibly nonracial issues, while implicit racial cues did not reliably activate racial thinking among Blacks.

Yet the differences between Blacks' and Whites' responses to explicit and implicit racial cues imply a degree of similarity across the two racial groups: the effect of racially coded political communication for both is moderated by ambivalence. For Whites, as others have shown, tension arises when they have to negotiate between attitudes of egalitarianism and those of racial conservatism. The root of Blacks' ambivalence, however, centers on tension in the definition of whose interests belong on the Black agenda. Connecting Blacks' in-group attitudes and their positions on public policies hinges on a tension between belief in a common racial group interest and negative representations of some subsets of the group. Thus, when an issue is linked to a marginalized subset of the in-group, the role of Black group identification in determining support for that issue is attenuated; the issue, despite implication of its racial meaning, is treated as beyond the "boundaries of Blackness."

Finding that the effect of racial cues on Blacks' policy positions is moderated by ambivalence when those cues make particular representations of the racial group salient raises several important questions for future research. First are questions about the work of subgroup specific cues. In the context of the racial politics of Black and White, the expectation for Whites is that implicit racial cues activate negative attitudes about the out-group. Yet this expectation is predicated on the notion that attitudes about differences between the in-group and the out-group are generally negative. The question remains whether it might be possible with subgroup specific cues to tap positive attitudes about the out-group—whether some particular portrayal of Blackness could resolve the tension between egalitarianism and racialized thinking for Whites. Moreover, while conflicting attitudes about the in-group did the moderating work among Blacks, the question remains whether conflicting attitudes about the out-group could do that same work. That is, outside of the realm of racial politics, where a political discourse that has highlighted the tension between out-group resentment and the norm of equality provides the limit on anti–out-group politics, are subgroup-specific cues possible sources of ambivalence that might moderate the effectiveness of out-group–based politics?

Finally, although the findings presented in this paper demonstrated when race matters and when it doesn't for African Americans' thinking about ostensibly nonracial issues, it also highlighted how much more there is to know about the roles race plays in Blacks' political decision-making. Most centrally, it opened questions about when and how race matters for issues that offer a more universal benefit to the Black community, such as affirmative action or reparations for slavery. With such inherently racialized issues, we might expect that race would be a chronically salient feature of Blacks' political thinking. Yet if issue frames characterized such policies as benefiting only certain marginal subsets of the Black population, could the broader in-group meaning of the policy be deactivated? The results presented in this paper would suggest that this might be possible, but that the effectiveness of such framing might hinge on whether these issues really could be discussed without explicit references to race. While there are limitations on identity politics among Black Americans, group identification is easily invoked when politics take on any explicit tension between Black and White.

APPENDIX A: QUESTION WORDING

SUPPORT FOR THE WAR IN IRAQ

Iq1. Do you favor or oppose having U.S. forces take military action against Iraq? Those who favor the use of military action against Iraq are at point 1 and those who oppose the use of military force are at point 7 and, of course, some other people have opinions somewhere in between at points 2, 3, 4, 5 or 6. Where would you place yourself on this scale?

Iq2. Do you favor or oppose having U.S. forces (including U.S. ground forces) take military action against Iraq?

Iq3. What do you think is more important—for the United States to move quickly against Iraq, even if that means acting without international support; or for the United States to gain international support, even if that delays action against Iraq?

All items were recoded to range from 0 to 1 with 1 equaling greater support for the use of military force. The items were then additively scaled.

(Blacks: Mean=.24; Standard deviation=.23; Cronbach's *alpha*=.69)
(Whites: Mean=.34; Standard deviation=.24; Cronbach's *alpha*=.81)

SUPPORT FOR INCREASED SPENDING ON FOOD STAMPS

Fs1. Do you think that federal spending on Food Stamps should be increased, decreased, or kept about the same?

Fs1a. Do you think that federal spending on Food Stamps should be increased/decreased greatly or just a little? 1=Increased greatly, .75=Increased a little, .5=Kept about the same, .25=Decreased a little, 0=Decreased greatly

(Blacks: Mean=.69; Standard deviation=.29)
(Whites: Mean=.47; Standard deviation=.29)

IN-GROUP IDENTIFICATION

Do you think that what happens generally to Black/White people in this country will have something to do with what happens in your life? 1=a lot, .66=something, .25=not very much, 0= nothing at all. Blacks were asked about Blacks and Whites were asked about Whites.

Iraq War Experiment
(Blacks: Mean=.75; Standard deviation=.34)
(Whites: Mean=.74; Standard deviation=.29)

Food Stamps Experiment
(Blacks: Mean=.70; Standard deviation=.33)
(Whites: Mean=.72; Standard deviation=.30)

The wording of this measure is identical to the measure of linked fate used by Dawson (1994). Although this measure was originally designed to measure Blacks' closeness to their racial group (Dawson 1994) other researchers have similarly tailored such measures to capture Whites' closeness to their racial group (Kinder and Winter 2001).

OUT-GROUP RESENTMENT

In the Iraq War experiment, out-group resentment was measured by the reverse coding of the White/Black feeling thermometer. Blacks were asked how they felt about Whites and Whites were asked how they felt about Blacks. The thermometer scores were then coded so that 1=Cold and 0=Warm.

(Blacks: Mean=.35; Standard deviation=.35)
(Whites: Mean=.29; Standard deviation=.23)

In the food stamps experiment, out-group resentment is measured by the respondents' willingness to make stereotypical attributions to the racial out-group. Subjects were asked to rate on a seven-point scale how well the words hardworking, intelligent, and lazy described either Blacks or Whites as a group. The responses to each of these questions was measured on a seven-point scale and coded to run from 0 to 1 where high values represented negative responses. The items were then additively scaled.

(Blacks: Mean=.59; Standard deviation=.27; Cronbach's *alpha*=.48)
(Whites: Mean=.56; Standard deviation=.21; Cronbach's *alpha*=.54)

IDEOLOGY

Ideology is measured by the following question: We hear a lot of talk these days about liberals and conservatives. On a 7-point scale, where 1 is very liberal and 7 is very conservative, where would you place yourself on this scale, or haven't you thought much about this? For this analysis, this variable was recoded to run from 0 to 1 with 1 representing a very conservative self-placement.

Iraq War Experiment
(Blacks: Mean=.50; Standard deviation=.29)
(Whites: Mean=.44; Standard deviation=.25)

Food Stamps Experiment
(Blacks: Mean=.53; Standard deviation=.27)
(Whites: Mean=.51; Standard deviation=.24)

DOVE/HAWK

Dove/Hawk dispositions were measured by a single item which asked: Which do you think is a better way for us to keep the peace—by having a very strong military so that other countries won't attack us, or by working out our disagreements at the bargaining table? (1=Bargaining Table, 0=Strong Military).

(Blacks: Mean=.66; Standard deviation=.47)
(Whites: Mean=.77; Standard deviation=.42)

INDIVIDUALISM

Ind1. What do you think makes most poor people poor? Most of them are poor because ... 0=They don't get the training and education they need. 1= They don't try hard enough.

Ind2. Do you agree or disagree with the following statement: Most people on public assistance could get by without it if they really tried.

(Blacks: Mean=.40; Standard deviation=.29; Cronbach's *alpha*=.23)
(Whites: Mean=.39; Standard deviation=.29; Cronbach's *alpha*=.51)

EQUALITY

Eq1. Do you agree or disagree with the following statement: Our society should do whatever is necessary to make sure that everyone has an equal opportunity to succeed.

Eq2. If people were treated more equally in this country we would have many fewer problems.

(Blacks: Mean=.85; Standard deviation=.19; Cronbach's *alpha*=.51)
(Whites: Mean=.69; Standard deviation=.24; Cronbach's *alpha*=.56)

FEELINGS TOWARD THE POOR

Poor People feeling Thermometer—0=Cold, 1=Warm

(Blacks: Mean=.71; Standard deviation=.24)
(Whites: Mean=.58; Standard deviation=.19)

Acknowledgment: This chapter was originally published in the *American Political Science Review* 101 (2):339–54. Copyright © 2007 by the American Political Science Association. Reprinted with the Permission of Cambridge University Press.

Chapter 6

One of Our Own: Black Female Candidates and the Voters Who Support Them

Tasha S. Philpot and Hanes Walton, Jr.

While the number of African-American elected officials has increased over the last four decades, Blacks remain underrepresented at all levels of government. Even more striking is the relatively small number of Black women who achieve electoral success in the contemporary political arena. For instance, Black women make up less than 3 percent of U.S. Representatives and there are no Black women in the U.S. Senate (CAWP 2005). Why are there so few Black female elected officials? Does race or gender help or hinder the electoral prospects for Black female candidates? These questions remain largely unanswered. While scholars have examined race (Reeves 1997; Sigelman et al. 1995; Terkildsen 1993; Citrin et al. 1990) and gender (Sanbonmatsu 2002; Sapiro and Conover 1997; Zipp and Plutzer 1985; Kahn 1996) as moderating variables that determine a candidate's electoral success, few have examined the intersection of the two.

We attempt to address this omission by examining who are the likely supporters of Black female candidates. While there is evidence to suggest that both Blacks and women experience structural barriers while running for public office, we are primarily interested in understanding what happens once Black women appear on the ballot. In doing so, we hope to illuminate some of the factors that help explain the relatively few Black female elected officials. Similar to previous studies, we argue that, inasmuch as Blacks vote along racial lines, African-American voters will be more likely to support Black female candidates. In contrast, since gender consciousness is more tenuous, gender will not predict support for a Black female candidate. Finally, we argue that gender and race interact to create a separate consciousness whereby race trumps gender but the intersection of the two trumps both. In other words, we argue that Black women candidates find their greatest support among Black women voters.

In what follows, we discuss the literature on voting for Black and female candidates. We then bridge these two literatures to discuss the unique position of Black female voters and candidates. Finally, we test our hypotheses using national survey data, experimental data, and local aggregate election data. This study contributes to our understanding of electoral politics in two important ways. First, we demonstrate that candidates belonging to two marginalized groups need not be doubly disadvantaged. Second, we demonstrate that voters do not necessarily use one identity at the expense of the other when making political decisions. Rather, multiple identities can interact to create a separate single identity that can be used to evaluate candidates.

THE CASE OF THE AFRICAN-AMERICAN CANDIDATE

Since the passage of the Voting Rights Act in 1965, the United States has seen an increase in the number of Black elected officials. Nevertheless, "although blacks constitute 11% of the nation's voting-age population, less than 2% of all elected officials in the nation are black" (Barker et al. 1999, 291). Historically, more than 11,000 people have served in Congress. Yet, just over 100 of them have been Black (Walton and Smith 2003, 169). Although African-American representation in public office is greater at the state and local levels of government, Blacks still remain underrepresented.

The relatively few African-American elected officials can be attributed, in part, to the difficulty these candidates face getting elected. First, scholars have found a relative reluctance among White voters to vote for Black candidates (Reeves 1997; Terkildsen 1993; Williams 1989). For instance, Williams (1989) found that although Whites report a willingness to vote for a qualified Black candidate, they were far more likely to believe that a White candidate would be more effective and more qualified than a Black candidate. Similarly, Reeves (1997) also found that racially conservative, less educated, male, and older White voters are less likely to vote for Black candidates, especially in a racially charged election. Some recent evidence suggests party may mitigate the effects of race. Using exit poll data from U.S. House elections, Highton found that there was "little support for the hypothesis that white voters discriminate against black candidates in House elections" (Highton 2004, 11). White voters were no less likely to vote for the Democratic candidate when he or she was Black than they were if the candidate was White. The same held true for Black Republican candidates. Of course, this data can only capture those opinions of voters that showed up at the polls. There is reason to suggest that discrimination may be masked by an unwillingness to participate. For instance, Gay finds that "the election of African Americans to Congress is accompanied by a lower level of political engagement among whites" (Gay 2001, 589). If this is the case, reluctance to vote for a Black candidate would not appear in vote choice but in the decision to vote at all.

That is not to say that all Whites are unwilling to vote for Black candidates. The electoral success of J.C. Watts (R-OK), Alan Wheat (D-MO), Cynthia McKinney (D-GA), and Sanford Bishop (D-GA) demonstrates that Black candidates can win congressional elections in majority White districts. In addition, there have been a number of Black mayors (e.g. David Dinkins, Ron Kirk, and Tom Bradley) elected in predominantly White cities (Barker et al. 1999).

Regardless of support from White voters, African-American candidates typically rely on overwhelming support from Black voters to get elected. For instance, Adler discusses the electoral prospects of Black mayors. He argues that "to win at the ballot box African-American candidates needed virtually unanimous support from African-American voters; these mayors typically captured more than 90 percent of the votes cast by African Americans" (2001, 12).

Along these lines, it is generally understood that Black voters support Black candidates. To be sure, ideology and viability of the candidate matter (Tate 2003). Nevertheless, a growing body of literature has been devoted to examining the impact of district composition on electoral prospects of Black candidates (Swain 1993; Canon 1999), the impact of Black candidates on Black turnout (Gay 2001) and Blacks' evaluations and orientations toward government as a consequence of being represented by an African American (Tate 2003; Bobo and Gilliam Jr. 1990; Fenno 2003). For instance, using the 1987 General Social Survey, Bobo and Gilliam find that Black participation increases in cities with Black mayors. Moreover, African-American participation rates in these cities exceed that of Whites (Bobo and Gilliam Jr. 1990).

For the most part, these studies assume that Black voters vote for Black candidates. Ironically, few studies have been devoted to examining

Black-vote choice at the individual level. One exception is Tate's examination of support for Jesse Jackson in 1984 and 1988. She found that Blacks in the 1984 National Black Election Study (NBES) gave Jackson, on average, a feeling thermometer score of 74. In contrast, Whites in the 1984 American National Election Study rated Jackson at 40 on the same scale. It comes as no surprise then that 57 percent of the NBES sample indicated they supported Jackson in the Democratic presidential primary, compared to 27 percent for Mondale (Tate 1993).

Black voting behavior, especially as it relates to support for Black candidates, is thought to be a function of a sense of group identification. In general, scholars argue that "people identifying with various groups do bring different perspectives to bear on the political world, perspectives that focus more heavily on those issues most explicitly linked to each group's economic and social interests" (Conover 1984, 774). Consequently, research has found that Blacks in particular use what happens to the group as a proxy for individual self-interests (Dawson 1994; Gurin et al. 1989; Tate 1993). The higher one's level of group consciousness, the more likely he or she is to vote for a Black candidate or support policies designed to ameliorate racial inequality. Although it was once predicted that group consciousness would dissipate as Blacks experience greater social and economic heterogeneity (Wilson 1978), Black group consciousness remains high (McClerking 2001; Dawson 1994). Thus, it is likely that Blacks will continue to overwhelmingly support Black (Democratic) candidates.

To sum, Black candidates receive the greatest support from Black voters. There is also evidence to suggest that Black candidates can also gain the support of White voters. White support, however, is highly contingent on racial attitudes and overall perceptions of African Americans. As a result, Black support for Black candidates exceeds White support. The boundaries of this claim, however, will be explored shortly.

THE CASE OF THE FEMALE CANDIDATE

Women constitute just over half of the American electorate, yet the percentage of elected officials who are female is nowhere near 50 percent. Duerst-Lahti and Verstegen (1995) argue that "when we look at the proportions of women holding public-leadership posts over time, women have in fact not been literally present beyond occasional tokens" (215). Over the past decade, however, there has been an increase in the number of women officeholders. Before the 1992 elections, women constituted only 5 percent of the U.S. Congress. As Duerst-Lahti and Verstegen note, the 1992 elections resulted in the doubling of this proportion, which "by far [was] the biggest single expansion of the number of women in Congress, especially, in the Senate" (1995, 221). Still, the proportion of women serving in public office lags behind their proportion in the general electorate.

Some scholars have attributed the lack of female political elites to the relative reluctance on the part of women to run for public office. Like African-American candidates, however, there is also a relative reluctance to support female candidates. Female voters (and voters more generally) perceive women candidates and legislators to be especially responsive to woman's issues like child care and women's rights (Kahn 1996; Sanbonmatsu 2002; Huddy and Terkildsen 1993b). As a result, women have a greater propensity to support female candidates, all else being equal (Sanbonmatsu 2002). In most elections, however, all else is not equal. Thus, the results of several decades' worth of studies examining the electoral prospects of female candidates are inconclusive. Support for female candidates can be contingent on issue salience (Paolino 1995), the particular office sought (Huddy and Terkildsen 1993a), and individual candidate characteristics (Ekstrand and Eckert 1981). Voter partisanship and the extent to which the female candidates are identified as supporting women's issues also affects vote choice (Zipp and Plutzer 1985).

Support for female candidates is also influenced by the electoral context. Duerst-Lahti and Verstegen point to the "Year of the Woman" as an illustration of the catalyzing effect of female candidates. The "Year of the Woman" marks the 1992 election in which "women stepped forward to run [for elected office] in record numbers and were supported by record numbers of women" (Duerst-Lahti and Verstegen 1995, 221). Using the 1992 American National Election Study, Sapiro and Conover examine the extent to which gender mattered in the 1992 elections. They found that "women were more attentive to election news in [gender-mixed elections] than in all-male contexts" (1997, 507). Contrary to their expectations, Sapiro and Conover also found that "the mobilizing impact of female candidates was especially strong for women who [did] not especially identify with feminism" (ibid). Likewise, Zipp and Plutzer found that "sex is related to voting for a female candidate primarily among self-identified Independents in races in which the woman is identified as supporting issues which are important to women" (1985, 194). However, they found that "strong female candidates can attract the crossover votes of both men and women, while weaker ones can lose the votes of men and women" (ibid).

Finally, support for female candidates is contingent on the race of the voter. Sigelman and Welch found that "white men are about as likely as white women to support female candidates" (1984, 473). They also found that Black women were more supportive of female candidates than

Black men, with Black women being the most supportive of both sexes and races.

Again, there is mixed evidence supporting the notion that men and women support female candidates at different levels. Despite the prevalence of a gender gap—a small, but persistent difference between men and women in support for parties, candidates, and issues (Frankovic 1982; Wirls 1986; Norrander 1999a, 1999b; Kaufmann 2004; Hutchings et al. 2004; Kaufmann and Petrocik 1999)—women are not necessarily predisposed to support female candidates. Perhaps this is because gender consciousness does not exist to the extent that African-American consciousness does (Gurin 1985). While group identification is positively correlated with support for "women's issues" overall levels of group identity are not particularly high (Conover 1988). One explanation is that:

> [T]he structure of relations between men and women profoundly inhibits the development of group consciousness among women. Specifically, the frequent and intimate interaction that typically occurs between men and women interferes with women's development of a sense of solidarity and their recognition of group deprivation. Thus the extent and intensity of group consciousness among women is less than for some other groups (such as racial minorities)
>
> Conover 1988, 67

Nevertheless, in almost every instance where there is a gender gap in support for female candidates, it is because there is a marginal preference among female voters for women seeking elected office.

THE CASE OF THE BLACK FEMALE CANDIDATE

As Mansbridge and Tate argue, "Race and gender are intimately intertwined in the lives of Black women in the United States. Race constructs the way Black women experience gender; gender constructs the way Black women experience race" (1992, 488). Historically, Black women have found themselves marginalized by both the Black and the female struggle for equality (King 1975). For instance, during the fight for universal suffrage, Black women often found themselves torn between racist White women and sexist Black men (hooks 1981). Around the time of the passage of the Fifteenth Amendment, White women campaigned to have their right to vote granted before that of Black men, citing the inherent inferiority of Blacks (Walton and Smith 2003). As a result, "African American women were pushed to the periphery of any discussions, or were acknowledged only nominally, despite the fact that they existed as persons who were both female and black" (Locke 1997, 384). Black women also found themselves outside of the mainstream during both the Civil Rights Movement and the women's movement of the 1960s and 70s. The male leadership of civil rights organizations such as the Student Nonviolent Coordinating Committee and the Black Panthers believed that issues specific to Black women should come second, if at all, to issues of the race more generally (Gay and Tate 1998; Anderson-Bricker 1999; Perkins 1999). Likewise, throughout the women's movement, Black women often found themselves in separate feminist organizations from White women. Black feminists criticized their White counterparts for neglecting issues of both race and class (Roth 1999).

Because they are "doubly bound," it is reasonable to posit that Black women have developed a Black female consciousness, separate from that of Black men and White women. Limited support for this claim is evident when examining Black women's orientation toward politics.[1] Still, scholars have found that Black women differ from both Black men and White women in terms of their levels of political participation (Baxter and Lansing 1983; Burns et al. 2001). Further, Gay and Tate (1998) found that Black women who were both gender- and race-identifiers evaluated Black leaders and political events differently than their low-identified counterparts. Interestingly, Gay and Tate's study does not include analyses of gender differences across racial lines. Inasmuch as a joint race and gender consciousness is more likely to occur among Black women, however, there is reason to suspect that Black women's evaluations would also differ from that of White women and men of both races.

We argue that Black women also differ in terms of their support for candidates, particularly Black female candidates. First, it is important to note that Black female elected officials are a relatively new feature of the political landscape. It was not until 1968 that the first Black woman, Shirley Chisholm, was elected to Congress. "Prior to the late 1960s the only period of widespread black involvement in politics was the period of Reconstruction in the South when women were still denied the franchise. Black women, therefore, did not experience with black men this brief stint of voting and officeholding, which was mostly restricted to the South" (Prestage 1977, 401).

Nevertheless, there has been an upward trend in the number of Black female elected officials. According to a report issued by the Joint Center for Political and Economic Studies, the net increase in the number of Black elected officials (BEOs) between 1999 and 2000 were all women. In general, the number of Black female elected officials "has risen from

160 in 1970 (then 10.9 percent of all BEOs) to a record number of 3,119 in 2000 (34.5 percent)" (Bositis 2000, 9). The proportion of female BEOs is relatively constant across levels of government, with the exception of the county level where the number of Black female elected officials is substantially lower (Bositis 2000). Even so, Black women, who constitute slightly less than 7 percent of the U.S. population, remain underrepresented. For instance, in 2005, Black women held less than 1 percent of statewide elective executive offices. In contrast, White women held approximately 24 percent of these positions. Likewise, only 3 percent of state legislators are Black women, compared to White women who constitute 18 percent of state legislators. Note, however, that Black women have been fairing better than Latina and Asian-American elected officials who are women at both the state and national level (CAWP 2005). According to the Center for American Women and Politics, seven Latinas currently serve in the U.S. House of Representatives, three hold statewide elective execute offices and 69 serve in state legislatures. Moreover, only 24 Asian-American women serve as state legislators, one is a member of Congress, and none hold statewide elective execute offices (CAWP 2005). Regardless of color, there is room for improvement when it comes to female elected officials in general.

As a result of their few numbers, very little empirical work has been done on Black female elected officials. What exists is mostly speculation about how Black female candidates will fare given the examples provided by Black candidates and female candidates and the general treatment of Black women in the larger society. Scholars, however, disagree over the extent to which Black female candidates receive more than their fair share of opposition from voters. Some argue that Black female candidates face both sexual and racial discrimination, making it even more difficult for them to be elected than Black men and White women (Bryce and Warrick 1977; King 1975; Anderson-Bricker 1999). In contrast, Tate argues that Black women, relative to White women, are better able to mobilize voters along both racial and gender lines. She speculates, however, that Black female candidates are more likely to find their support from other Blacks. Similar to the arguments posited earlier, she contends that "the 'women's vote' in contrast to the 'Black vote' has historically been far more elusive because women, for a variety of reasons, are less likely than Blacks to vote as a bloc" (Tate 2003, 64). Thus, she concludes that Black women, like all women, cannot necessarily count on the female vote.

The small amount of empirical data available tends to support Tate's argument. For instance, Clayton and Stallings (2000) use the election of Eva Clayton (D-NC) in 1992 to the United States House of Representatives as a case study. They found that Eva Clayton achieved a broad base of support from both Blacks and Whites, with African Americans being the strongest supporters.

While Clayton and Stallings provide the foundation for understanding the electoral prospects of Black female candidates, the story is not complete. Namely, we do not know the extent to which the pattern of support for Black female candidates found in their study extends beyond North Carolina's first district. Since Clayton and Stallings relied primarily on county-level data, which did not allow them to control for sex of voters, we also do not know what role gender played in the decision to support a Black female candidate. Thus, the goal of this article is to examine a variety of races featuring Black female candidates to see if a discernable pattern of support emerges based on the gender and race of voters, both at the individual and at the aggregate level.

Similar to Sigelman and Sigelman (1982), we argue that voters create a hierarchy of candidate preferences based on their own group membership. The closer a candidate resembles the voter, the more supportive of the candidate the voter will be. Applying this logic to Black female candidates, we argue that Black women will be the greatest supporters of Black women candidates, while White men will the least supportive of Black female candidates. On its face, this argument suggests that Black men and White women should be equally likely to support Black female candidates because each group shares one common identity. We argue, however, that Black men will be more supportive than White women since race consciousness tends to be stronger than gender consciousness. In other words, African Americans are more likely to see themselves as a group than women are. Therefore, there should be a greater perceived connection between Black male voters and Black female candidates along racial lines than between White female voters and Black female candidates along gender lines. More concisely stated, we hypothesize that the level of support in ascending order for Black female candidates is as follows: White male, White female, Black male, Black female.

DATA AND METHODOLOGY

We approach testing our claims about support for Black female candidates from a number of different methodological directions. Specifically, we utilize three data sources: an experiment, precinct-level election data, and exit poll data. Below is a description of each study.

The experimental component of the research design gauges reactions to a description of a fictitious campaign that was embedded within the 2005 Party Image Study, a project examining politics and political parties more generally. Participants in the 2005 Party Image Study were nonstudent subjects recruited from a number of locations, including an art fair and hotel lobbies, in Michigan and Texas. In total, 469 subjects were recruited for the experiment, including 226 Blacks and 210 Whites.[2] The mean age of the sample was 42, 62 percent of the sample was female, 58 percent of the sample was college educated, and the median income of the sample was between $40,000 and $49,999. The entire questionnaire took approximately 20 minutes to complete. Once subjects completed the study, they were given $10 in cash for their participation.

In addition to answering a number of questions about their ideology, partisanship, and issue positions, respondents were randomly assigned to read one of three paragraphs about an upcoming mayoral election featuring a Black female candidate. Each of the three paragraphs was identical except for the race and gender of the Black female candidate's opponent. Below is the exact wording of the paragraph:

> A recent poll indicates that the two front-runners in this year's nonpartisan mayoral race are City Councilmember Sharon Johnson and *businessman/businesswoman Claude/Claudine* Barker. Johnson, a 38-year-old lawyer, has served on the City Council for six years. If elected, Sharon Johnson will become the city's first, Black female mayor. Her opponent, 45-year-old *Claude/Claudine* Barker, is a relative newcomer to politics. Barker, who is a *Black male/White male/White female*, is an active member of the city's chamber of commerce and has served on its board of directors. Both candidates have indicated that tackling the city's economic problem is their number one priority. Barker's plan includes providing tax incentives to business owners interested in relocating downtown with the hopes of revitalizing the central city area. Johnson, on the other hand, advocates the creation of job training programs that would prepare workers to meet the changing needs of today's economy.

The italicized words denote the words that were manipulated across conditions. In the first condition, subjects read that the Black female candidate, Sharon Johnson, was running against Claude Barker, an African-American male. Claude Barker is a White male in the second condition. Lastly, in the third condition, Johnson's opponent is Claudine Barker, who is a White female. After reading about the campaign, subjects were then asked, "Based on what you read, if the election was held today and you had to choose between the two candidates, who would you vote for?" Responses were coded 1 if subjects chose Johnson and 0 if they indicated that they would vote for Barker. We then compared the mean level of support for Johnson among Black women, Black men, White women, and White men. In addition, we examined whether this support was contingent on the race and gender of Johnson's opponent.

The advantage of using a contrived scenario about a Black female candidate is that it allows us to control for spurious relationships that might interfere with our ability to discern the connection between race and gender in support for a candidate. In particular, these data allow us to examine support for Black female candidates when all else (including incumbency status, campaign spending, prior political experience) is held equal. Nevertheless, using experimental data limits our ability to generalize beyond this hypothetical situation. In reality, political candidates launch campaigns under a variety of circumstances. Therefore, we supplement the experimental data with data from actual elections.

To examine the electoral support for Black female candidates, we also rely on voting and registration data from the City of Atlanta. The City of Atlanta provides a unique opportunity to explore the current subject because of its unique political history and its place in the struggle for African-American political incorporation. As Affigne notes, "the city of Atlanta holds a prominent place in the history of Black America, the development of Black social thought, and the scholarly analysis of urban life in the United States. Crucial events of the nation's antebellum economic development, Civil War, Reconstruction, Civil Rights Movement, and post–civil-rights Black political emergence all occurred in Georgia's largest and most important city" (Affigne 1997, 71). Atlanta also has a long history of electing and reelecting Black mayors (Philpot and Walton 2005). In recent years, it has also witnessed the entry of Black females into its mayoral elections and elected its first female mayor in 2001. Finally, Atlanta is one of the few cities that collect registration information by gender *and* race. Thus, we are able to examine whether the level of support for a Black female candidate in a precinct was related to the race and gender of the registered voters in that precinct. The first dependent variable we examine is the change in voter turnout by precinct from 1997 to 2001. This variable was created by subtracting the percentage of registered voters that voted in 1997 from those that voted in 2001. We also examine the vote share in a precinct received by the two Black female candidates in the 2001 Atlanta mayoral contest—Shirley Franklin and Gloria Bromell-Tinubu. We include independent variables measuring the percentage of Black men, Black women, White men, and White women registered in a precinct. Because voter turnout and vote choice are continuous variables, we use ordinary least squares to estimate the models.

As is the case with aggregate data, these data do not allow us to make conclusive arguments about individual-level phenomena. Therefore, to complement the Atlanta data, we also rely on an additional individual-level data source. Specifically, we utilize 1996 and 1998 exit poll data collected by the Voter News Service to examine vote choice during two electoral cycles. These two studies were chosen because, combined, they feature a relatively large number of respondents, including large subsamples of African Americans. Further, both polls included the state and congressional district number for each respondent, enabling us to add information about the race and gender of the candidates for which respondents voted.[3] Lastly, these data are drawn from a national sample, enabling us to generalize beyond a particular region within the United States.

Using this information, we examined support for a Black female candidate given the race and gender of the voter.[4] Here, the dependent variable represents a reported vote for a Black female candidate in a U.S. House race. Responses were coded 1 if the respondent voted for a Black female and 0 if the respondent did not.

Our primary independent variables are the race and gender of the respondents. First, the variable Black was coded 1 if the respondent was African American and 0 if the respondent was White. We also included a dummy variable for the sex of the respondent, coded 1 for female and 0 for male. Finally, we included the interaction between the two in order to test the hypothesis that Black women were more likely to support a Black female candidate. This variable was coded 1 if the respondent was a Black female and 0 if otherwise.

To control for contextual factors related to each House race, we include dummy variables for whether the Black female candidate was an incumbent (1) or nonincumbent (0), whether she faced an opponent that was a Black male (1) or non-Black male (0), a White female (1) or non-White female (0), and whether she held elected office prior to running for Congress (1) or was a political novice (0). We also control for the region of the race. Included is a dummy variable, coded 1 for South and 0 for non-South. Because we combine exit poll data from two separate elections, we also include a variable for whether the race occurred during a midterm election (1) or during a presidential election year (0). Finally, we include a party match variable that indicates when a respondent and a candidate have the same party identification (1) and when their party identifications differ from one another (0).

To account for other differences among voters, we control for a number of background characteristics and political predispositions. Specifically, we include measures of the respondents' age, income, and whether the respondent received a college degree. We also include the respondents' self-reported ideology, coded 1 if the respondent was liberal, .5 if the respondent was a moderate, and 0 if the respondent was conservative. Similarly, we coded respondents' party identification 1 if they were Democrats, .5 if they were independents, and 0 if they were Republicans. Finally, because the dependent variable was dichotomous, we estimated the model using logistic regression.

ANALYSES

Looking first at the experimental data in Table 6.1, we find that Black women tend to be the biggest supporters of Black female candidates. Regardless of whom her opponent was, Black women overwhelmingly supported Johnson, the fictitious Black female candidate. This support ran from 78 percent when Johnson's opponent was a Black male to 85 percent when her opponent was a White male. Black males also supported Johnson at similar levels, although their support was contingent on her opponent. When Johnson's opponent Barker was described as a Black male, only 60 percent of Black men preferred Johnson over Barker. The difference between Black men and Black women's support for Johnson in this condition was statistically significant. The gap between levels of support for a Black female candidate among Black men and Black women disappears when Johnson's opponent is White. Over 80 percent of both groups support Johnson when she faces a White opponent, regardless of whether the opponent is a White male or White female.

In contrast, White respondents supported Johnson at much lower rates than their Black counterparts. When White women read about Johnson running against a Black male candidate, their mean level of support for Johnson was 67 percent. Although this constituted a 17-percentage point difference from Black women's support for Johnson, this difference was not statistically significant. In the treatment group where the Black

Table 6.1   Mean support for the Black female candidate

	Black Females	Black Males	White Females	White Males
Black female vs. Black male	78	60**	67	61*
Black female vs. White male	85	81	68**	62**
Black female vs. White female	82	84	63**	53**

Note: Values are mean levels of support for Johnson (Black female candidate) over her opponent. Difference-of-means tests were conducted by comparing Black female subjects' responses to the responses of other groups. Starred values indicate statistically significant differences.

** p < .05, * p < .10.

Source: 2005 Party Image Study.

female candidate is challenging a White male candidate, 68 percent of White female respondents preferred Johnson over Barker. Similarly, support for Johnson was 63 percent among White women when Johnson faced a White female candidate. The differences between Black female respondents and White female respondents in these conditions were statistically significant. When White male subjects read about the contrived election, their support for the Black female candidate is 61 percent when Johnson runs against a Black male and 62 percent when Johnson's opponent is a White male. These levels of support are significantly different from that of Black women. White male support for Johnson, however, is lowest when the Black female candidate faces a White female candidate. The percentage of White men that prefer Johnson over Barker drops to 53 percent. The almost 30 percentage point difference between Black women and White men in this condition is statistically significant.[5]

Looking next at the Atlanta data, Table 6.2 presents the election returns for the 2001 Atlanta mayoral election. Shirley Franklin, who previously served as a city administrator during the Andrew Young and Maynard Jackson Administrations, received just under half of the votes cast. Her strongest competitor, Robert Pitts, a Black male and a long-time city council member received roughly 33 percent of the vote. Newspaper accounts of the election attributed Franklin's success, in part, to a well-organized and well-funded campaign. Reportedly, Franklin "raised more money than any other female candidate for public office in Georgia's history" (Chunn 2001). Shirley Franklin's campaign received donations from Quincy Jones, Vernon Jordan, Bill Richardson, and Ed Rendell (Miller and Judd 2001). At the local level, Franklin's campaign disclosure report revealed that just under half of her individual contributors were women and that she received substantial support from people of all races (Chunn 2001).

Gloria Bromell-Tinubu, the other Black female candidate, also ran in the 1997 mayoral race. Although, Bromell-Tinubu had previously

Table 6.2   The number and percentage of votes in the 2001 Atlanta mayoral election

Candidate	Total votes	Percentage
Shirley Franklin	40,724	49.4
Robert Pitts	26,856	32.6
Gloria Bromell-Tinubu	12,970	15.7
Trudy Kitchin	295	0.4
G.B. Osborne	225	0.3

Source: Adapted from the "Fulton County Municipal General Election," City of Atlanta, November 13, 2001.

served on the Atlanta city council and Georgia's board of education, her
campaign was not as well-funded as Franklin's, and she had less political
experience than the two frontrunners in the election (Philpot and Walton
2005). A professor of economics at Spellman College, she ran a more
energetic grassroots campaign and managed to capture 12.9 percent of
the vote in 1997 and 15.7 percent in 2001, placing third in both elections. She also received campaign endorsements from the Georgia Green
Party, the Teamsters Local 528, and the Atlanta chapter of the Georgia
Women's Political Caucus (Miller 2001). Together, the Black female candidates received roughly two-thirds of the vote.[6]

But what role did race and gender play in the 2001 Atlanta mayoral
election? To answer this question, we first look at the change in voter turnout from 1997 to 2001. In general, voter turnout does increase modestly
in 2001. Looking at Table 6.3, however, we see that race did not play a
major role in the increased turnout. Turnout was not contingent on the
number of registered Black voters in a precinct. This was true regardless
of gender; there was no statistically significant relationship between the
percentage of Black female registered voters in a precinct and voter turnout
in that precinct. This is consistent with Gilliam and Kaufmann's (1998)
findings that Atlanta voter turnout, in general, increases in elections where
there is not an incumbent (as was the case in the 2001 election) and is not
necessarily a function of race. On the other hand, voter turnout in a precinct
did increase as the number of female voters in a precinct increased.

Table 6.3   Voter turnout and Black female vote share by race and sex

	Voter turnout	Black female vote share
Black voters registered (%)	.056	−.685*
	(.06)	(.14)
Female voters registered (%)	.201*	−1.604*
	(.09)	(.21)
Black female registered voters (%)	−.181	2.021*
	(.12)	(.26)
Constant	.025	1.220*
	(.04)	(.10)
R^2	.12	.70
N	141	166

Note: Coefficients are OLS estimates. Standard errors appear in parentheses.
Omitted category is the percent of White male registered voters in a precinct.
* $p < .05$.
Source: Adopted from the "Fulton County Municipal General Election," City of
Atlanta, November 13, 2001 and the "Fulton County, Georgia Count of Voters by
Precinct and District," October 2001.

With respect to vote share, the results presented in Table 6.3 suggest that Black women were the strongest supporters of the Black female candidates. The two candidates' marginal vote share increased the most when the percentage of Black female registered voters increased in a precinct. Surprisingly, support for Franklin and Bromell-Tinubu *decreased* as the percentage of White female and Black male registered voters increased in a precinct. Note that the rate of decrease was larger for White women than Black men. Nevertheless, contrary to our expectations, the Black female candidates did better in precincts with higher levels of White male registered voters than they did in precincts with higher levels of Black male or White female registered voters.

To illustrate this point, we use the Atlanta data to calculate the mean vote share of the two Black female candidates based on the racial composition of a precinct. In precincts where Black females make up the majority of the registered voters (n=89), Franklin and Bromell-Tinubu received approximately 79 percent of the vote share. In contrast, they only received an average of 54 percent of the vote in precincts where Black males comprised the majority of registered voters (n=3). Finally, in precincts where White men (n=2) and White women (n=8) comprised the majority of registered voters, Franklin and Bromell-Tinubu's vote share was 67 and 30 percent, respectively.

Finally, we examined the extent to which the pattern of support for a Black female candidate translated across contexts by exploring vote choice in the 1996 and 1998 congressional elections. Model 1 in Table 6.4 looks at support for a Black female candidate when we do not consider campaign-specific variables. Using White males as the baseline, we see similar, although not identical results. First, respondents' race mattered; African Americans were more likely to vote for a Black female candidate. Specifically, being a Black male increased the probability of voting for a Black female candidate by 8 percentage points. Similar to the Atlanta findings, being a White female decreased the likelihood of voting for a Black female candidate by 4 percentage points, although this effect was not statistically significant. Respondents that were Black and female, however, were significantly more likely to vote for a Black female candidate. There was a 10-percentage point difference between Black women and White men's probability of voting for a Black female candidate. In other words, while there was no statistically significant difference between White men and White women in the probability of voting for a Black woman running in a U.S. House election, there was a substantial difference between that of Black women and White men.[7]

Model 2 in Table 6.4 reveals that any race and gender effects completely disappear once we control for contextual factors. First, incumbency was

Table 6.4   Voting for a Black female house candidate

	Model 1	Model 2
Black	1.004**	.517
	(.31)	(.38)
Female	−.297	−.169
	(.21)	(.24)
Black * female	.765*	.445
	(.41)	(.48)
South	.588**	.010
	(.20)	(.30)
Ideology	.920**	.542*
	(.27)	(.32)
Party identification	.439*	−.130
	(.23)	(.29)
Income	−.124*	−.134*
	(.07)	(.08)
College degree	.079	.115
	(.21)	(.24)
Age	.069	.150**
	(.05)	(.06)
Mid-term election		−.065
		(.30)
Incumbent		1.042**
		(.51)
Party match		1.912**
		(.24)
Held previous office		.773*
		(.47)
Black male opponent		−1.221**
		(.31)
White female opponent		.643
		(.83)
Constant	−.857**	−1.487**
	(.39)	(.45)
N	643	643
Log-likelihood	−379.25	−299.29
Pseudo R^2	.14	.32

Note: Coefficients are logistic regression estimates. Standard errors appear in parentheses.
** p < .05, * p < .10.
Source: VNS National Exit Polls, 1996 and 1998.

a substantively large and statistically significant. Respondents were 16-percentage points more likely to vote for a Black female if she was an incumbent. This is consistent with previous research (e.g. Jacobson 1997) that demonstrates the power of incumbency status when predicting vote choice. Whereas Democrats were more likely to vote for a Black female candidate in Model 1, party identification was not a statistically significant predictor of voting for a Black female candidate in Model 2. What mattered more was that the candidate and the respondent have the same party identification; support for Black female candidates received a 10-percentage point boost when the candidate and the voters' party identification converged. Also significant was whether the Black female candidate held previous elected office prior to running for Congress. Black female candidates with prior political experience garnered a statistically significantly, although modest (2 point) increase in support from voters. Finally, the race of the candidates' opponent was a significant predictor of vote choice. Respondents' probability of voting for a Black female candidate decreased by 4 percentage points when she ran against a Black male. Having an opponent that was a White female, however, did not make a difference.[8]

In summary, the race and gender composition of the electorate matters with respect to the electoral success of a Black female candidate, although our findings come with a few caveats. In our fictitious race, Black women respondents unconditionally preferred the Black female candidate. Black men matched Black women's support for the Black female candidate so long as her opponent was not a Black male. White men and White women both supported the Black female candidate with less vigor than Blacks. Their levels of support did not appear to be contingent on gender. White men and White women's preference for the Black female candidate did not significantly differ from one another.

With respect to the Atlanta data, the Black female candidates received a greater percentage of the vote in precincts with greater numbers of Black female registered voters. Consistent with the experimental data, the percentage of Black male registered voters was negatively correlated with the Black female candidates' vote share. On average, support for Franklin and Bromell-Tinubu was lower in districts with high percentages of Black male registered voters than that of both Black female and White male registered voters. Keep in mind, that the other frontrunner in the 2001 Atlanta mayoral election was a Black male. Again, the findings suggest that Black male support for a Black female candidate is contingent on the race and gender of her opponent. Unlike the experimental data, the results of the analyses of the aggregate data also show that the Black female candidates were significantly less well-off in precincts with higher levels of White female voters, even when compared to the vote share in precincts with a greater number of White males.

Lastly, an examination of the electability of Black female U.S. House candidates sheds further light on the complex relationship between race and gender. Without taking into account any campaign-specific factors, the pattern of support found in the other two data sources holds. Black female U.S. House candidates did better among Black women. Substantively, the probability for voting for a Black female candidate was highest among this group.[9] Black men were also more likely to vote for a Black female candidate than White men or White women. Finally, as they did in the experimental and aggregate data, the results of the exit poll data reveal a lack of gender consciousness among White women— when it came to Congressional elections, White women were no more or less likely to vote for a Black female candidate than White males.

Interestingly, none of these differences matter when we control for incumbency, previous political experience, and the similarity between the candidates' and the voters' party identification. If there is an initial reluctance on the part of White voters to vote for a Black female candidate, it subsides when the candidate is an incumbent or has held public office prior to running for Congress. Also, race and gender matter less when the candidate and the voter share the same party identification.

CONCLUSION

We began this study by asking the question: Does race or gender help or hinder the electoral prospects for Black female candidates? Our answer is yes and no. First, it is important to note that when it comes to examining the electoral prospects of Black female candidates, it is difficult to disentangle the effects of race and gender. For Black women, race and gender do not operate separately from one another. By the nature of where they lie at the intersection of race and gender, Black women experience a political reality separate from that of White women and Black men. As evidence, we found that Black female candidates garner support from Black women at extremely high levels. Here, race and gender strengthened support for Black female candidates.

Beyond Black women voters, there are other ways in which race and gender operate in the electorate. The substantial difference between the level of support between Blacks and Whites suggests that race does play a significant role in the decision to vote for a Black female candidate. If we assume that the difference between Black and White voters is driven, at least in part, by Whites' relative reluctance to vote for a Black female candidate, then race does hinder the electoral prospects of Black female candidates. The findings suggest, however, that Black female candidates receive equal levels of support among Whites relative to Blacks when she has amassed a bit of political experience. Here, the background of the candidate allows her to transcend her race and gender among White voters. On the flip side, because of their race, Black females are able to mobilize Black voters, regardless of gender.

From this perspective, race helps the electoral prospects of Black female candidates, while gender plays little to no role.

Thinking more broadly, our findings have implications for the study of group politics. The foundation for understanding politics in terms of the battle over group interests was laid by the writers of our founding documents. It was argued that the incorporation of a variety interests in the political debate would temper decision making (Wills 1982). The assumption was that people have a number of overlapping interests, so much so that one group could never dominate politics. Gay and Tate describe this pluralist perspective:

> [E]ach individual bears multiple, often competing, allegiances. No one is wholly constituted as a factory worker; she is also a female, a Jew, a parent. Only a fraction of her political identity and attitudes could be expressed through union affiliation, for example. The priorities of any one group are not expected to figure prominently in her interpretations of politics. Furthermore, the argument goes, the absence of internal cohesion (a consequence of overlapping memberships) limits the effectiveness with which any group can assert its claims—countering the threat posed by the proliferation of interest group activity.
>
> Gay and Tate 1998, 171

This argument rests on the notion that, when faced with competing loyalties, individuals will try to strike a balance between the two.

In the area of Black politics, this has not been the case. Scholars, for instance, have found that race consistently factors more heavily than class in political evaluations and attitudes of African Americans (Dawson 1994; Tate 1993). That this phenomenon occurs even though Blacks experience more economic and educational heterogeneity contradicts pluralist theorists (e.g. Dahl 1961) who argue that racial/ethnic identities become less salient as groups become more assimilated. Research has also demonstrated that Black women use race at the expense of gender in their political evaluations (Gay and Tate 1998; Mansbridge and Tate 1992). Taken together, this research suggests that, rather than striking a balance between two identities, Blacks frequently use their racial identity, while neglecting other identities.

Our research, however, reveals that neither the pluralist perspective nor the Black politics perspective conveys the entire story. We argue that being a Black woman and identifying as such is not simply adding what it means to be Black to what it means to be a woman. Instead, we argue that by the nature of their status in American society, Black women have created an identity that is greater than the sum of its parts. This, in turn, guides their political decision-making whereby they evaluate candidates based on the potential benefit yielded to Black women rather than Blacks and/or women. Stated more generally as it relates to group politics, rather than choosing a political outcome that minimally satisfies both identities simultaneously or an outcome that satisfies one identity at the expense of another, individuals in some cases will choose a political outcome that maximizes the utility for those standing at the intersection of the competing identities. We provide evidence that demonstrates that Black women's evaluations of Black female candidates cannot simply be explained by their race or gender, independently of one another. As scholars continue to explore the relationships between competing groups in society, we contend that this line of thinking should be extended to other individuals that simultaneously possess overlapping and competing interests, especially where these interests are both inescapable and subordinate. This includes, but is not limited to, homosexuals who are also racial/ethnic minorities.

While the findings of the current study are enlightening, we find it necessary to point to some of the limitations of our research. First, we treat objective group membership and group attachment as interchangeable. But as Conover notes, objective group memberships is "a necessary, but not sufficient, condition for identification" (1984, 761). A more precise test of our hypotheses would examine whether the relationship between objective group membership and candidate preference is strengthened when voters exhibit higher levels of group consciousness, as well as the moderating role of racial and gender attitudes. We speculate that such analyses would serve to bolster our evidence.[10] Similar to studies examining support for Black candidates in general (e.g., Dawson 1994; Tate 1993), we hypothesize that African-American support for Black female candidates would be even higher among Blacks that exhibit a sense of linked fate with other Blacks. Likewise, Black women that identify with a Black feminist ideology would be even more likely to support Black female candidates. Finally, we expect to see an increase in support for Black female candidates among those White women with a sense of gender consciousness.

We also recognize some of the limitations with the data we use. By themselves, the experimental data, the Atlanta data and the exit poll data cannot conclusively test the hypothesized relationship between the race and gender of voters and support for Black female candidates. To be sure, the Atlanta data allow us to examine actual vote returns. Because of the nature of aggregate-level data, we cannot make individual-level inferences. While these data allow us to discern whether the characteristics of the registered voters in a precinct related to support for the Black female candidate, we do not know whether these registered voters actually cast ballots for this candidate. Moreover, the Atlanta data do not allow us to control for contextual factors related to vote choice. In contrast, the experimental data allow us to control for contextual-level factors by holding constant the background, experience, and other confounding elements related to candidate preference. They also allow us to delineate the relationship between support for a Black female candidate and the race and gender of her opponent absent any campaign spending and partisan differences. The major drawback of experimental data, however, is that they restrict the ability to generalize. Likewise, the exit poll data also allow us to control for a variety of sociodemographic and contextual factors. These data, however, rely on self-reported vote choice, rather than actual vote choice. Yet, the three data sources taken together allow us to triangulate on the true relationship between gender and race of a voter and support for a Black female candidate. That these three very different datasets yield similar patterns of support for Black women running for public office enables us to be fairly confident in the results. Moreover, examining both local and national elections allows us to speak to the generalizability of the findings.

Lastly, this study only constitutes one piece of a much larger puzzle. There are still many questions left unanswered. For instance, in addition to voters, what other obstacles do Black women face in their quests for electoral success? Are there differences in the way Black women are recruited to run for public office? Once in office, do Black women behave differently than White women or Black men? Does their gender or race or both guide their legislating? In other words, do Black women differ from others in the way they substantively represent their constituents? Already, there is evidence to suggest that Black women in state legislatures differ from Black men and White women in terms of their policy priorities (Barrett 1995). Exploring these questions further should be among the avenues pursued by scholars in the future.

Nevertheless, we believe that the current study contributes to our understanding of race, gender, and electoral politics. Often, scholars explore the impact of race and gender on candidate evaluation separately. In this study, we have demonstrated that this approach leads to a miscalculation of the effects of each. Just like the relationship between gender and candidate evaluation is contingent on race, the relationship between race and candidate evaluation is moderated by gender. Here, we have illuminated some of the nuances of these relationships.

Acknowledgment: This chapter was originally published in the *American Journal of Political Science* 51 (1):49–62. Copyright © 2007 by the Midwest Political Science Association. Reprinted with the Permission of Blackwell Publishing.

CHAPTER 7

RACE, IDENTITY, AND CANDIDATE SUPPORT: A TEST OF IMPLICIT PREFERENCE

JAS M. SULLIVAN

RACIAL IDENTITY (IN ITS VARIOUS CONCEPTIONS) has been an important explanatory variable in African-American politics. For example, with respect to policy preferences, Tate (1993) found a relationship between racial group identification and African Americans' opinions on affirmative action; Kinder and Winter (2001) found a correlation between racial group closeness and African Americans' support of social welfare programs; and White (2007) found that explicit and implicit racial verbal cues activate racial thinking about policy issues. Research has also shown a relationship between racial identity and other political orientations. Specifically, Tate (2003) found that "African American identification was significantly related to African American political interest and to voter participation in congressional elections; however, it was unrelated to political knowledge and to political efficacy" (142). Olsen (1970) and Verba and Nie (1972) found that African Americans with strong senses of racial identity or group consciousness participated at higher rates in politics. Dawson (2001) found that linked fate—believing that one's fate is connected to that of the group—is a strong predictor of economic nationalism, support for African American feminist orientations and ideology, allowance for more women to become members of the clergy, and warmth for lesbians. Thus, Dawson (1994) concluded that Black identity continues to be stronger than identities based on class, gender, religion, or any other social characteristics.

Given the explanatory power of racial group identification, it should be no surprise that group-based considerations also influence Blacks' support for political candidates (see Philpot and Walton in this volume). But whether this support is unconditional has not been fully explored. For instance, does an implicit positive preference exist among African-American voters for an African-American candidate who does not mention a race-specific policy over a White candidate who emphasizes a race-specific policy that is highly favored by African Americans? This is the question I address in this chapter. I argue that Blacks prefer coethnic candidates over White candidates, even when there is policy congruence between them and the White candidate.

THEORIES OF RACIAL IDENTITY

Racial identity is an ambiguous and socially constructed concept. It implies a "consciousness of self within a particular group" (Spencer and Markstrom-Adams 1990, 292). It refers to the "meanings a person attributes to the self as an object in a social situation or social role" (Burke 1980, 18), and it relates to a "sense of people-hood, which provides a sense of belonging" (Smith 1989, 156). While there is a level of uncertainty and confusion that renders it difficult to develop a standard definition (Herring et al. 1999; Phinney 1990), according to the symbolic interactionism theory, "racial identity is treated as one of the many identities contained within self" (White and Burke 1987, 311), and it is given fundamental and overriding importance in the United States.

Racial identity formation is produced by the everyday "interactions and challenges" (Davis and Gandy 1999, 367) that an individual encounters. It is affected by socioeconomic status and situational context (Cornell and Hartman 1998). It is "dynamic and changing over time, as people explore and make decisions about the role of race in their lives" (Phinney 1990, 502). In other words, racial identity is "achieved through an active process of decision making and self-evaluation" (Phinney 1990, 502). Thomas (1971), Cross (1971), and Banks (1981) have proposed the idea that racial identity development is a "progressional process which occurs in a hierarchical sequence from racial unconsciousness to racial pride and commitment" (Gay 1985, 49). For example, Cross's (1978) five stages to identity development include the following: preencounter, encounter, immersion-emersion, internalization, and internalization-commitment. In essence, these stages represent a process by which people come to a "deeper understanding and appreciation of their race" (Phinney 1990, 500). Even so, a deeper understanding may not translate into a greater acceptance of their racial identity; nevertheless, it has an effect on behavior.

Within this broad category of racial identity, scholars have specifically explored African-American identity and its impact on social behavior. Scholars have conceptualized African-American identity in a variety of different ways, including racial categorization (Jaret and Reitzes 1999), common fate or linked fate (Gurin et al. 1989; Dawson 1994), racial salience (Herring et al. 1999), closeness (Allen et al. 1989; Broman et al. 1988; Conover 1984), Black separatism or racial solidarity (Allen and Hatchett 1986; Allen et al. 1989), racial self-esteem (Porter and Washington 1979), Africentrism (Grills and Longshore 1996), and racial awareness and consciousness (Jackson 1987). Others suggest that African-American identity has "multiple dimensions" (Sellers et al. 1998). Consequently, several different psychometric scales have been used to tap the different dimensions of African-American identity. The psychometric scales most often employed range from one question to over sixty questions, depending on how African-American identity is conceptualized.

The purpose of this research is to add another means of assessing racial identity, particularly as it relates to candidate preference. Accordingly, I utilize Implicit Association Test (IAT) to investigate whether there exists an implicit positive preference among African Americans for an African-American candidate who does not mention race-specific policy over a White candidate who emphasizes a race policy. I expect African Americans will implicitly be more likely to prefer the African-American candidate who does not mention race policy, even though there is policy congruence between African-American respondents and the alternative White candidate who mentions support for the race policy. This expectation is based on the similarity-attraction theory discussed in the political and social psychology literature (see Brown and Lopez 2001 for a review of this research). It argues that individuals are more comfortable with others who are like themselves. According to this view, attraction is a positive function of the extent to which two individuals share beliefs about important topics. Furthermore, perceived similarity (i.e., the degree to which we believe another's characteristics are similar to ours) is often sufficient to attract us to others. For example, Byrne and Nelson (1965) asked participants to rate a stranger and varied the stranger's proportions of similar attitudes on four levels. They found a linear relationship between similar attitudes and attraction. Newcomb (1957), in a housing study on a college campus, found that similarity in background, attitudes, and values predicted friendship formation. In addition, Sigelman and Welch (1984) examined the effects of the similarity-attraction on electoral behavior and found candidate preferences of Whites were based on perceived similarities such as race and gender.

The race of the candidate conveys information about the similarity between that candidate and her prospective supporters. Instances where voters possess limited information and the cost of information is high, they make political decisions based on their previous political knowledge (for example, see Downs 1957; Stokes and Miller 1962; Tversky and Kahneman 1974; Conover and Feldman 1989). In essence, voters use political and social stereotypes to judge candidates about whom they have limited information. The major implication is the race of the candidate reflects an important cue for the voter, whether African American or White.

I expect, however, that respondents will explicitly say that they prefer the White candidate who expresses support for race policy. Why the difference in the responses on implicit versus explicit? The thought here is that respondents are not going to be honest about their preferences when asked directly on a survey. Based on previous research (Davis 1997), I expect that Blacks will find it more socially desirable to say that they have a willingness to prefer the White candidate who supports affirmative action policy (which is highly favored by African-American respondents in this study) over the African-American candidate who does not mention any race policies.

DATA AND METHODOLOGY

As mentioned earlier, I utilize an Implicit Association Test. The IAT enables researchers to assess unconscious cognitions. The IAT provides a measure of automatic associations (Greenwald, Nosek, and Banaji 2003, 197). It is an indirect measure of attitudes. The measurement is based on two properties: First, it is a measure of strength of association (Lemm and Banaji 1999). Second, the IAT is based on the assumption that it should be easier to make the same behavioral response to concepts that are strongly associated than to concepts that are weakly associated (Greenwald et al. 1998; Lemm and Banaji 1999). According to Lemm and Banaji (1999), "The underlying idea of the IAT is simple: if two concepts are associated in memory, they will be easier to associate in judgment of behavior compared to concepts that are less associated in memory" (223). The procedure for the IAT requires respondents to "identify stimulus items and categorize them into one of four superordinate categories. Association strengths are measured by comparing the speed of categorizing members of the superordinate categories in two different sorting conditions (Nosek, Greenwald, and Banaji 2005, 167). The IAT is based on a response-latency indicator obtained in the process of pairing an attitude object with specific attributes or an evaluative dimension that may not be purely evaluative. That is, "the test exposes implicit biases by detecting subtle shifts in reaction time that can occur when test takers are required to pair different set of words or faces" (Banaji, Bazerman, and Chugh 2003, 4).

In this research, the IAT is utilized to measure respondents' implicit preferences for either Mary Williams, the African-American candidate who does not mention race policy, or Yvonne Jones, the White candidate who mentions race policy. First, respondents were provided a vignette and names of the candidates. The vignette stated the following:

> Mary Williams (African American) and Yvonne Jones (White) are running for political office. If elected, Mary Williams would focus on military and economic policies. If elected, Yvonne Jones would focus on strengthening Affirmative Action in education, military, and economic policies. Mary Williams and Yvonne Jones have undergraduate and law degrees. Before entering politics, each served in the United States military and was practicing attorneys. As for political experience, Williams and Jones have both served as city councilwomen and presently, as State Senators for their respective states. Both are married and have two children.

After reading the vignette, participants in the IAT were asked to classify, as quickly as possible without making mistakes, the targets (represented by names of Williams or Jones) with attributes (represented by positive or negative words).

The IAT procedure involved a series of seven trials. The first trial required participants to categorize target concepts (names of the candidates: Mary Williams vs. Yvonne Jones) into their proper categories; the second trial required participants to correctly categorize attribute concepts as either positive or negative; the third and fourth trials were target + attribute combined tasks in which respondents were required to categorize them into their proper categories; the fifth trial reversed the target concept and asked respondents to accurately categorize it in its proper category; and finally, the sixth and seventh trials were reversed target + attribute combined tasks, in which respondents were required to categorize them into their proper categories. Before each of the blocks was presented, respondents were provided instructions on how to proceed. Depending on the trial, the target and attribute categories appeared at the top-right and top-left corners of the computer screen. The stimulus items appeared in the middle of the screen.

For example, for trial 1, the target concept Williams would appear on the top-left corner of the screen, and the target concept Jones would appear on the top-right corner, and positioning of these changed depending on the trial—that is, in trial 1, target concept Williams would always appear on the top-left corner, and target concept Jones would always appear on the top-right corner. The stimulus (either the names Williams or Jones) would appear in the center of the screen. After each correct response, the next stimulus appeared. A correct response was one that corresponded to the categorization identified.

After performing the IAT, respondents completed a single-item measure of explicit attitude toward Mary Williams and Yvonne Jones. Specifically, they were asked, "How cold or warm do you feel toward Mary Williams and Yvonne Jones?" The feeling thermometer asked participants to rate both Williams and Jones on a thermometer that ran from 0 to 100 degrees. Ratings between 50 degrees and 100 degrees meant that they felt favorably and warm toward that person. Ratings between 0 degrees and 50 degrees meant that they did not feel particularly favorably and were cool toward that person.

The IAT was administered via computer. First, participants were given background information about the research, approximate length of the survey (15–20 minutes), and gave their informed consent. Once the survey was visible on the screen, participants were not allowed to go backward or forward between the pages to change their responses. However, participants were allowed to stop entering responses at any time. After respondents completed the IAT, they were queried about their racial identity and were asked questions related to competition, inequality, their demographics, and political preferences. After the completion of the study, participants were thanked for their participation.

Respondents were recruited from political science and sociology courses. For their participation, respondents were provided 15 extra-credit points. A total of 123 African-American college students from a southern university participated in the research. However, 29 participants were excluded from the analysis due to incompleteness of survey and high level of error rates.[1] Among the 94 respondents included in the analysis, 29 were male and 65 were female. The majority of respondents were between the ages of 19 and 22. With respect to social class, 14 percent indicated they were in poverty, 46 percent were working class, and 28 percent were middle class; the remainder reported being in the upper-middle class and wealthy class. Regarding political party and ideology, there were 3 Republicans, 14 Independents, and 77 Democrats while 19 were conservative, 45 neutral, and 30 liberal.

For the IAT effects, I calculated the speed and accuracy with which Williams can be paired with positive or negative attributes, versus the speed and accuracy with which Jones can be paired with the same positive or negative attributes. The greater the speed and accuracy of pairing Williams +Good/Jones+Bad versus Williams+Bad/Jones+Good, the greater the assumed positive implicit preference toward Williams relative to Jones. A higher and positive values indicate an implicit preference for Williams relative to Jones. Once this measure was calculated for each respondent, a one-sample t-test was run to see whether the observed IAT difference was statistically significant. For explicit effects, I subtracted Williams's and Jones's thermometer scores to get a thermometer difference score and then ran a t-test to assess the statistical significance of the differences. Positive values represent preference for Williams; negative values represent preference for Jones. For both the implicit and explicit evaluations, I also calculated Cohen's effect size d to measure the magnitude of the effect size of the implicit and explicit measures. *Cohen's d* is conceptually defined as "the magnitude of an effect independent of sample size and is widely utilized in empirical research and meta-analysis in the behavioral sciences" (Green et al. 2007, 4). The range for *Cohen's d* is from small (0.20) to medium (0.50) to high (0.80).

RESULTS

The findings presented in Figure 7.1 reveal respondents' implicit (or automatic) preference for Williams, the African-American candidate who did not mention race policy, relative to Jones, the White candidate who

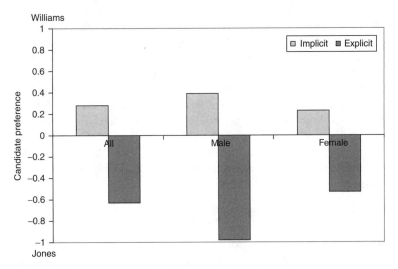

Figure 7.1   Implicit and explicit candidate preference, by gender.

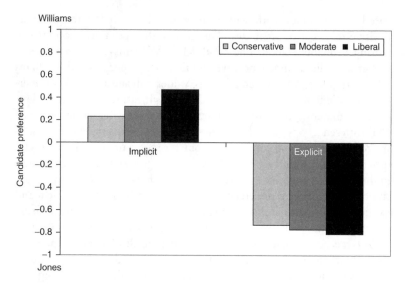

Figure 7.2   Implicit and explicit preference, by political ideology.

did mention race policy. In contrast, this figure also shows that when respondents were explicitly asked their preferences, they favor Jones over Williams. The differences in both the implicit and explicit evaluations are statistically significant at the $p < .05$ level.

I also explored whether candidate preferences were moderated by respondents' gender and political ideology. These results are also presented in Figure 7.1. With respect to gender, both males and females had a significant unconscious preference for candidate Williams over candidate Jones. Explicitly, both males and females had a preference Jones over Williams. This preference was much larger for males, however.

The same pattern holds, regardless of ideology. As Figure 7.2 indicates, conservatives, moderates, and liberals all significantly preferred Williams over Jones. This preference became stronger as we move from conservative to liberal, with liberals preferring Williams the most. Explicitly, there was the expected preference for Jones over Williams. Again, the preferences became stronger as respondents' ideology moved from conservative to liberal.

CONCLUSION

As expected, African-American respondents were more likely to have a preference for someone like themselves (racially) than the White candidate whose racial policy position was congruent with their own.

It appears racial similarity (or perceived similarity) has attracted respondents to the African-American candidate. This finding is in line with social psychology research, which has shown that similarity-attraction influences human behavior.

Another possible explanation is that African-American respondents may have made the assumption that the African-American candidate supports affirmative action policy, even though there was no mention of it in the vignette. Based on existing public opinion polls, their assumptions are not farfetched. A public opinion survey conducted by the NAACP in 2007 found that 81 percent of Blacks thought that affirmative action programs are needed today to help racial and ethnic minorities overcome discrimination. Therefore, it could have been possible that the respondents assumed that the Black candidate shared the majority of Blacks' support for affirmative action.

Why the difference in the implicit and explicit preference? Were African-American respondents conflicted in their preference? This difference in preferences shows there are problems with self-reports of attitudes. In using explicit measures, the assumption is that "people are aware of their attitudes, beliefs, and values that guided their behavior, and that they would be willing to reveal them if asked appropriately" (Kihlstrom 2004, 195). However, while people are aware of their own attitudes, they may not always be willing to share them with researchers, especially on topics that are personal or highly charged (Greenwald and Banaji 1995). Under such cases, respondents are prone to response management. Response management is likely to occur when an accurate response is seen as either impolite or prejudice (Dovidio and Fazio 1992), jeopardizes one's image of self (Gaertner and Dovidio 1986), or is considered atypical (Haire 1950). While it is difficult to pinpoint the reasons for the difference, there seems to have been both this internal conflict and response management.

While the findings from this study are interesting, there are some limitations. The first major limitation is that the sample includes only those between the ages of 19 and 25. Therefore, the results are only generalizable to that specific age group and not the entire African-American population. Another limitation is the sample size. Certainly, the sample size could be much larger. Nevertheless, this was an exploratory study and a first step in a long line of IAT research being conducted on the impact of racial identity and candidate preference. Subsequent studies need to utilize a larger, more representative sample.

PART 3

CONTEMPORARY ISSUES IN THE PSYCHOLOGY OF BLACK POLITICAL ATTITUDES AND BEHAVIOR

CHAPTER 8

RELIGION THROUGH A RACIAL LENS: THE EFFECT OF RACE ON RELIGIOUS INTERPRETATION

ERIC L. MCDANIEL

RECENTLY, THE REPUBLICAN PARTY HAS ATTEMPTED TO ATTRACT THE BLACK VOTE by appealing to religious values. Blacks, being highly religious, would appear to be a receptive group for such a strategy. However, this appeal has been unsuccessful. This failure goes beyond the political sphere, as the Religious Right has also tried but failed to bring Blacks into their fold (Calhoun-Brown 1998). Why do these appeals seem to fall on deaf ears in the Black community even though the basic moral and family values message would seem so consistent with the group's core commitments? One explanation seems obvious: the Black community rejects religious appeals from the Right either because they do not believe they are sincere, or because their nonreligious political interests override their religious commitment. There is, however, another possible explanation, and it is one I hope to explore in this chapter.

I argue that religious appeals have failed to persuade Blacks because they have a fundamentally different understanding of religion and its implications for politics than do Whites. The African-American understanding of religion differs significantly from the White understanding, because it has been shaped in the context of the Black experience. Consequently, Blacks have a different conceptualization of Christianity based upon a divergent interpretation of religious texts. So, while both Blacks and Whites may hold the Bible in the same regard, these divergent interpretations lead to diverging political attitudes. The purpose of this chapter is to discuss this phenomenon. The chapter will explore the intersection of race and religion in order to explain how different interpretations of scripture uniquely and distinctly shape political behavior.

THE BLACK RELIGIOUS CONTEXT

As Hanes Walton (1985) points out in *Invisible Politics*:

> Black political behavior is informed by unique forces. It is a variant form of American political behavior. It is inspired and shaped *by some features and currents that do not form the basis of all American political behavior because it is rooted in the black experience in America*
>
> 8; emphasis in original

These same forces have been integral in the development of Black religion. Just as Hanes Walton notes that Black political behavior is similar to mainstream political behavior, but different, Black Christianity is similar to that of Whites, but different. This is best explained by Lincoln and Mamiya (1990) in their discussion of the Black Sacred Cosmos. They argue that the facets of Black religion seen today were developed as part of the struggle for Blacks to define and identify themselves in the American context. The Black Sacred Cosmos stresses the same biblically orthodox beliefs as Whites, but places greater emphasis on certain theological views. Blacks are far more likely to stress the issues of freedom, social justice, equality, and community.

Although many would argue that churches foster the integration of marginalized groups into larger society, scholars of Black religion argue that this is not the case for Blacks. Those who have examined the religion of Blacks have found that it has kept them out of mainstream society by providing a shield from larger society. While some have seen this as detrimental to Black development in the United States (Frazier [1964] 1974), others have heralded it as the grand defense of the race and its interests. Scholars have noted the fact that Black religion fostered a counter culture to mainstream American culture. Its purpose was not only spiritual care, but social care as well. As Gunnar Myrdal (1944) states: "The chief function of the Negro church has been to buoy the hopes of its members in the face of adversity and to give them a sense of community" (875).

Black churches, historically the sole Black-owned property in America, were used to bring together the group and critique mainstream

White society. As Fredrick Harris (1999) points out in his discussion of an "oppositional civic culture," Black religion—while fostering a connection to larger American society—is still highly critical. Harris argues that while churches provide civic skills they also provide "oppositional dispositions to challenge their marginality" (40). Reese and Brown (1995) come to similar conclusions as they find that certain messages sent in Black churches encourage Blacks to understand their inequality as a systematic consequence rather than individual inefficiencies.

Examinations of the religion of slaves as well as free Blacks during antebellum America show a critical analysis of America from a religious standpoint (Harding 1969; Raboteau 2001, 1978; Washington 2004). Albert Raboteau (2001) demonstrates this by contrasting the crossing of the Atlantic Ocean for British Colonists and Africans:

> British colonists had spoken of their journey across the Atlantic as the exodus of a New Israel from bondage in Egypt to the Promised Land of milk and honey. For African Americans the opposite was true: whites might claim that America was a new Israel, but blacks knew that it was Egypt because they like the children of Israel of old, still toiled in bondage (44).

Frederick Douglass (1999), in his attack on a Christian interpretation that would justify slavery, openly points out the contradictions in this religious interpretation:

> They would be shocked at the proposition of fellowshipping with a sheep-stealer; and at the same time they hug to their communion a man-stealer, and brand me with being an infidel, if I find fault with them for it (108).

This sentiment can also be seen in the works of David Walker, Henry Highland Garnett, and others (Harding 1969). In the South, this outlook would lead to the religiously inspired revolts of Gabriel Prosser, Denmark Vesey, and Nat Turner (Sidbury 2003). Even after slavery, the years of separation forced upon Blacks maintained the role of the church as a critic of mainstream America.

This has led Blacks to develop a strain of religious interpretation that was distinctively different from that of Whites. Similar to Whites, the Black Christian understanding places a strong emphasis on the individual's responsibilities to society. The two part company because Black Christianity also emphasizes society's responsibility to the individual. While Black clergy will admonish the immoral activities of the individual, a society that does not do its best to protect the individual is seen as immoral as well. For Blacks, religion is not simply a guide for individual behavior in society, but also for the moral responsibilities of the community toward the individual (Paris 1985). The most obvious example of this is Black Theology, which provides a religious interpretation that better identifies with the Black experience (Cone 1997). Cone and others argue that God is on the side of the oppressed and it is the duty of every Christian to overcome oppression. Black Theology, a variant of Liberation Theology, emphatically places immorality in the hands of the individual and the community. While most Black clergy do not fully embrace this theology (Lincoln and Mamiya 1990), elements of Black Theology can be seen throughout the Black church and in turn Black religion (Cone and Wilmore 1993). In what follows, I will demonstrate the political implications of this worldview.

RELIGION AND INFORMATION PROCESSING

Religion is closely linked to political thought processes because religion provides a guide for achieving the good life, both on EARTH and in the afterlife. Religion provides ways of understanding and legitimizing the world that surrounds us (Leege 1993; Berger and Luckmann 1963; Berger 1969). Religion gives the individual a guidebook for understanding how the world operates and how to operate in the world. By providing rituals and belief structures, religion helps define the individual's place in the world, which in turn shapes his behavior. By providing an understanding of how the world works, religion plays a strong role in how individuals process information and formulate opinions. Religion, therefore, can be understood as one pathway to decision making (Ellison and Sherkat 1997).

Differences in religion, as well as the importance of religion, factor into how information is processed and into the creation of the religious schema. By providing guideposts in life, religion allows individuals to better cope with the world. Studies of the connection between religious belief and well-being argue that religion provides an ordering of the world and the self in a way that makes life less stressful (Ellison 1994). In this case, religion provides a schema that allows the person to negotiate his world better.

With respect to political decision-making, the salience of religious precepts is necessary, but not sufficient in understanding how religion factors into how people make sense of the political world. In order to gauge whether and how religion influences individuals' political decision-making, we not only need to know whether they consider religion to be important to their lives, we must also pay attention to the prior step: religious interpretation. As several scholars have shown, interpretations of scripture are not constant among members of a particular denomination, let alone across religious traditions. Members of a religious group, due to their unique experiences and interests, will develop different interpretations of religious texts and symbols (Bartkowski 1996; Boone 1989; Fish 1980). This means that while "religion" as a group affiliation is likely to affect policy beliefs in a statistical sense, actual religious schema within a given tradition in the end may vary. Therefore, while broad religious categories may capture certain experiences, different religious interpretations may make some experiences more salient than others.

This is especially true for Blacks, who continue to be one of the most religious demographics in American society and whose experiences in the United States rival no other group. Several studies have shown that Blacks, compared to Whites, are far more active in attending religious services, taking part in private religious activities, and report higher levels of biblical orthodoxy (Taylor et al. 2004). This is not only a factor of Protestantism, this has also been found to be true of Black Catholics (Cavendish et al. 1998).

As a result, religion influences many facets of Black life. For instance, studies have shown that religion plays a strong role in maintaining and supplementing Black well-being (Taylor et al. 2004; Ellison and Gay 1990; Mattis et al. 2004). Blacks who are highly religious are less likely to suffer from stress and esteem issues compared to their less religious counterparts (e.g. Mattis et al. 2004). Further, religious beliefs on the part of Blacks boost communal attachments (Ellison 1991; Wilcox and Gomez 1990; Allen et al. 1989). Mary Patillo-McCoy's (1998) work on a Black neighborhood in Chicago shows that religion and the church permeate almost all aspects of some Black communities. Additionally, she finds that this connection to religion and the church is used throughout the community to mobilize its inhabitants.

RELIGION, RACE, AND POLITICS

How, then, does religious interpretation influence Black politics? Already studies that have compared religious Whites and Blacks on their social and political attitudes have found differences at both the individual and organizational level. To be sure, examinations of attitudes about inequality and other social issues have found religious Blacks to be systematically different from Whites on many of these issues (Calhoun-Brown 1998; Gay and Lynxwiler 1999; Hinojosa and Park 2004; Hunt 2000, 2002; Leege and Kellstedt 1993). Likewise, scholars have found that while Black and White religious congregations have the same level of social activism, they focus on different issues (Chaves 2004; Cavendish 2000; Chaves and Higgins 1992; Tsitsos 2003).

These studies, however, have only captured race's direct effect on political attitudes and orientations. In other words, the observed differences between Blacks and Whites are not necessarily attributable to those with salient religious worldviews. Indeed, Black-White differences persist regardless of religious beliefs. I argue, however, that race additionally has an indirect effect on Black politics.

Using the same analogy employed by McDaniel and Ellison (2008), the experiences of a group act as a prism in regards to religious instruction. These experiences refract religious teachings, creating divergent interpretations. Because race has continually shown to be the most salient issue in the lives of African Americans (Gurin et al. 1989; Dawson 1994), I argue that race serves as the refracting lens that creates Black religion. In turn, this Black religious schema or worldview acts as mechanism for collecting information and making decisions, including those related to politics.

Therefore, race not only anchors Blacks' political attitudes, it can also cancel out or magnify religion's effect on certain political attitudes as well. From this standpoint, race conditions the effect of religion on Black decision-making. This, I contend, serves as an additional division between Blacks and Whites with similar religious orientations.

DATA AND METHODS

To test my argument, I chose the 2000 Religion and Politics Survey, because it addresses respondents' views on political, social, and religious issues, allowing for a well-developed analysis of religious beliefs and practices as well as political attitudes. The survey is a collection of 5,603 telephone interviews conducted between January 6 and March 31, 2000. Of these 5,603 interviews, 570 of the respondents identified themselves as Black. The principal investigator of the study is Robert Wuthnow and the survey was obtained through the American Religion Data Archive (www.thearda.com).

The dependent variables for this analysis are questions that relate to various policy concerns as well as partisanship and vote choice. The policy issues are questions related to the level of interest the respondent has in improving several policy issues including: gender equality, racial equality, rights for homosexuals, protecting the environment, and poverty. Each of these is a three-point measure ranging from zero to one, with one indicating very interested and zero indicating not interested. The partisanship measure is identifying as a Republican. Vote choice is measured by gauging whether respondents voted for a Republican candidate in the 1996 election or intended to vote for a Republican candidate in the 2000 election. Each of these measures is dichotomous.

One of the primary independent variables is religious beliefs. Because religion is multidimensional, this study incorporates several different measures of religious beliefs and rituals. This study is mainly concerned with religious orthodoxy. Religious orthodoxy relates to the inerrancy of the Bible and taps directly into religious beliefs. Orthodoxy has been shown to be a religious belief system that promotes conservatism because it relates to traditional values and belief structures and has a strong emphasis on individualism (Guth et al. 1997; Leege and Kellstedt 1993; Ellison and Musick 1993). An orthodoxy scale (alpha=.57) was created based upon this understanding. The measure includes whether or not the respondent believes that the Bible should be taken literally; whether or not the respondent believes that the Bible contains errors, and whether or not the respondent feels that the Bible was inspired by God. The orthodoxy measure is a three-point additive index ranging from zero to one. Also included is a measure of respondents' level of religiosity. To do so, I utilize items tapping into devotionalism and church attendance. The church attendance measure is a basic self-reporting of how often the respondent attends church services. Devotionalism relates to the private religious practices of individuals such as praying and reading the Bible. The devotionalism measure (alpha=.77) is a twelve-point scale, ranging from zero to one, comprised of the frequency with which an individual prays and reads the Bible, along with how important it is for them to develop their spirituality in their adult life.

The other primary independent variable is race. For this analysis, race is a dichotomous variable with one indicating Black and zero indicating White. Because of the small number of Hispanics, Asians, and other racial groupings, the analysis will just be limited to those who identify as White or Black.

To account for the racial differences in the effects of orthodoxy, an interaction term was created. The interaction term is the multiplication of the orthodoxy measure and race. The results from the interaction term indicate the differences between the effects of orthodoxy on Blacks compared to Whites.

To better understand the effects of religiosity on Black and White political attitudes, this study also controls for basic demographics and political ideology. Demographics are controlled for using age, education, sex, whether or not the respondent works fulltime, and level of urbanicity in which a respondent lives. Political ideology is controlled for using a seven-point, liberal-conservative scale, where zero indicates strong liberal and one indicates strong conservative.

Before beginning with the analysis of the interaction of race and religious beliefs, it is important to point out that the interpretation of these results is slightly different from other regression models. The coefficients for the variables orthodoxy and Black are not their direct effect on the dependent variable, but their effect on the dependent variable when one or the other is set at zero. In this case, the coefficient of orthodoxy is the effect of orthodoxy when Black is equal to zero, meaning that it represents the effect of orthodoxy on Whites. In the case of the Black coefficient, it represents Blacks with a zero orthodoxy score. Because of the interaction term, the effects of Black and orthodoxy are now contingent upon each other. Analyzing these lower-order terms as being independent of each other would lead to a faulty understanding of the results (Braumoeller 2004; Freidrich 1982). The calculation for the coefficient for orthodoxy's effect on Blacks is the coefficient of orthodoxy, plus the value of Black multiplied by the coefficient of the interaction term. For this chapter, the coefficients for orthodoxy's effect on Blacks will be calculated using the linear combinations command in STATA version 8, which calculates the coefficients as well as the standard errors and confidence intervals. To further interpret how race and religion interact, I will also use predicted probabilities and predicted values. These will be calculated using the spost command in STATA (Long and Freese 2001).

RESULTS

The analysis of the effects of the interaction between race and orthodoxy begins with an examination of attitudes toward policy areas (see Table 8.1). An examination of the interaction terms finds that the only case where religious orthodoxy has a significantly different effect on Blacks relative to Whites is in the case of equal rights for homosexuals. The coefficient for Whites it is –.720 and is statistically significant (at $p<.05$), for Blacks it is –.265 and not statistically significant. In this case, the effect of orthodoxy on Blacks is significantly weaker and does not appear to be working as systematically as it does for Whites.

To substantively illustrate the relationship between religious orthodoxy and attitudes toward equal rights for homosexuals, I calculate the linear predictions as both groups move from low orthodox to highly orthodox. While the low-orthodox Whites appear to see this as a salient issue more than low-orthodox Blacks, highly orthodox Blacks see this as more of an important issue than highly orthodox Whites. Looked at another way, the difference between low- and high-orthodox Blacks is not as great as the difference between low- and high-orthodox Whites. This provides some evidence to support the argument that race moderates the relationship between orthodoxy and political attitudes.

Table 8.1 The effect of race and orthodoxy on political attitudes

	Protecting environment	Gender equality	Equality for homosexuals	Racial equality	Protecting the poor
Black * orthodoxy	0.103	0.239	0.455**	0.146	-0.145
	(0.20)	(.23)	(.25)	(.23)	(.23)
Orthodoxy	-0.364***	-0.398***	-0.720***	-0.405***	-0.157**
	(0.08)	(0.08)	(0.08)	(0.08)	(0.08)
Black	-0.165	0.335**	-0.347**	0.750***	0.569***
	(0.15)	(0.17)	(0.14)	(0.18)	(0.17)
Age	0.203**	0.303***	-0.151	-0.167*	-0.013
	(0.10)	(0.10)	(0.10)	(0.10)	(0.10)
Education	-0.094	-0.003	0.334***	0.255***	-0.161**
	(0.07)	(0.07)	(0.06)	(0.07)	(0.07)
Works fulltime	0.043	0.162***	-0.045	-0.009	-0.103**
	(0.04)	(0.04)	(0.04)	(0.04)	(0.04)
Female	0.005	0.474***	0.401***	0.186***	0.266***
	(0.04)	(0.04)	(0.04)	(0.04)	(0.04)
Conservatism	-0.602***	-0.639***	-0.697***	-0.608***	-0.797***
	(0.07)	(0.07)	(0.06)	(0.07)	(0.07)
Urban	0.070	0.211***	0.220***	0.159***	0.048
	(0.06)	(0.06)	(0.05)	(0.06)	(0.06)
Devotionalism	0.457***	0.363***	0.204*	0.619***	0.887***
	(0.12)	(0.12)	(0.11)	(0.12)	(0.12)
Church attendance	-0.233***	-0.133*	-0.383***	-0.022	0.003
	(0.08)	(0.08)	(0.07)	(0.08)	(0.08)
Log-likelihood	-3568.126	-3477.343	-4049.546	-3609.786	-3340.977
N	4098	4081	3999	4075	4084

Notes: * p ≤ .1; ** p ≤ .05; *** p ≤ .01.
Source: 2000 Religion and Politics Survey.

While the interaction term is not significant for the other variables, it is important not to make the assumption that orthodox Blacks and Whites are necessarily on the same page when it comes to the importance of these issues. An examination of the actual effect of orthodoxy on Blacks finds that in most cases the effect is not significant, meaning that for Blacks the effect of orthodoxy is not as systematic as it is for Whites on these issues. In addition, an examination of the Black coefficient, which indicates the effect of being Black when orthodoxy is at zero, shows that Blacks start from a different position than Whites on many of these issues. The only issue where it appears that low-orthodox Blacks and low-orthodox Whites are not significantly different is in their support for the environment.

If orthodoxy were to work as systematically for Blacks as it does for Whites, it would still have to overcome the main effect of being Black. Figure 8.1 shows the predicted probability of stating that gender equality, racial equality, and policies protecting the poor are very important. Here, as orthodoxy increases for both groups they become more conservative. However, because Blacks start at a significantly more liberal position, the effect of orthodoxy has been muffled.

The examination of partisanship and vote choice, found in Table 8.2, yields the same results. It appears that orthodoxy does not work differently for Blacks in terms of party identification and vote choice in the 1996 and 2000 elections. But again, as was shown above, this does not mean that there is a convergence on the part of the White and Black orthodox.

An examination of Figure 8.1 still shows that being Black mutes the effects of orthodoxy on partisanship and vote choice. While 36 percent of orthodox Whites identify as Republican, less than 10 percent of orthodox Blacks do. In terms of vote choice in the 1996 election, less than 3 percent of orthodox Blacks indicated voting for Dole, while close to 28 percent of orthodox Whites reported voting for him. Finally,

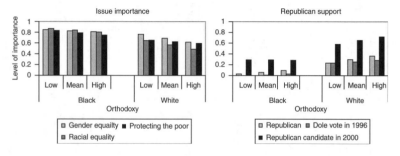

Figure 8.1   Issue importance and Republican support, by race and orthodoxy.

Table 8.2   The effect of race and orthodoxy on partisanship and vote choice

	Identifies as republican	Vote for Dole in 1996	Intend to vote Republican in 2000
Black * orthodoxy	0.195	1.095	−0.424
	(0.34)	(0.73)	(0.28)
Orthodoxy	0.374***	0.155	0.388***
	(0.09)	(0.10)	(0.10)
Black	−1.143***	−2.458***	−0.738***
	(0.27)	(0.63)	(0.21)
Age	−0.142	0.280**	−0.450***
	(0.12)	(0.14)	(0.13)
Education	0.357***	0.643***	0.125
	(0.08)	(0.09)	(0.09)
Works fulltime	−0.010	0.001	0.006
	(0.05)	(0.06)	(0.06)
Female	−0.094**	−0.255***	−0.134***
	(0.05)	(0.05)	(0.05)
Conservatism	1.204***	1.513***	1.301***
	(0.08)	(0.10)	(0.09)
Urban	0.001	−0.202***	−0.257***
	(0.07)	(0.08)	(0.07)
Devotionalism	0.095	−0.060	−0.022
	(0.14)	(0.16)	(0.15)
Church attendance	0.438***	0.453***	0.326***
	(0.09)	(0.11)	(0.10)
Constant	−1.672***	−1.819***	−0.302**
	(0.11)	(0.14)	(0.12)
Log-likelihood	−2121.682	−1598.458	−1720.897
Correctly predicted	73.93	75.69	70.88
N	3967	3221	3019

Notes: * p < .1; ** p < .05; *** p < .01.
Source: 2000 Religion and Politics Survey.

in terms of the 2000 election, close to 72 percent of orthodox Whites indicated that they would vote for a Republican candidate, while slightly over 28 percent of orthodox Blacks indicated the same. The results from this figure show overwhelmingly that while orthodoxy does move Blacks in a more conservative direction, they never reach the level of conservatism as their White counterparts.

CONCLUSION

When considering how religion plays a role in shaping people's thought processes and eventual attitudes, it is important to pay attention to how differences in religious interpretation can generate different cognitive structures. Because the religious interpretation of Blacks is significantly different from that of Whites, White religious appeals to religious Blacks in many cases fall on deaf ears. The Black understanding of religion was shaped in the context of the Black experience. Because the Black experience has been shaped in confrontation to mainstream society, the religion of Blacks took the same tone.

The results from these analyses have shown that the effect of orthodoxy is contingent upon race. Even when orthodoxy does effect Blacks the same way it does Whites, further analysis has shown that in many of these cases, the effect of orthodoxy is not as systematic as it is for Whites. Finally, when examining the actual effect of orthodoxy on the final outcome of Black attitudes, it is subdued by Blackness. Being Black mitigated the conservatizing effects of orthodoxy. What is evident in this analysis is that orthodoxy does not overcome the effects of race. The results clearly show that the grasp race has on Black attitudes is stronger than religious beliefs.

So what can we take away from this preliminary but illuminating study? In the end, the findings suggest that being born Black is more salient than being born-again. The religion, religious context, and experiences of Blacks prevent orthodoxy from affecting them the same way it does Whites. Because of this, it is difficult to see how the Republican Party and the Christian Right will make sufficient gains in the Black community. Their strong emphasis on religious and traditional values is attractive, but it still does not address historical and contemporary racial disparities. Until these groups develop a platform that includes remedies for racial inequality, Blacks will remain reluctant to give them their support.

SOME LIKE IT HOT: TOWARDS A POLITICAL CLIMATE EXPLANATION OF RACIAL DIFFERENCES IN POLITICAL INTEREST

RAY BLOCK, JR.

> *It is perplexing that political scientists have not shown more recent interest, as it were, in political interest.*
> Campbell, Galston, Niemi, and Rahn in Macedo et al. 2005, 35

POLITICAL INTEREST—defined here as the extent to which citizens profess an awareness of, are curious about, or pay attention to politics and public affairs (Bennett 1986)—sits quietly at the very core of the political participation literature. Democratic theorists place a great deal of value on political interest (see Bennett 1986). As van Deth (2000) notes, scholars debate over the degree, not the necessity, of mass-level interest in politics. In fact, political interest was so important to the ancient Greeks that their word for "idiot" refers to political apathy rather than mental deficiency.[1] In addition to its key role in normative democratic theory, interest is a reliable determinant of political action. Research consistently demonstrates that interest in politics relates to greater political participation, a finding that holds true for numerous types of political acts (Verba, Schlozman, and Brady 1995; Leighley and Vedlitz 1999). The relationship between interest and activism has been confirmed so many times that, as Milbrath and Goel (1977) observe, authors no longer bother to report it. For these and many other reasons, it is safe to conclude that political interest is "interesting."

As the opening passage indicates, despite its normative and empirical importance, research on political interest is surprisingly underdeveloped; as a result, many assumptions about political interest remain unexamined. Some of the least-tested assumptions deal with the impact of race on political interest. For example, studies show that, compared to Blacks, Whites generally express more interest in politics (Matthews and Prothro 1966; Verba, Schlozman, and Brady 1995). However, Bennett (1986) acknowledges that this is "usually, but not always" the case: there are times when Blacks' interest levels match or even surpass those of Whites (72; see also Block 2006; 2007).

Why are Whites usually more politically interested than Blacks, and why do Blacks sometimes take more interest in politics than do Whites? Currently, there are no explanations for these Black-White differences in interest levels—differences I characterize as constituting a "race gap" in political interest. Nevertheless, one can draw inferences from the research on racial differences in political participation. Because interest and activism represent different facets of a broader construct best described as "political involvement," it is possible that similar processes explain why Blacks and Whites differ in the extent to which they involve themselves in politics, be that involvement physical or psychological. To account for the interest gap, it is useful to revisit the work of sociologist Nicholas L. Danigelis, who, in his critique of research on Black activism, provides the intuition for a "political climate" theory of racial differences in political involvement. Despite several attempts (Danigelis 1978; 1982), the author admits that his theory awaits a proper exploration, partly because it is difficult to quantify the abstract and many-sided concept of climate (Danigelis 1977). In this chapter, I apply some of Danigelis' arguments to the study of the interest gap. Pooled survey data from the 1952 through 2008 American National Election Studies (ANES) allow for a more comprehensive test of the implications of Danigelis' theory, and the evidence lends support to the author's expectations.

EVIDENCE OF A RACE GAP

There is good reason to believe that Blacks and Whites pay different amounts of attention to politics, for there is a wealth of research spanning numerous disciplines chronicling racial differences in levels of psychological involvement. Delli Carpini and Keeter (1996) and Iyengar (1986) find that Whites perform consistently better than do Blacks on tests of general political knowledge. Political socialization scholars often mention White-over-Black differences in political efficacy (Abramson 1972; Kleiman 1976; Wu 2003). Likewise, Tate (2003), Hetherington (1998), and Owen and Dennis (2001) confirm a racial gap in levels of political trust. Additionally, Campbell, Gurin, and Miller (1954) find that Whites convey a stronger sense of civic duty than do Blacks.

Taken together, this body of evidence suggests that Blacks are less politically engaged than Whites are. Compared to Whites, Blacks tend to know less about politics, be less trusting of government, feel less obligated to participate, and have little confidence that their actions will make a difference. Based on these findings, one would anticipate racial differences in political interest as well. After all, interest in politics is a key measure of psychological engagement (Bennett 1986; Block 2006; Brody 1978; van Deth 1990), and it should behave similarly to other engagement variables. From this line of reasoning comes the expectation that levels of political interest will be higher among Whites than among Blacks.

Preliminary analyses bear out this expectation. Figure 9.1 reports racial differences in political interest levels using pooled data from the 1952 to 2008 ANES. I compare Blacks' and Whites' responses to two commonly asked questions from the ANES. The first question measures respondents' general interest in politics:

Some people seem to follow what's going on in government and public affairs most of the time, whether there's an election going on or not. Others aren't that interested. Would you say you follow what's going on in government and public affairs most of the time, some of the time, only now and then, or hardly at all?

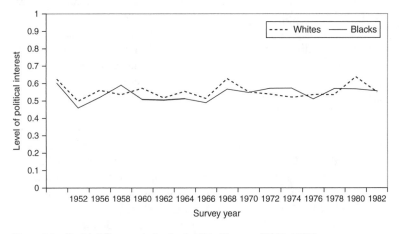

Figure 9.1   Racial differences in levels of political interest (1952–2008).

Notes: Data points are average levels of political interest by race and over time.
Source: 1952–2008 American National Election Studies.

The second question gauges respondents' interest in the current presidential campaign:

Some people don't pay much attention to campaigns. How about you? Would you say that you have been very much interested, somewhat interested, or not much interested in political campaigns (so far) this year?

I measure interest in politics as an additive index of general and campaign interest.[2] I scale this index so that it ranges from zero (weak political interest) to one (strong interest). The solid line in Figure 9.1 traces the trends in political interest among those ANES respondents who self-identify as "Blacks" or "African Americans" (not of Hispanic origin), while the dashed line displays interest trends for those respondents who classify themselves as (non-Hispanic) "Whites" or "Anglo Americans."

One of the strongest findings in Figure 9.1 is that the political interest trends for Blacks resemble those for Whites. Regardless of race, the same visual pattern persists: interest in politics ebbs in the early 1950s and bottoms out in the late 1950s to early 1960s; then it rises to a peak in the mid-1960s, where it plateaus until the mid-1970s; interest drops off temporarily in the late 1970s and increases in fluctuations from the 1980s to the end of the period. Correlation analyses corroborate the association between interest trends. A weak statistical correlation would suggest that Blacks' and Whites' interest trends are moving independently of one another, while a strong correlation suggests that the trends move in tandem or in opposition. Figure 9.1 reveals a strong, positive, and statistically significant[3] association ($r=.66$) between Blacks' and Whites' interest levels, which suggests that these trends have parallel trajectories.

A closer look at Figure 9.1 shows that there are some small but predictable racial differences in levels of political interest. Whites generally express greater interest in politics than do Blacks, a pattern that holds for most of the survey years. Means difference tests for the entire period confirm these racial differences in levels of political interest measures are statistically significant. In addition to the overall test, I examine the differences of means for each year. While there are years when the interest gap changes—mainly in the early 1960s, the mid-1980s, the late 1990s, and, of course, in 2008, and I will discuss these later—the results generally show that the White-over-Black gap in political interest is the rule rather than the exception. These results, while impressionistic, lend some credence to Bennett's observation that Whites are "usually, but not always" more interested in politics than are Blacks (Bennett 1986, 72). What accounts for these racial differences? I address this question in the next section.

Explaining the Race Gap: A Political
Climate Theory

Danigelis acknowledges that the race gap in political involvement changes over time and across geographic regions, and he attributes these fluctuations to shifts in America's racial context, what he calls the "political climate."[4] Danigelis focused on the effect of climate on African Americans' activism in his 1977 essay, "A Theory of Black Political Participation in the United States", but it is clear from his subsequent papers (see Danigelis 1978; 1982) that he seeks to explain *racial differences in political involvement*. Distilling his argument to its essence, Danigelis assumes that the participation gap increases when the political climate is "unfavorable" (i.e., during those periods when structural factors demobilize Blacks). The race gap decreases in climates that are more "favorable": when there is widespread encouragement for (or, at the very least, a lack of widespread opposition to) minority involvement (see Danigelis 1977).

Danigelis' makes several assumptions about racial group differences in the impact of political climate on political involvement. For example, the author accepts the premise that Whites are generally more politically involved than Blacks are. This is not a controversial assumption, for, as I show in the previous section, the claim that Whites tend to outdo Blacks in levels of political involvement is widely documented. A related, perhaps less explicit, assumption pertains to racial differences in the effect of climate on political involvement. For Danigelis, a "warmer" climate is one that promotes the political inclusion of all racial and ethnic groups, and a racial context that is unwelcoming (cooler) toward African Americans is likely to suppress Blacks' involvement (Danigelis 1977). However, the author does not consider the effect (if any) of climate on Whites. It would be odd to expect an unfavorable climate to discourage Whites, so one can anticipate that an increase in climate will either have a positive impact on Whites' involvement or have no impact at all. Even if "context matters" for both racial groups, it is safe to assume that changes in political climate will matter more for Blacks than they will for Whites. Put another way, Blacks and Whites should respond differently to the political climate. Although it stimulates African Americans' political involvement, a more favorable racial climate should have less of an impact on Whites. It is because of the differential effect of an improving political climate that we will observe a decrease in the race gap.

Extending the concept of political climate from political behavior to psychological involvement, racial differences in interest levels should vary depending on the political climate. If Danigelis' theory is correct, then we should observe the largest interest gap in the coolest (least favorable) political climate, and this gap should decrease (and possibly reverse) as the climate becomes more favorable toward African Americans. To summarize, Danigelis' theory predicts that *an increase in the favorability of the political climate will "close" or "flip" the White-over-Black gap in political interest.*

In a personal communication with the author on May 5, 2006, Danigelis admits that, despite the richness of his theory, a precise measure of political climate awaits development. Danigelis' 1977 essay made several suggestions but presented no empirical analyses. In 1978, he conducted the first test of his theory, but he limited his definition of political climate to perceived racial discrimination among Blacks. Danigelis refers again to political climate in his 1982 article, but only in passing; the focus of this article was on the interactive effects of race and class on political involvement. The challenge of Danigelis' theory lies in gauging political climate. After all, how does one quantify Zeitgeist? In the next section, I propose two operational definitions for this elusive concept.

MEASURING POLITICAL CLIMATE

As noted in the previous section, Danigelis characterizes political climate as a spatial and temporal concept: it is difficult to refute the claim that some places are more racially inclusive than others are, and Figure 9.1 demonstrates that America's tolerance toward Blacks was greater in some years than in others. Danigelis' characterization suggests that geographic region (a reliable measure of spatial context) and survey year (a standard item for examining time trends) may serve as spatial and temporal measures of political climate. Of course, I acknowledge that geographic region and survey year are crude representations of something as hard to pin down as the racial context. Nevertheless, in the absence of more precise alternatives for measuring climate, I feel comfortable making the claim that these indicators, while imperfect, are suitable proxies for climate. Admittedly, this is a step backward theoretically, but this is a necessary step back if we are to proceed forward empirically. Below, I examine the role of these indicators of spatial and temporal context on racial differences in political interest.

One possible measure of spatial climate is geographic region. For example, there are numerous studies showing that, compared to the rest of the nation, southern states have traditionally been less favorable to African Americans. Black-White relations in the South, with its history of racial conservatism, are more blatantly volatile than are those in the relatively progressive nonsouthern states, where prejudice and discrimination take subtler forms (Key 1954; Glaser and Gilens 1997; McClerking and Philpot 2008; Schuman et al. 1997; Steeh and Schuman 1992; Tuch and

Hughes 1996; Tuch and Martin 1997). Perhaps because of these regional differences, Danigelis consistently finds the White-over-Black gap in political involvement to be greatest in the South (Danigelis 1978).

Figure 9.2 replicates Danigelis' findings by displaying racial differences in average levels of political interest, sorted by whether or not respondents live in what the ANES calls the "political South." Southern respondents are those residing in the eleven states of the CONFEDERACY: Alabama, Arkansas, Florida, Georgia, Louisiana, Mississippi, North Carolina, South Carolina, Tennessee, Texas, and Virginia. Respondents who do not live in these states are referred to as nonsoutherners. As Figure 9.2 shows, Whites are generally more interested in politics than Blacks, and this pattern is clearest in southern states. For Whites in the South, the mean level of self-reported political interest is .55, while the average interest level among Blacks is .50; this leads to a difference of .05, which is a statistically significant race gap. The interest gap in nonsouthern states is also statistically significant, but it is noticeably smaller: average interest levels for Whites and Blacks are .56 and .54, respectively (which is a gap of only .02). Consistent with Bennett's (1986) analysis, I too find that interest levels tend to be slightly higher among nonsoutherners than they are for southern respondents. The South has a history of having disproportionately low poverty levels, particularly in states like Arkansas and Mississippi (Mink and O'Connor 2004). Given the abundance of research that links political involvement to factors like income and education (see Verba, Schlozman, and Brady 1995), it makes sense that, regardless of race, nonsouthern respondents report higher average levels of political interest.

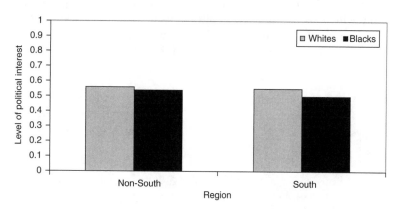

Figure 9.2 Racial differences in levels of political interest, by geographic region.

Note: Data points are average levels of political interest by race and geographic region.
Source: 1952–2008 American National Election Studies.

Danigelis (1982) describes geographic region as a spatial context that complements the temporal dimension of political climate. As shown earlier, there are instances when Blacks' interest levels meet or exceed those of Whites, and these trend changes occur at predictable moments. For example, in Figure 9.3, which reports trends in political interest levels by race and geographic region, political climate is least tolerant in the years leading up to the Civil Rights Movement,[5] and the race gap in political interest is widest during this period. Political interest trends spiked in 1964, and, for the first time, the mean level of Blacks' political interest was higher than the mean for Whites. Regardless of the region, the difference between these means is historically meaningful despite it not being statistically significant, which suggests that the interest gap closed in 1964. This rise in racial climate, and the disproportionate increase in Blacks' attentiveness, might reflect the hypervisibility of race at the height of the Civil Rights Movement. In an automated content analysis of political science journals, McClerking and Philpot (2008) show that both scholarly and popular attention shifted to race relations during the Civil Rights Movement. Furthermore, while there were many milestones during the movement, those happening in 1964 must have been particularly fascinating for African Americans.[6]

If the mid-1960s represent a politically warm period—arguably the warmest in the nation's history—then many scholars (particularly Walton 1997) consider the Reagan through the (H. W.) Bush era of the early 1980s to early 1990s a cooler temporal climate. Not surprisingly, the trends in Figure 9.3 resemble those of Figure 9.1, for they show that Whites regain the advantage in the race gap in political interest. There is, however, a notable exception: interest rises considerably among nonsouthern Blacks and African Americans in the overall samples outdo Whites in interest levels. This shift overlaps with Jesse Jackson's first campaign for the presidency in 1984. Many would argue that Jackson had little chance of winning the election; however, his decision to run

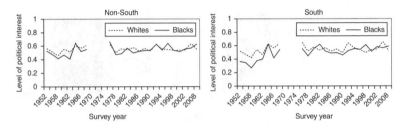

Figure 9.3   Racial differences in levels of political interest, by geographic region and race.

Note: Data points are average levels of political interest by race, geographic region, and over time.
Source: 1952–2008 American National Election Studies.

received tremendous media exposure, which, in turn, heightened racial group consciousness and bolstered grassroots political motivation. As a result, Blacks followed politics more closely that year than they had previously (for detailed treatments of the impact of Jackson's campaign on Black political involvement, see Gurin et al. 1989; Tate 1993).

Another period worth mentioning is the year 2008. Regardless of region, the White-over-Black gap in political interest reverses in this year. Obviously, this trend change reflects the excitement that Barack Obama's presidential campaign inspired. Obama was not the first candidate of color to pursue the presidency (his decision to run follows Shirley Chisholm's candidacy in 1972 and Jesse Jackson's runs in 1984 and 1988), but the former Illinois Senator was the first one to achieve the nation's highest elected office. Given the enormous media attention of the 2008 election and the historical magnitude of the possibility of his victory (see Block 2009; Sinclair-Chapman and Price 2008; Walters 2007), it is not surprising that the race gap changed. In fact, one would expect the reverse gap in political interest to be even larger.

To summarize, I integrate research from political science and sociology to explain racial differences in political interest. The results bring the contours for this race gap into sharper relief. They show that Blacks and Whites do pay differential amounts of attention to politics, which is a finding that many expected but few tested systematically. Utilizing two measures of political climate (measures that, despite their crudeness, perform adequately for testing Danigelis' claims), I demonstrate that the width of the White-over-Black gap in political interest depends on the favorability of the political climate, for this race gap can close or reverse as the climate improves. In fact, one of the fundamental conclusions to be reached from this chapter is that what we know about the race gap in political interest depends on when and where we look for racial differences. More importantly, the analyses lend support to the Danigelis-inspired claim that the racial gap in political interest may indeed depend on the political climate.

DISCUSSION AND CONCLUSIONS

The racial gap in political interest speaks to the broader issue of minority representation, for the citizens who are least politically attentive are often those to whom politics does not attend. Currently, the research on this topic is limited. Excepting the works of Matthews and Prothro (1966) and Verba, Schlozman, and Brady (1995), few scholars examine racial differences in political interest levels; and those who do rely on crosssectional surveys, which can only tell us about interest differences at one point in time. To my knowledge, only Bennett (1986) looks at the race gap over time, and his research is largely descriptive. What the literature lacks is a more comprehensive study of racial differences in interest levels.

This chapter adds to our understanding of the race gap in political interest, and, in so doing, it contributes both to the race politics and the participation literatures. Scholars give many reasons for group differences in political involvement. Rather than catalog these reasons here—curious readers can consult Bobo and Gilliam (1990), Gutterbock and London (1983), and Leighley and Vedlitz (1999) for typologies. I find it more useful to group these explanations by topic. For example, one could categorize the studies in this line of research by whether they emphasize the importance of personal characteristics or contextual forces. In addition to offering what is currently the most extensive analysis of racial differences in political interest, this chapter provides further evidence that macro-level factors can help to explain why some citizens are more politically involved than others are.

CHAPTER 10

DIVIDE AND CONQUER: HOW PARTISAN RACE CUES POLARIZE THE ELECTORATE

VINCENT L. HUTCHINGS AND NICHOLAS A. VALENTINO

RACE HAS HISTORICALLY been the most enduring sociopolitical cleavage in American society (Myrdal 1944; Hutchings and Valentino 2004). Debates over how to address the issue of slavery nearly derailed the delicate compromise necessary for ratification of the Constitution in the eighteenth century and ultimately led to America's deadliest war in the nineteenth century. In the twentieth century, the issue of race precipitated one of the most far-reaching social movements in our nation's history and ultimately led to the dismantling of Jim Crow racism in the South.

Still, the racial divide in American politics has not been fully eradicated. Even in the first decade of the twenty-first century, Black and White Americans differed sharply in their political views. This is most evident in their presidential candidate preferences and in their party allegiance. For example, exit polls indicate that in the 2008 presidential election, 95 percent of African Americans voted for Democratic nominee Senator Barack Obama whereas 43 percent of Whites voted for the Republican nominee, Senator John McCain. Moreover, in a particularly bad year for Republicans, a slight plurality of Whites remains committed to the GOP. According to the 2008 American National Election Study (ANES), 45 percent of Whites identified with the Republican Party compared to 44 percent who identified as Democrats. Among Blacks, only

5 percent identified as Republicans and about 85 percent identified as Democrats. This racial divide in political perspectives has not diminished over time and there is little reason to expect that it will decline in the foreseeable future, in spite of the election of the nation's first president of African descent (Hutchings 2009).

By many accounts, both journalistic and scholarly, politicians have sought to exploit these racial divisions for political gain (Edsall and Edsall 1991; Kinder and Sanders 1996; Reeves 1997). This has gone on throughout much of American history (Mendelberg 2001), but what is perhaps most interesting is the extent to which this practice continues even *after* the collapse of Jim Crow racism in the 1960s. The post–Civil Rights Movement version of racial partisan appeals is often more subtle than the blunt efforts from the nineteenth and early twentieth century. Along with former Georgia governor George Wallace, and Republican Presidential nominee Barry Goldwater, one of the earliest pioneers of this new form of racial campaigning was Richard Nixon. Nixon's infamous "southern strategy" from his 1968 and 1972 presidential bids involved appeals to southern Whites, not on the discredited basis of Jim Crow racism, but rather on the grounds of "law and order" and other racial code words. In short, this strategy relied on appeals to those concerned with preserving the racial status quo but without overt appeals to racism. In practice, candidates seeking to court these voters would highlight their opposition to "busing" or "welfare" or "crime" even as they proclaimed their support for the principle of racial equality.

As indicated in more detail below, these appeals appear to have been, at least in some cases, successful. But what is the cost of such a strategy? At present, the literature on overt and covert racial appeals has focused principally, indeed almost exclusively, on the extent and process by which such appeals mobilize support among Whites. However, we still know little about how partisan racial appeals affect Black Americans. The aim of this chapter is to explore this understudied topic in more detail. In particular, we examine whether African Americans are immune to such appeals (owing to their overwhelming support for the Democratic Party and their ostensibly chronic preoccupation with racial concerns) or if exposure to racial cues succeed in exacerbating the racial divide by driving Blacks and Whites further apart.

EXPLOITING RACIAL DIVISIONS IN THE POST–CIVIL RIGHTS ERA

Politicians have sought to exploit racial divisions since before the passage of the 15th amendment granting voting rights to African-American males (Klinkner and Smith 1999; Williams 2003). However, some have argued that with the sweeping changes brought about by the Civil Rights Movement, such appeals are no longer effective in American politics (Thernstrom 1987; Thernstrom & Thernstrom 1997). The Thernstroms raise three criticisms regarding the effectiveness of racialized campaign strategies. First, they argue that such appeals, often characterized as implicit or covert, are simply too subtle for most Americans to recognize. That is, the use of so-called racial "code words," such as "law and order" or "welfare queen," do not strike most Americans as pertaining solely to African Americans and, thus, are not recognized as racial appeals. Second, critics argue that if the voters did recognize such appeals as racially motivated they would almost universally reject them. That is, since the successes of the Civil Rights Movement, virtually all Americans regard political efforts to appeal to racial sentiments as unacceptable. Finally, even if Whites appear to respond to racial messages, it is not because of the racial content of the message that they are persuaded, but rather because of the (nonracial) elements—such as the elements highlighting the value of individualism.

A growing literature suggests that conclusions regarding the demise of racialized campaign appeals may be premature (Gilens 1999; Hutchings et al. 2004; Mendelberg 1997, 2001; Reeves 1997; Valentino et al. 2002). Essentially, these scholars argue that subtle appeals to race can in fact alter mass political decisions. The power of such appeals lies in their ability to activate racial thinking among voters even though the appeals are ostensibly not about race at all. Mendelberg (2001) lays out this theory in detail. She offers four axioms that undergird the phenomenon of "racial priming." First, Mendelberg maintains that, at least in the post–Civil Rights era, most Whites are *ambivalent* on matters of race. On the one hand there is genuine commitment to the norm of racial equality. On the other hand, there is also genuine resentment about the demands made by Blacks as well as lingering anti-Black stereotypes. Second, Mendelberg notes that oftentimes voters cannot recognize the racial subtext of campaign appeals. In fact, she argues this is precisely why they are effective. As long as the appeal is sufficiently subtle, or *ambiguous*, then it can activate or prime the latent resentment many Whites hold against Blacks without appearing to violate Whites' genuine commitment to the norm of racial equality.[1] Third, these subtle racial appeals are effective because they make latent racial attitudes more *accessible* in memory. In effect, subtle appeals are effective *because Whites are not even aware* that they are bringing their racial attitudes to bear on their political decisions (the process is automatic or *unconscious*).[2] Finally, and consistent with the argument of critics, Mendelberg argues that if voters do become *aware* of such appeals they will reject them because of the violation of the norm of racial equality (and their sincere desire not to violate this norm). Thus, she argues that if voters recognize the racial appeal then it will cease to be effective.

PARTISAN RACE CUES AND THE AFRICAN-AMERICAN VOTER

Although the literature on racial priming and racial appeals has demonstrated the power of elite racial cues in the context of election campaigns, this research suffers from a glaring omission: the failure to consider the impact of such appeals on the attitudes of Black Americans (Gilens 1999; Hutchings et al. 2004; Mendelberg 1997, 2001; Valentino et al. 2002; although see Hutchings, Valentino, Philpot, and White 2006). It is perhaps understandable that scholars have not addressed this issue. As indicated above, African Americans' allegiance to the Democratic Party has scarcely fluctuated over the past forty years. Moreover, if racial considerations are chronically salient among African Americans—as many scholars have assumed—then partisan racial appeals should not have much of an effect on Black attitudes about the major party political candidates (Dawson 1994; Lau 1989; Lublin 2004). In short, most seem to believe that near-monolithic Black support for the Democratic candidate is all but assured regardless of the campaign strategies adopted by the candidates.

However plausible this perspective may be, there is a growing body of literature that suggests it is overstated. A number of recent works have shown that Black attitudes on various public policy debates are neither immutable nor invariably infused with racial considerations (Bobo and Johnson 2004; Harris-Lacewell 2004; Hutchings et al. 2006; Hurwitz and Peffley 2005; Tate 2003; White 2007). Either through question wording experiments embedded in sample surveys (Bobo and Johnson 2004; Hurwitz and Peffley 2005; Tate 2003) or laboratory experiments (Harris-Lacewell 2004; Hutchings et al. 2006; White 2007) this research has shown that Blacks do respond to racialized political frames, implying that such considerations are not chronically salient. For example, Bobo and Johnson (2004) and Hurwitz and Peffley (2005) both find Black attitudes about the criminal justice system become more liberal after exposure to arguments highlighting the disproportionate penalties faced by African Americans. Similarly, Tate (2003) shows that Black support for majority-minority districts is heavily influenced by the racial content of the arguments supporting such districts. Finally, Harris-Lacewell (2004), White (2007), and Hutchings and his colleagues (2006) demonstrate in a series of laboratory experiments that Blacks' ideological views, policy preferences, and even their candidate evaluations can be significantly influenced by the nature of the racial cues they receive.

With the exception of the work by Hutchings and his colleagues, none of the work cited above considers attitudes about political candidates.[3] Still, although candidate preferences may seem to be less pliable, it is possible that the reverse is true. That is, although debates concerning particular issues often remain on the nations' agenda for many years, political candidates—and given term limits, especially presidential candidates—are often much more transitory. In 2000, for example, Vice-President Al Gore had been a national figure at least since 1988 when he first ran for the Democratic nomination for president, but then-Governor George W. Bush was a relative unknown on the national stage. It is not at all clear that Blacks viewed him as a "traditional" Republican and, indeed, his obscure political background allowed Bush to campaign credibly as an unconventional, or "compassionate," conservative (see Philpot 2007). Consequently, we argue that implicit racial appeals should have influenced a range of candidate attitudes for White *and* Black voters in 2000. Specifically, Blacks' preference for Gore relative to Bush should be smaller in the absence of implicit racial appeals and greater when they are present in campaign communications. Moreover, this should hold true both for overall candidate support as well as related attitudes, such as which candidate is most competent in particular issue areas and which candidate will best represent particular social groups.[4]

DATA AND METHODS

Our interest in this chapter is to determine whether implicitly racialized campaign appeals influence political judgments. One of the most effective ways to examine campaign effects is through the use of experimental methods. The principal advantage of this strategy is that it allows the researcher to isolate and manipulate the factors that might produce changes in political preferences (Kinder and Palfrey 1993). Much of the previous work on racialized campaign appeals have relied upon laboratory experiments (Mendelberg 1997, 2001; Valentino et al. 2002). While this approach maximizes the strength of one's causal inferences, laboratory experiments sacrifice external validity—the ability to extrapolate to a larger population. In contrast, cross-sectional sample surveys are ideal for estimating means and trends in a population, but they are less effective at determining precise causal impact. Ideally, both strategies would be combined so that one could both isolate causal factors and confidently extrapolate the findings to a larger population (see for example Gilens 1999; and Reeves 1997). This is the strategy we adopt for this chapter.

The data for these analyses are drawn from an innovative survey experiment conducted in the spring and summer of 2000 in the tri-county metropolitan area of Detroit.[5] Respondents in these face-to-face interviews were selected at random. The chief goal of this study was to manipulate the salience of racial cues embedded in standard political advertisements and then expose our respondents to a video stimulus. The questionnaire and political advertisements for this Detroit Area Study (DAS) were stored on a laptop computer that interviewers carried into the respondents' homes. Approximately 10 minutes into the interview, the laptop was turned over to the respondent to view the advertisements and to answer some questions about politics immediately following.[6] Out of 652 initial contacts, 314 interviews were completed, of which 568 were eligible, for a response rate of $314/568 = 55.3$ percent.[7] The following analyses focus only on respondents who self-identify as either Black or White. After excluding all other respondents, the sample size drops slightly to 302.[8]

All subjects viewed three separate advertisements. Subjects in the control group viewed three common product commercials. Subjects in each of the three treatment groups viewed one of the product ads followed by a political ad of our own design and yet another product ad.[9] The political ads we designed focus on the candidacy of George W. Bush. In each of the three different versions of the ad, the male narrator begins by invoking Bush's "dedication to an America with strong values," and then contrasts Bush with Democrats who would "spend your tax dollars on wasteful government programs." The narrator continues, "George W. Bush will cut taxes, because you know best how to spend the money you earn." The second half of the narrative focuses on health care, with the claim that Bush will reform an "unfair system that only provides health care for some, while others go without proper treatment because their employer can't afford it."

The experimental manipulation in the Bush ads is carried entirely in the images that accompany the narration. In the "race-neutral" version of the ad, the only recognizable people in the ad are George W. Bush and his wife. For example, we inserted racially neutral visuals, such as the Statue of Liberty, the U.S. Treasury building, and empty residential streets, over this narrative. When health care is invoked, racially ambiguous images of the medical profession appear.[10] Consequently, this ad contains no visual race cues while still advancing the "wasteful government spending" message. In the second and third versions of the ad, visual racial cues are inserted in place of the formerly group-neutral symbolism. For example, in what we refer to as the "Black + White" version of the ad, images of White Americans are added to the neutral version just as the narrator says, "you know best how to spend the money you earn." In addition, a White mother and child are inserted just as the narrator states, "others go without proper treatment, because their employer can't afford it." Bush is also shown interacting with a group of White supporters at the end of the ad. Additionally, this version of the ad includes a brief image of an African American counting money, followed by a Black mother and child in an office setting, just as the narrator says "Democrats want to spend your tax dollars on wasteful government programs." When the narrator invokes the health care system that "only provides health care for some," a Black mother and child are shown in a hospital setting. All other images in the ad are identical to those in the visually "neutral" version. In what we will refer to as the "White cues" condition, all African-American visual images in the "Black + White" version are removed, so that only White Americans appear in this ad.

The three versions of the Bush political ad were meant to vary the type of racial implications one might draw from the message. The neutral version gives the audience no obvious indication about which group or groups in society benefit from higher taxes and increased spending on social welfare programs and, alternatively which group or groups bear the burden of such policies. The "White cues" version of the ad indirectly indicates to viewers that Whites are disproportionately responsible for generating tax revenue yet do not benefit in the form of social welfare expenditures. The "Black + White" campaign appeal implies not only that Whites bear this burden, but that the primary recipients of the governmental benefits are African Americans. As the racialized message is starkest in this version, we anticipate that the effects will also be largest in the "Black + White" version.[11] Finally, it is worth repeating that all of these messages are conveyed without any verbal references to race or to what some have shown are "racially coded" issues such as crime or welfare (Gilens 1999; Gilliam and Iyengar 2000; Mendelberg 2001). We believe our emphasis on implicit cues mimics what actually occurs in contemporary political discourse. Moreover, by focusing on less racially charged issues we adopt a conservative test of our theory.

RESULTS

Our first test involves the impact of our political ads on levels of support for George W. Bush. We measure this in two ways: presidential vote choice and the feeling thermometer.[12] The three experimental conditions are represented by dummy variables along with interactions for each of these conditions with respondent race.[13] If our expectations are confirmed, then the interactions should be negatively signed, indicating that African Americans are less supportive of Bush after exposure to the Bush political ad. This should be especially true where the racial cues are most prominent, albeit implicit, as in the Black + White condition. The results for Whites, on the other hand, should be either mildly positive, suggesting greater support for Bush after exposure to the racialized ads, or essentially zero, owing to internal divisions among Whites. The second column in Table 10.1 presents these results for the vote choice. In general, our expectations are not confirmed. That is, the interactions between race and the experimental conditions are not negative nor are they statistically significant. In short, Blacks' voting decisions are unaffected by the racial cues embedded in our Bush ads. As those who argue for the chronic salience of race among African Americans might have expected, irrespective of which ad they are exposed to, Blacks are roughly 16 percentage points less supportive of Bush than are comparable Whites. Whites' candidate preferences are also unaffected by the ads, as all of the coefficients on the treatment conditions are negligible in size and fall well short of statistical significance.

The third column in Table 10.1 presents the results for the George W. Bush feeling thermometer. Here our results are more in keeping with expectations. The "Black + White" condition by race interaction is highly significant, both statistically and substantively. To appreciate the size of these effects, the analyses presented in Table 10.1 have been converted into bar graphs, as shown in Figure 10.1. The first square on the left-hand side of the figure represents the estimated feeling-thermometer scores for Bush among Whites and Blacks, respectively, holding all other variables in the equation at their mean or median. Here, we find that racial differences are minor and, in any case, not statistically significant. Among those respondents who viewed the neutral version or the "Whites only" version of the Bush ad, as represented by the second and third pairs of bars, there is scarcely any change. However, when the racial cues are more prominent, as in the "Black + White" version of the ad, racial divisions become extremely pronounced. Specifically, in the ad where the implicit race cues are most striking, White support for Bush grows by 4 points whereas Black support declines by 22 points. The result is a racial gap of 21 points on the 101-point feeling thermometer. Clearly, Blacks and to a lesser extent Whites, are responding to the visual racial cues embedded in the political appeal as the narrative content of the message does not vary across conditions.

The impact of partisan race cues may extend beyond candidate support. It is possible that these messages also convey to voters the priorities and characteristics of the candidate. Specifically, we examine whether the racial cues contained in our ads influence perceptions of how the

Table 10.1   Effects of implicit racial cues on presidential vote choice, Bush thermometer, candidate responsiveness to social groups, and effectiveness handling economy

	Vote choice	Bush thermometer	Represent Whites	Represent Blacks	Represent business	Handle economy
Intercept	.71***	67.16***	.56***	.41***	.75***	.72***
	(.03)	(4.64)	(.05)	(.05)	(.05)	(.05)
Neutral condition	.03	–.859	.08*	.06	.04	–.02
	(.04)	(4.99)	(.05)	(.05)	(.05)	(.06)
Whites only condition	.00	–2.93	.13**	.04	.04	.02
	(.04)	(4.77)	(.05)	(.05)	(.05)	(.05)
White & Black condition	–.05	4.08	.11*	.09*	.06	.04
	(.07)	(4.87)	(.05)	(.05)	(.05)	(.05)
Black	–.16**	5.37	.15**	–.02	–.04	.06
	(.05)	(6.77)	(.07)	(.07)	(.07)	(.08)
Neutral * Black	–.01	.27	–.17*	–.07	–.12	–.06
	(.07)	(9.34)	(.09)	(.10)	(.10)	(.10)
White condition * Black	.04	–.54	–.11	–.07	–.06	–.13
	(.07)	(9.96)	(.10)	(.10)	(.11)	(.11)
White & Black condition * Black	.03	–25.78**	–.30***	–.05	–.21*	–.19*
	(.07)	(9.31)	(.09)	(.10)	(.10)	(.10)
Party identification	–.19***	–15.44***	–.03*	–.08***	–.06***	–.19***
	(.01)	(1.87)	(.02)	(.02)	(.02)	(.02)
Education	–.03	–1.97	.03	–.14***	–.08**	–.06*
	(.02)	(3.39)	(.03)	(.03)	(.04)	(.04)
Female	–.01	.87	–.03	.07**	–.11***	–.04
	(.02)	(3.04)	(.03)	(.03)	(.03)	(.03)
Race of interviewer	.05*	–2.20	–.01	–.03	.01	.03
	(.02)	(3.00)	(.03)	(.03)	(.03)	(.03)
Adjusted R square	.53	.23	.05	.10	.19	.30
N	293	293	293	292	293	293

Notes: * p ≤ .05; ** p ≤ .01; *** p ≤ .001 for one-tailed test, except constant.

presidential candidates will represent particular social groups, and how well they will manage the economy. We focus on three social groups in this chapter: Whites, Blacks, and business groups.[14] The results of these analyses are presented in Table 10.1. We find that our ads—particularly the "Black + White" version—succeed in exacerbating racial divisions on each issue with the important exception of the responsiveness to Blacks variable. Even on the representing Blacks question, our White respondents are more likely to view Bush more favorably, relative to Gore, after they have viewed the ad with both Black and White implicit cues. Among Blacks, however, the effects are essentially indistinguishable from zero. The inability of our ads to shape these views may be due to the lack

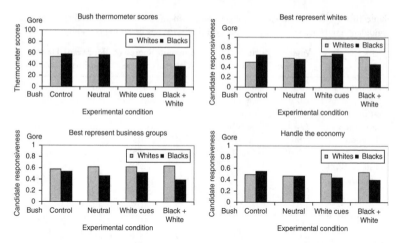

Figure 10.1   Estimated Bush thermometer and candidate responsiveness, by race and experimental condition.

of variance in these perceptions. Across all conditions, only 15 percent of Whites viewed Bush as more likely to represent Black interests, with 56 percent reporting the Gore was most responsive to this group. Among Blacks, perceptions are even more skewed. Only 5 percent viewed Bush as more likely to represent the interests of their group. Fully 57 percent viewed Gore as the more responsive candidate, with 37 percent viewing him as "much better" than Bush. Racial differences are not as sharp for representing Whites, business, and handling the economy.

The results from Table 10.1 are most clearly illustrated by converting them into figures. The upper-right-hand quadrant of Figure 10.1 presents the results for candidate responsiveness to Whites.[15] Here we find that, in the control condition, Blacks are significantly better inclined than Whites to view Bush as more likely to represent Whites' interests, relative to Gore. This likely reflects the widespread view among African Americans that the contemporary Republican Party is primarily designed to reflect White interests, rather than (or, perhaps at the expense of) Black interests (Dawson 1994; Gurin, Hatchett, and Jackson 1989). However, among those respondents who viewed the "neutral" version of the Bush ad, significant racial differences begin to emerge. In this condition, Blacks become somewhat *less* convinced that Bush is the more effective candidate on this dimension even as Whites become somewhat more convinced that the Texas governor would more effectively represent their interests. As a result, the racial gap present in the control condition all but disappears in the neutral condition. How is it that racial perceptions are divergent here even though the ad contains no racial imagery? Although our data only allow us to speculate, it is possible that in some cases political rhetoric alone is sufficient to activate racial considerations if the issues raised are associated with race in the minds of the voters (Edsall and Edsall 1991; Gillian and Iyengar 2000; Valentino et al. 2002).

When the Bush ad contains "White cues" only, the implicit racial message for White respondents seems almost unmistakable. Relative to the control group, Whites' perceptions of candidate responsiveness to their group move 13 percentage points in the direction of George W. Bush. Blacks are scarcely affected at all, suggesting that the message conveyed in this condition is very much in keeping with what they assumed to be the case in the absence of any Bush ad. Interestingly, the 15-point racial gap present in the control condition reemerges in the "Black + White" condition, only in this condition it is Whites who are more convinced that Bush is more responsive to their group, relative to Gore. This stark turnaround suggests that African Americans are reacting to the Black as well as the White cues in this ad. That is, in the "Black + White" condition, and to a lesser extent the "neutral condition," Blacks appear to view Bush as promoting White interests *at the expense of Blacks*. Perhaps as a reaction to the implicit suggestion of racial conflict, Blacks give Bush lower scores across the board on representing groups in society.

In the lower-left-hand corner of Figure 10.1, we shift from an examination of racial groups to perceptions of an economic group. Our expectation is that when candidates convey an implicit, and traditional, partisan message on race, they may also solidify stereotypes about their responsiveness to other groups. In particular, we focus on business groups in this figure. In the control condition, racial differences in perceptions of candidate responsiveness are negligible. More substantial, and familiar differences begin to emerge in the next two conditions, but these effects fall short of statistical significance. Once again, we find that the "Black + White" treatment produces the largest racial gap in perceptions, with Whites adopting the most favorable view of Bush whereas African Americans move strongly, and significantly, in the direction of Al Gore.

Finally, in the lower-right-hand corner of Figure 10.1, we move away from attitudes about social groups and instead focus on perceptions of which candidate will best handle the economy. As in the previous figure, racial differences in the "neutral" and "Whites only" treatments do not differ, statistically, from the control group. However, in the "Black + White" condition the racial groups become significantly polarized around perceptions concerning who would best handle the economy. Clearly Blacks, who shift 15 percentage points in the direction of Al Gore, relative to the control, infer from the implicit racial messages in this ad that George W. Bush would not only mismanage race relations, but also the national economy. So again, Blacks and not Whites seem to be punishing Bush for promoting the idea that Black and White group interests are in conflict. In short, implicit racial cues have implications beyond racial perceptions.

CONCLUSION

First and foremost, this chapter has shown that implicit racial cues embedded in standard political messages can affect both Black and White Americans. We found strong support for this proposition in the area of candidate support and with regard to perceptions of candidate responsiveness and policy traits. Assumptions that African Americans' political views are chronically influenced by racial considerations, and thus immune from the effects of racial framing, were shown to be inaccurate. In many cases, Blacks' political judgments were not racially distinctive unless they were presented with the subtle racial messages contained in our ads. When such cues were present, the racial divide in political perceptions increased substantially, at times rivaling the effects of partisan identification.

Although our results demonstrate convincingly that implicit racial appeals can influence African Americans, those who have argued that racial considerations are constantly salient among this group are not wholly wrong. Our analyses suggest that, in the case of the presidential vote choice and perceptions about candidate responsiveness to Black interests, implicit racial cues are not terribly persuasive. That is, the lion's share of African Americans are already so predisposed to support the Democratic candidate, and are virtually monolithic in their belief that Republican candidates do not have their best interests at heart, that no political advertisement is likely to influence these views. The research presented in this chapter indicates that Blacks are not nearly so unanimous in terms of judgments about group leadership and more general measures of candidate approval. Here, they are susceptible to the persuasive power of implicit racial cues.

In many ways, this research only scratches the surface on the issue of the ways in which African Americans are influenced by the racial content in various political frames. Our work shows that such cues can be effective, but there remain a number of unanswered questions in this nascent literature. For example, although we demonstrate significant persuasion effects in this chapter, it remains to be seen whether the racial attitudes of Blacks can be primed by particular racial appeals (implicit or explicit). If racial appeals can prime the racial attitudes of African Americans, then are their in-group or out-group attitudes most likely to be activated (see for example White 2007 reprinted in this volume)? Further, are some Blacks more likely to be susceptible to these media effects and, if so, which ones? All of these questions need to be addressed in future research on the role of racial messages in campaign appeals. In the end, we believe that to fully understand the role of race in contemporary American politics, researchers need to consider not only the views of Whites, but also those of Blacks as well as an increasingly multiracial and multiethnic citizenry.

CHAPTER 11

AFRICAN-AMERICAN ACTIVISTS' PERCEPTIONS OF RACISM AND EMPOWERMENT

KENNETH FOSTER, SR.

> "Racism is an integral, permanent, and indestructible component of this society."
>
> Derrick Bell, *Faces at the Bottom of the Well*

RACISM IS A PERSISTENT REALITY THAT PLAGUES ALL AMERICANS. The fact that it has morphed into a more covert and insidious phenomenon has caused many to deny its persistence. African Americans are least likely to be able to engage in such denial. In fact, many take on roles of activists for human and civil rights as a response to racist discrimination. The primary goal of this study was to examine the relationship between African-American activists' experiences with racism and their personal sense of empowerment.

The author hypothesized that an individual's perception of racism can foster a need for and sense of that individual's attitudinal and behavioral empowerment. This hypothesis asserts that such individuals perceive racism as a pervasive threat to their psychological and physical well-being and that their empowering attitudes and behaviors are at least in part a response to this threat. This behavior can, therefore, be also viewed as a coping strategy.

Research has demonstrated that racism—a stressor experienced by African Americans—is on the one hand negatively correlated with health behaviors and symptoms, and certain belief systems. On the other hand, there exists empirical data demonstrating a positive relationship between prior experience with racism/racial prejudice and, among other outcomes, Africentric awareness. This research project describes some of the conditions under which certain African Americans, as a reaction to racism, become empowered to engage in individual and/or collective action that benefits themselves and others.

Racism is the belief that race is a primary determinant of human worth or potential. Racist behavior can range from making verbal slurs, such as "nigger," or denying people their basic freedoms, including access to and use of public resources, to inflicting physical harm, including death. African Americans have been the primary targets of racist discrimination, at least in the United States, since slavery. Historically, torture and lynching were common, sanctioned behaviors. The resulting psychological effects continue to take a measurable, albeit debated, psychological toll. Although overt physical practices of racism have abated appreciably, blatant incidents continue to occur. For example, on June 7, 1998, in Jasper, Texas, James Byrd, an African American, was offered and accepted a ride by three White men[1]. He was then beaten, chained to the back of the truck and dragged several miles. Mr. Byrd's torso, head and one arm were eventually recovered a mile apart along a road littered with his blood, tissue and bone. Three months later, a volunteer fire department, in a predominantly White New York neighborhood, sponsored a Labor Day parade that included a parody of the Jasper incident.

OUTCOMES AND/OR EFFECTS OF RACISM

It is utterly exhausting being Black in America: physically, mentally, and emotionally … There is no respite or escape from your badge of color.

Marian Wright Edelman

The broader psychological question relating to the current study is: what impact does racism, whether subtle or overt, actually have on an individual's subjective well-being? African Americans cannot escape the stressful effects of issues related to race. Whether highly assimilated or immersed in the double consciousness of being both African and American, Blacks feel the sting of up-front racism as well as the subtle, more common "microaggressions" either directly or indirectly on a regular basis (Du Bois 1903; Early 1994; Feagin and Sikes 1994; Foster 2004; Harris 2009). When asked if his diagnosis of AIDS posed the greatest life challenge to him, the late Arthur Ashe responded that there was a more formidable challenge: "Being black is. No question about it. Even now, it continues to feel like an extra weight tied around me" (Shuster 1993).

Not only is there overwhelming evidence of the negative and often debilitating effects of racism on the mental and physical health of African Americans but the very systems that are supposed to provide ways to ameliorate these effects in some instances exacerbate the problem. These systemic inequalities contribute to a pervasiveness of distrust for such institutions by Blacks (Jones 1993; Nickerson, Helms, and Terrell 1994; Rubens 1996; Stevenson 1994; Terrell, Terrell, and Miller 1993; Whaley 2004). While there is a continually growing corpus of literature illuminating the deleterious effects of racist discrimination on African Americans (e.g., Carter 2007; Clark and Clark 1947; Foster 2004; Franklin 1991; Landrine and Klonoff 1996b; Priest 1991; Steele 1997; Utsey 1998; Ward 1996), there is comparatively little evidence of outcomes that are psychologically empowering.

Racism, like empowerment, manifests in various forms, depending on people, settings, goals, etc. At least one researcher (Jones 1997) posits that the complexity of racism is justification for viewing the phenomena in terms of *racisms*—a set of various, often overlapping constructs. He defines racism thus:

> Racism builds on the negative-attitude view of prejudice but includes three other important criteria: First, the basis of group characteristics was assumed to rest on biology—race was a biological concept. Second, racism has, as a necessary premise, the <u>superiority</u> of one's own race. Third, racism rationalizes institutional and cultural practices that formalize the hierarchical domination of one racial group over another. Therefore, although racism shares certain aspects of prejudice, it takes on a decidedly broader and more complex meaning (11).

So it is that racism can be and is studied and discussed in its myriad forms, including institutional racism (Branch 2008; Jones 1997; Parham 1993), scientific racism (Herrnstein and Murray 1994; Landrine and Klonoff 1996b; Rubens 1996; Stevenson 1994), and gendered or sexuality-based racism (Ali 2007; Leavitt 1998; Mays and Cochran 1993; Stevenson 1994; West 1993).

Many people today believe or at least advocate the notion that racism has become a relatively innocuous, individual-based issue and not the persistent, pervasive phenomenon that it once was. In addition, there are many African Americans, mostly middle class and neoconservative, who likewise perceive racism as being all but eradicated in the United States (Corcoran and Thompson 2004; Robinson 1995; Steele 1990). For example, Robinson (1995) believes that racism is no longer an impediment to racial progress but that there now exists a counterproductive attitude among discontented Black and White liberals, whiners and naysayers to an ostensibly emerging fair, cooperative society. Relatedly, some scrutinize racist and/or perceived racist events, offering routinely alternative explanations (e.g., Harris 2009; Schacht 2008), suggesting the onus perpetually is on the target or perceiver to "prove" the event to be racist.

Some broad observations have been made about psychological responses to racism. For instance, Feagin and Sikes (1994) reported that:

> Racial stress can stimulate important coping mechanisms. Individual reactions ... may range from constructive adaptation to a breakdown of normal functioning. Significantly, many victims of discrimination have marshaled resources that were not previously obvious or strengths of which they were not aware (275).

Much of the "constructive adaptation" in which Blacks engage is defensive in nature and strategies are geared toward survival rather than affirmative empowerment or activism. For instance, coping mechanisms include careful assessment, often resulting in less than direct confrontation. Even direct confrontation, however, does not in and of itself constitute an enduring activist posture. In turn, this study sought to address the following question: given the obvious psychological, emotional, and somatic toll of racism, under what conditions and to what extent might a positive outcome, such as empowerment or activism, result from a negative stressor, such as experiencing racial discrimination?

There are, of course, variations among African Americans in the ways in which they cope with racist events. As pointed out by Landrine and Klonoff (1996a), coping style and skills probably moderate the negative impact of such racist events. This probably occurs in much the same way that they moderate the impact of generic life events and hassles (Billings and Moos 1981). Similarly, social support (e.g. Cohen and Wills 1985) and personality traits such as hardiness (Kobasa 1979) are likely to moderate the negative impact of racist discrimination. For some, the response to racism may be a sense of powerlessness; for others, the response is an attendant empowering behavior. In fact, activism is often viewed as the only viable response to oppression. Researchers have begun to study the factors that mediate the relationship between racism and well-being. Looking at African-American coping responses, according to Moritsugu (personal communication, 1998), four notable themes emerge: Compassion, Perspective, Consideration of the end goals, and Flexibility.[2] Gail Wyatt (personal communication, 1997) agreed with the importance of being flexible. Racism, she explained, demands a multitude of responses that, as much as anything, depend on how you are feeling that day: "You have to know how to cope, what kind of strategies you need on a daily basis. ... If you think racism is going to punch you, then you have to know how to let some things alone so you can come back and punch it the next day."

For many African Americans, the response to racism may be a sense of powerlessness, learned hopelessness (Seligman 1975), despair, and/or negative health behaviors and symptoms (Landrine and Klonoff 1996a). For some, their response includes participation in social groups or organizations that can help foster a sense of empowerment. The empirical question, however, remains: for whom and under what conditions does the latter occur? For the purposes of the current study, empowerment refers to "a process by which individuals of lesser power gain control over their lives and influence the organizational and societal structures in which they live" (Segal, Silverman, and Temkin 1995, 215–227). To this definition, however, it should be added that the goal is *greater* control over one's life and *positive* influence on their environment.

One researcher (Rappaport 1987) suggests that empowerment is the process toward which the primary energies of community psychologists, social workers, and others should be directed and through which most of the goals for social and individual change will be most appropriately accomplished. For instance, among many providers to mentally disabled clients, empowerment has become a *program principle* (Cohen 1989) and this principle underlies group self-help designs, mechanisms, and consequences. Rappaport (1981) asserts further, as do others (Zimmerman 1990) that empowerment should not be treated simply as "some personality variable" that would neglect the construct's social relationship.

One of the glaring gaps in the psychological literature—albeit less glaring within Black or Africentric psychology—is the paucity of research comparing and contrasting differences in worldview and cosmology based on culture, race, and/or ethnicity. Ogletree (1976) points out that Blacks in the United States may in fact be much more like non-Western groups in their worldview and orientation to correlates to empowerment, such as locus of control (Hsieh, Shybut, and Lotsof 1969). This suggests alternative explanations for cultural aspects that are not sufficiently appreciated by Eurocentric social scientists. For example, an Africentric orientation, not unlike that of Native American and other indigenous peoples, posits a general philosophical assumption that humans do not, should not, and cannot control the forces of nature and that the collective, not the individual, holds social primacy (Azibo 1997; Brook and Pahl 2005; Cross 1991; Harris 1992; Morris 2000; Myrdal 1944; Nobles 1989; Thompson and Spacapan 1991).

Undergirding empowerment is the construct of power. Power is also central to the concept of racism in that racism can be seen as a function of power. Empowerment is a process of developing power to "obtain resources on multiple levels to enable [people] to gain greater control over their environment" (Hasenfeld 1987, 478–479).

African-American women and men have a well-documented history of activism. History provides evidence that the formation of self-help, educational, economic, and political groups predates the arrival of the Mayflower (Aptheker 1983; Robinson 1995; Young 2007). Even during slavery, individuals and groups empowered themselves to resist those who would deny their dignity and humanity. Aptheker (1983), for example, documented some 281 slave revolts, and this did not take into account the resistance posed by human captives that occurred during the Mid-Atlantic Passage.[3] Activism was and continues to be a behavior often viewed by the activist as not only possible but as a necessary response to social constraints. As pointed out by Weis, Fine, Shepard, and Foster (1998):

> In the face of American society telling African Americans that they could not do certain things, not actualize the American Dream, an oppositional culture developed wherein Blacks were told within the community that they could do a great many things, irrespective of dominant ideology about Blacks (67).

The stories that parents share and the warnings that they impart about the pitfalls of growing up Black in a White-dominated society are crucial to individual development. This process, however, does not necessarily include the process of modeling advocacy geared toward challenging, limiting, or removing those pitfalls.

DATA AND METHODS

At this juncture, it seems important to do two things: 1) restate the main research questions/hypotheses; and 2) contextualize the study findings with some of the data. This qualitative research project collected data on and describes conditions—including racist discrimination—under which African Americans choose to engage in activist behavior. It was hypothesized that such individuals perceive racism as a pervasive threat to their psychological and physical well-being and that their activist attitudes and behaviors are, at least in part, a response to this threat.

A sample of 20[4] African-American activists (8 females, 12 males) were recruited from various locations in New York, New Jersey, Pennsylvania, Washington, D.C., and South Carolina. Each of these individuals was involved in one or more specific forms of social activism. In each case, the decision to engage in activist behavior was made prior to being involved in their current professional activities, much of which involves what might easily be referred to as activism.

A semistructured interview was used to collect data on individuals' perceptions of and experiences with racism and empowerment and their beliefs about how these factors impact their lives, either negatively or positively. Interviews were audio-taped and were an average of 45 minutes in length.

About 75 per cent of the participants are middle class, with only one individual having an annual household income of less than $35,000. All but one were born and reared in the Southeastern United States or the Midwest. One participant was born and reared in Jamaica, West Indies.[5] Half of them are married, four are single, five divorced or separated, and one was a widow. Among those who are parents, they have an average of two children.[6] All have attended college; seven have obtained a bachelor's degree, and eight hold advanced degrees. Their average age at the time of the interviews was 48. The professions represented within this sample included: administrator, copy editor, clergy, radio broadcaster, community police officer, credit relations analyst, realtor, and a technical operations specialist. There was also a concentration of individuals situated within the field of education, including three directors of academic programs, a history professor, a director of an urban education research project, and a volunteer for an education legal defense group.

RESULTS

DEFINING RACISM

Respondents defined racism in basically one, two, or a combination of three ways: 1) discrimination based on race; 2) the unequal distribution of social, economic, and political power in society; 3) a manifestation of ignorance characterized by strong dislike or hate. It should be noted that some participants offered multiple perspectives on the definition of racism. As a result, the number of individual perspectives was greater than the total number of participants. Possibly the most straightforward way to define racism was discrimination based on race. Half of the participants did just that. For example, Darryl,[7] a former schoolteacher who now is an outspoken broadcast journalist for a noncommercial, progressive radio station, offered this:

> I would think that it's the systematic denial of people's basic rights, based on the color of this skin. And I say systematic because if someone just doesn't like me, that just might be their preference. They don't have to like me. But if they're in a position to deny me my rights, then that's the difference.

Yvette, an operations specialist for a multinational corporation in Aiken, South Carolina, helped to spearhead a labor struggle that resulted in a class action suit brought by African-American employees at her plant. She defined racism as: "The dislike or hatred of another human being within a different race." Ophelia, who is an executive director in northern New Jersey, was equally succinct: "When people are denied access ... for no other reason but race." Lucien, a history professor, offered a multidimensional definition:

> I would look at it as a relationship with at least three different dimensions. Those being individual racism, institutional or systemic racism, and internal racism. And what captures the essence of racism is the inequity that exists between the races and was perpetuated against individuals.

When asked whether Blacks can be perpetrators of racism, Belinda, who holds a Ph.D., found herself dissecting the construct as she spoke:

> I don't think ... I know, at this point there are times when White folks want to act like there are racists among African Americans, we can't be racists. We can be prejudiced. We can dislike people, but ... you know ... the majority population controls everything ... how any of us think, act, or react.

On the other hand, Katherine, a copy editor at a major national magazine and part-time radio journalist offered this:

> You know, it's funny. No one has ever asked me that before and I don't know if I've ever really thought about ... what it actually is. Everybody says because we don't have any power we can't be racist. But, I think, in some ways we can. I think racism is the active dislike and when I say active, even if I'm not in a position of power there may be things that I can do to exclude them from my life. So I think ... to define it you have to include the word exclusionary.

One fourth of the participants in this study offered ignorance as integral to their definition of racism. Nissa, a researcher at a teacher's college, who happens to be in an interracial marriage, sees racism as follows:

> When people put you down or have low expectations for you, call you names, make you invisible. And when you feel it you know it is racism (laugh). When somebody does it, they most likely don't know what they just did but you feel it, you know it was just racism. You experience it on

an institutional level when people are oblivious to policy that they enact that doesn't recognize how racism is pervasive. When teachers in this institution say, "Well, we posted the job but no Black applicants applied," I would say it's racist to not go out and look for people just like they go out and look for [White] people in a White preschool."

Ted is a 55-year-old executive director of a program that introduces young minorities to higher education. As a young undergraduate, he helped to organize migrant farm workers in a rural New York town. He recalls being confronted by police who wanted to know the names of his clients. Adamantly refusing to comply, he was taken to jail. Although released after a relatively short period of time, he was acutely aware of the potential danger he faced that night, on a dark rural road. He also defined racism as multifaceted:

I think there's several levels ... I see it as ... really ignorance and intolerance taken to the next level. See, I think that people [exhibit] racial ignorance because they haven't been exposed [to people of color] ... don't care to be exposed. Then I think there's racial intolerance as a derivative of that. That you don't, you don't set yourself up to tolerate diversity or tolerate people of different races and different roles, or doing different things. But I think racism is also a conscious, asserted effort. ... Then you take the ignorance, you take the intolerance and put it together and make an assertive effort to harm someone, either psychologically, physically, emotionally, career-wise, based totally on their race.

Nate, an outspoken clergy, is chaplain at an AIDS hospice in Newark, New Jersey. He gave his definition of racism by way of describing a tragic situation that he was aware of. Such situations speak loudly to the extent of the emotions that sometimes come into play when race is a salient factor:

Well, let's look at the family that just tries to move into a new neighbor-hood ... I knew a couple that went down to Atlanta. ... And as they was driving around, they asked the question, where are the Black folk. ... They [Whites] shot his family.

EXPERIENCES WITH AND EFFECTS OF RACISM

It goes without saying that there are individual differences across persons. There also are, however, undeniable common threads. Nine participants reported racist experiences that occurred in the South, irrespective of whether they were living there at the time. Sixteen reported having experienced racism for the first time when they were children, on average 10 to 12 years old. Earl, a community police officer, recalls growing up in Asbury Park, New Jersey:

> There were things I felt, that I couldn't put a handle on. Like when my mother took me crosstown to go shopping. The stares, the humbleness that my mother had to assert to certain people. Automatically, I felt it was their [White folks] world. ... And watching my mother, and all that, I was wondering why she had to be so humble to these people. But the way they looked, the way they treated her when she was shopping. ... I knew there was a difference. And I actually felt inferior.

The impact of such experiences is often dependent upon the age at which it occurred. In other words, some of these men and women were exposed to racism but were at the time too young to understand what had transpired. For example, Ted recalls:

> I remember this little White girl named Stella who was a friend in the second grade. ... And I remember at some point I had to stop playing with Stella. But I never quite understood why. Later on in some conversation my mother brought it up, you know, that the family members on Stella's side wanted the playing to stop.

On the other hand, some were quite consciously and adversely affected, even at an early age. Some said that even though their seminal experience may not have been the point at which they decided to take a stand, it was nonetheless a defining moment. Carl, a history professor whose latest of three books offers an analysis of race and racism from a global perspective, said that the trauma of his earliest recollection of racism resulted in an aversion to traveling south again:

> I was about four or five and I went on a visit to my grandparents, down in Alabama. We were forced to go in the back door of a little convenience store ... people would drive by and call us nigger, and those were rather shocking [events] to me, being marked by our race. So I was traumatized. And I didn't go back to the south for another 18 years.

RACISM AS MOTIVATION FOR ACTIVISM

The study hypothesized, that for African-American activists, racism is a stimulus to which their response includes an enduring empowering posture manifest in their conscious activist behavior. In fact, when asked if racism was a motivator for their positive strides in life in general and their activist work in particular, nearly all answered in the affirmative. Only one participant replied specifically that racism was not a motivating force. Some were more deliberating in their answers; others were quick to respond emphatically that their work is, in varying degrees, a direct response to racial injustice experienced by themselves and others.

Ellen, the founding director of an Africentric, community-based organization, shared that her aunt told her that the way to deal with obstacles like racism was to outline a strategy of recognition, response, and goals. Her aunt's words, she said, were that you must, "meet, greet and defeat it." In fact, Ellen continues to meet, greet, and defeat the obstacles posed by racialized inequality. Her activist career dates back over three decades and includes serving as an interim secretary for Dr. Martin Luther King, Jr.

Earl links his decision to become an activist to his experiences in the Air Force:

> It [racism] was a motivator for me. A great motivator … I did a lot of reading … it helped me to understand much better the racism that I felt in the service, and the housing discrimination. I attempted to get an apartment, after I finished serving this country … I was refused the apartment, knowing full well there were vacancies there. So I, I knew.

During his tenure as the only community officer in a predominantly Black community, Earl has been instrumental in diminishing racially skewed hiring practices on the police force for which he works.

At the time of her interview, Yvette was embroiled in negotiating on behalf of her fellow workers, declining offers that would perhaps have benefited her individually. When asked if racism was a source of motivation in this and other activist behavior in which she has been involved, she responded:

> Sure. It has motivated me to take a stand for what I believe in because my children are not going to have equal opportunities if I don't. I am not afraid to speak up but I do it in a polite manner. I want my children to see me as a role model who is aware of her race and sometimes how I have to take a stand for what is right.

On the other hand, Rosalynn, an academic program director, seemed uncertain as to whether her work with young people was a direct response to racist discrimination.

I don't know if it's ... motivated me. I don't know if I'd give it that much control in my life. I think what I do is not so much to show White people what we're capable of doing, but more on the positive side to show our young Black kids what we're capable of doing. So, I'm not going to go to the negative and let that beat me up. It's more or less our young people need some role models. I don't consider myself a role model, but they need to know that ... Black people can get their Ph.D. My people can go to school. Because a lot of our kids now are giving up the notion of working hard. ... They don't see it; they don't want to hear it. And a lot of it [is] because even in the school district in this city, which is mostly Black and Hispanic, most of the teachers are White. So nothing has changed.

In spite of an outlook that seems at once pessimistic and optimistic, her interview exemplifies that there is for some activists a reinterpretation, a personal renegotiation, if you will, of the typical paradigm of racism and oppression. So it is that individuals like Rosalynn have chosen to regard racism as clear and present but not an inherent danger. This may in fact be yet another common trajectory or approach to activism. On the other hand, Melinda, also a program director, felt no uncertainty about her work being a response to racism:

Oh yes, in terms of my choices of a profession and what I do, and where I live, yeah. I mean, my initial thought was to be a civil rights attorney or a defense attorney. And, in the process of doing that, I ended up needing a job. I was working in Financial Aid, and learning that I could assist African Americans. I've been in this job ten years, you know ... I mean, we were talking about African-American and Latino folks who think they can't go to college, and come out of here, you know, with Associates Degrees, and know that they can be successful, [including] in four-year colleges.

Among the few who did not believe that racism, per se, helped to foster any positive outcomes in their lives, such as their activism, there is a need for further analysis. For example, Ted responded that racism had been, among other things, a debilitating force, particularly during his high school years:

No ... it has not been a motivator. I think it has been an unreal weight, you know, because... the thing that became Blackest the quickest in Washington [D.C.], you see, was the public school systems. Because everybody ... [had started] ... moving the kids elsewhere. ... But the other thing was, there was a lot of lack of resources. And ... because of that there were some things that would have sent me in a different direction.

When probed a little further about his high school years, however, Ted revealed the following:

> When I graduated from high school I decided I wanted to work with civil rights issues. I wrote to the Southern Christian Leadership Conference. And I went down and worked with Hosea Williams for that summer. ... And, so I had sort of developed this kind of working knowledge of what the power was ... and then when I looked at the decisions being made I could see how they impact us. I sort of knew. You saw Black faces all around you--super-intendents and all that kind of stuff. But you sort of knew that you weren't getting stuff that Merlin, Virginia, suburban kids were getting.

DEFINING EMPOWERMENT

When this group of activists grappled with defining the politically and emotionally charged concept of empowerment, they offered a variety of responses. While this was true for responses to questions asked before and after this one, the distinction lay in the fact that some of these men and women opted to put a different label on the term itself. This was consistent with the literature as well as a substantial amount of anecdotal data indicating African Americans prefer more descriptive terms, such as resistance.

Activism is a behavior often viewed by the activist as not only possible but a necessary response to social constraints. Angela Davis, speaking at the first national convention of the Black Radical Congress, said of her own experience that, "There wasn't this epiphany, there wasn't this moment" but that her behavior changed in a natural, progressive way. While many of the participants view their activist work as crucial, few if any openly refer to or see themselves as activists, per se. In fact, most would more readily view what they do on a daily basis as coping, as a means to an end or maintenance of their sense of well-being. So it is that there appears to be a circuitous connection between the constructs of coping, resistance, and empowerment.

Ellen, the founding director of a community-based organization, believes that organizations like the NAACP have made major shifts in their focus and purpose. In speaking of activists of the 1960s and 1970s, she describes the shifts:

> They're no longer on the battlefield for civil rights or racism fighters. Basically they're now part of the status quo. Hopefully they're going through a process of regeneration. And maybe what they're doing is important to get back in touch with what real needs are and what real people are but the caliber of leadership has really dropped.

She is, nonetheless, a card-carrying member of the NAACP. It is this apparent dichotomy that sheds light on the complex nature of many Black folks' struggles to remain connected and help maintain some semblance of a base or structure within which they can work to foster social change.

CONCLUSION

When the rallying cry, "Black is beautiful!" first reverberated on percolating college campuses and streets of urban America, it was seen by many as "the collective affirmation of Black identity (Speight, Vera, and Derrickson 1996, 37–52). More than an errant blip on the sociohistorical radar screen, this era represented a major shift in how Black people viewed themselves. In spite of the heightened emotional tenor of this unique period, the assumption of a collective affirmation should not be misconstrued as an affirmation of a unitary Black identity.

Racism in the United States persists as a problem that affects all Americans. Indeed Jones (1997) reminds us:

> Racism is a waste of human capital. ... So, taking racism as a composite label for all forms of disadvantage, discrimination, and bias, it is a problem for its victims, and it is a problem for the entire society. ... In short, the problem of racism was real (3).

It certainly is real to those who are denied a mortgage or a promotion or to those who have become accustomed to being followed in a store or the many whose relationship with the police is defined by being constantly under suspicion yet unable to get a timely response when they dial 911 for help.

There are a large number of people today, Whites and Blacks, who believe that racism is now a minor social aberration, a phenomenon reduced to little more than the sentiment or behavior of a few relegated to the fringes of our broader society. West (1993) asserts that, "This myopia stems from a sometimes unconscious belief that there are no psychic scars, that there was no history" (85). These beliefs render racism even more pernicious and problematic and exacerbate the search for an understanding of, or the ability to predict, the myriad psychological manifestations and ramifications.

This study illuminates the fact that for some African Americans, racism was a motivating force, a catalyst in the process of deciding to become a social activist. The ways in which this was done—that is, the manifestation and mobilization of Black Power in the 1960s and

1970s—clearly differs from the majority of activist movements today. A major difference lies in the venue: the former period was characterized by street-corner activism, knocking from door to door, usually in Black, working-class, or poor neighborhoods, that sought to challenge the dominant culture. In contrast, much of today's activism is carried out within the confines of the dominant culture, that is, schools and other federally and municipally funded and controlled settings. There is none-theless a current, undeniable trend that portends a growing resurgence of activist groups. These groups have been forming in efforts to access and assert the various forms of power that continue to be denied to African Americans (Clark, 1995; Saegert 1989). While these coalitions are in varying states of development, the common factor is that as people begin to *participate*, many find that they are not as powerless as originally per-ceived. Racism clearly plays a significant role in how empowered some African Americans become.

Most of the participants in this study are clearly middle-class African Americans, people who arguably do not personally share in all of the agonies of the underclass. This was significant in that most African Americans who believe that racism has abated appear to be members of the ostensibly privileged middle class. In addition, it might appear logical that those who Ellis Cose (1993) calls the privileged class would have less of a vested interest in the welfare of those who have not achieved similar levels of success.

Of all of America's hot-button issues, racism is certainly one of the most challenging. This is perhaps because it calls into question the very way in which each of us experiences the world, in general, and our society, in particular. This study did not question whether people expe-rience racism but how they experience it, and, equally important, why some people are able to thrive in the face of such adversity. And maybe the more important question is, or should be: why is more research not being done? As such, a primary goal of this study was to begin to lift up and unpack implicit and explicit hypotheses and theoretical insights about race and empowering behavior.

The role of psychology in the genesis and reification of scientific and other racisms is in fact integral to the persistence of institutional racism. In spite of the growing number of psychologists, many of them African Americans, who have chosen to challenge the historical hegemony, the discipline has historically been complicit in the formulation and expan-sion of deficit theory that has placed Blacks at the bottom of the human social totem pole.

Among the limitations to this study was the fact that it relies on self-report as the only source of data. As such, much of the data collected was reactive and responses were subject to biases including social desirability and other interval validity threats. Nonetheless, the qualitative methodology afforded the interviewer an opportunity not possible in quantitative inquiry to engage, probe, gain clarification, and the like. Standardized instruments with fixed responses are insufficient for collecting such an array of complex data that will inform this study.

Tatum (1992) discusses the need to use the university—including courses utilizing confrontational discourse—to address racism and break the oppressive cycle of considering discourse on racism to be taboo. This socially constructed taboo was a significant contributing factor to many people's (mostly White) belief that racism has been relegated to an isolated, individual phenomenon. In addition, social analysis, in general, and psychological research, in particular, continues to place the focus of racism discourse on the discriminated, with little attention placed on the discriminators (Hardiman 1982; Parham 1993).

Finally, several of the participants in the current research were working, as professionals and activists, within the arena of education. That there was this preponderance of such individuals in the study (i.e., this was a convenience sample) should not be misconstrued as implying any generalizable representation of the overall population of activists. Nonetheless, it was significant that these individuals chose academia as the venue within which they would choose to fight for social justice.

The charge of social science is to explore and move in new directions for future research. These things we must do in order to further our insight on how people traverse their individual and collective lives and the role each has in society's development and its simultaneously unfolding history. And so it is that continued investigations, especially longitudinal and intergenerational studies, will advance the theoretical and empirical discourse, help improve approaches to research, and contribute to increased social sensitivity and much needed social change. This change needs to have high on the agenda a push toward goals of transformation across the breadth of our broader society.

Acknowledgment: This research was supported in part by a Spencer Foundation grant.

DEPRESSING THE VOTE: THE ENVIRONMENTAL DETERMINANTS OF TURNOUT IN AFRICAN-AMERICAN PRECINCTS IN THE 2000 PRESIDENTIAL ELECTION

ERNEST B. MCGOWEN

FOR DEMOCRATS IN THE 505TH PRECINCT OF HOUSTON, Texas political information is no further than a trip to the mailbox or a walk around the block. Every few months, the precinct chair Scott Tillinghast and precinct election judge Stephanie Hrabar send out a joint newsletter entitled the "Precinct 505 Democrats Club." The name itself presumes some collegiality as if Democratic identification in this neighborhood has a social as well as political dimension. The newsletter normally has a national story, articles directed at the state and local party, and other information pertinent to the precinct including the next scheduled gathering. The 505th is far from a Democratic precinct; its nonpartisan city council representatives have Republican vote histories and the Republican state representative is going for his third term in November. To capsulate the issue, the description of the precinct convention comes with an inset in bold lettering:

> While the process may sound complicated, in Pct 505 we usually have barely enough voters to fill all of the vacancies for delegates to the Senate

District 15 convention. Chances are that if you come to the convention
and you want to be a delegate ... you will be.[1]

These precinct voters are confronted with a depressing political environment. Yet as part of a larger group, Harris County Democrats, their
electoral prowess is known statewide.

How does a politically isolated group maximize its political utility
when its immediate environment depresses the actualization of its political preferences? In other words, what is it that encourages Precinct 505
voters to transcend the boundaries of their precinct to connect with
the larger group of Harris County Democrats? These are the questions
I attempt to answer in this chapter. To do so, I focus on African-
American voters who live in predominately Black enclaves within larger,
predominately Anglo areas. The last few decades have witnessed a rise in
the residential mobility of African Americans. But although Blacks have
been increasingly able to move from central cities to suburban areas,
they remain quite segregated in predominantly Black suburban neighborhoods (Alba and Logan 1993). As a result, the most salient political
identity for the average African American is race, regardless of income
and education levels (Dawson 1994), despite earlier predictions to the
contrary (see Wilson 1978). Thus, many suburban Blacks find themselves
in a political situation similar to the one described in the opening paragraphs. How does this affect them politically? Because of their high levels
of group identity, suburban Blacks will have political preferences more
similar to their urban counterparts than suburban Anglos, despite living
in closer proximity to them. I argue that these Blacks, confronted with
political environments viewed as dissonant with preferences, will forego
the turnout decision for more salient forms of participation. When in the
voting booth, these voters will also be more likely to vote for President
and abandon the rest of the ballot, a phenomenon called roll-off.

To test my argument, I use aggregate data to compare the turnout
rates and vote preference of predominately Black precincts in majority-
Anglo congressional districts (CD) to the turnout rates of Black precincts
in majority-minority districts (MMD). I believe that voters in majority
African-American precincts located in Anglo CDs will face a political
environment of conflicting pressures each of which meters the turnout
decision. On average, Anglo-dominated congressional districts have higher
median incomes, home values, educational attainment, and occupational
prestige than minority-majority congressional districts. We would expect,
then, that African-American precincts located in these districts should
also have a higher average socioeconomic status (SES) than their MMD
counterparts and, by extension, higher aggregate turnout rates. I argue,

however, that the opposite is true. Despite a resource advantage, I contend that these voters will have a political marketplace that does not traverse in their most salient good—race. The average voter in this district will turn to more group conscious forms of participation or abstain altogether, resulting in lower aggregate turnout rates.

If we take a sociological view of participation, we see a conflicted voter. At its most direct, all avenues of participation are open and virtually costless due to higher levels of income and education. However, the African American in the majority–African-American precinct within the majority-Anglo CD must also recognize her minority status and will approach the political process as an outgroup member. Candidate choice will be between two candidates who are neither descriptively nor substantively representative with respect to race. Consequently, turnout in the local congressional race must be based on secondarily salient characteristics like income or party. Rather than expend resources to vote in an election that will yield minimum utility, I argue that it will be more rational for such voters to choose more salient forms of participation like volunteering to help the presidential candidate, working for a group-based petition organization, or even donating money to the coethnic candidate in the nearby urban minority-majority district.

Because this is an aggregate-level study, the opinions or motivations of individual voters within the precinct are immeasurable. This chapter, however, does not extrapolate its findings to the individual motivations of a voter in the precinct. Instead, it relies on a less rigorous assumption that the domination of a compact area, like a neighborhood or precinct, by a group of any salient characteristic will make them much more likely to form communal ties based around that characteristic. When this characteristic is phenotypic, community is easier to recognize and therefore more likely. Further, when the historic disenfranchisement and years of unabashed race-based conflict are added to the equation, community is almost certain. As a consequence, majority–African-American precincts in Anglo CDs will have like opinion and political attitudes with majority African-American precincts in MMD, even though their average SES differs.

LITERATURE REVIEW

Politically, residential segregation and the lineage of the 1965 Voting Rights Act produce a contemporary redistricting ethos firmly grounded in packing African Americans into minority-majority districts, where they have more opportunity to elect a coethnic representative (Swain 1993). As an unintended consequence, an African American living a moderate geographical distance from the majority of her group members will have a much lower likelihood of the same descriptive representation.

Verba, Schlozman, and Brady (1995) and countless others have shown that as political resources like income and education increase, people participate more. Further, increases in these resources lower the costs attached to voting, even if the material benefit is minimal (Downs 1967). For high-resource African Americans, voting would be as costless as Verba, Schlozman, and Brady and others suggest. Their models, however, do not account for the explosion of benefit derived from salient activities like working for the nearest coethnic candidate or group-based organizations located in the cultural centers from which they are separated. There is a long lineage in the African-American politics literature describing the congruence of African-American opinion regardless of socioeconomic differences and how group consciousness (Miller et al 1981) or linked fate (Dawson 1994) make up for resource deficits amongst the less-affluent voters in the group. The history of discrimination and disenfranchisement experienced by Blacks is consistently shown to be the root of both the high-linked fate, and the perpetuation of indigenous institutions like the long-standing churches and petition organizations that were at the forefront of the struggle for civil rights. I argue that these separated African Americans will attach lower utilities to voting in a political environment that does not address group salient goals and choose alternative forms of participation that reinforce group consciousness. Hence, while the turnout rates in presidential elections among these groups of Blacks will be on par with their White counterparts, their turnout in more local elections will be lower than suburban Whites and urban Blacks.

None of these ideas are inconsistent with the established participation literature, if you extrapolate from their theories. However, there has been little specific attention, especially in political science, paid to this growing group of democratic participants. The time-honored participation books like *Voting* (1954) and *The American Voter* (1960) and to some extent *Voice and Equality* (1995) or *Invisible Politics* (1985) have not adjusted their theories for this burgeoning population that does not fit neatly into any box. The Columbia and Michigan schools did not examine this population at all. Additionally, the rational choice, resource, and network theorists do not fully delineate the role of alternative participatory acts. Finally, Black politics empiricists attempting to examine this group lack complete data.

As a result, existing theories cannot explain the participatory habits of suburban Blacks. The most well-known theory of African-American participation is that when controlling for socioeconomic disparities, African American turnout is equal or higher than that for other groups (see Bobo and Gilliam 1990 for instance). This finding has long intrigued scholars in the race and ethnicity and participation communities because it flies in the face of the general resource argument. In an effort to close the gap, scholars have inserted the concept of group consciousness (e.g. Chong and Rogers 2005). The theory follows that blacks, who have lower-than-average resources, engage in networks where political participation is one of the most important group norms. These norms are reinforced by indigenous organizations and institutions that help lower participatory costs (Tate 1993; Calhoun-Brown 1996; Harris 1999). These studies can help explain why turnout is higher in areas where you would expect it to be lower but not why there would be depressed turnout in areas where extant theories would predict higher rates of participation. It is the aim of this project to extend both the race and ethnicity and general participation theories to the oft-overlooked African Americans in minority neighborhoods located in majority White congressional districts.

For my purposes, the participation discussion will be rooted in the rational choice theories of voting made famous by Downs (1957) and Riker and Ordeshook (1968). At its most basic, a citizen will cast a vote in an election if the benefit (material or psychological) from electing their preferred candidate multiplied by the chance that person will cast the tiebreaking vote for their candidate is greater than the costs associated with voting. This calculation has lead to the "paradox" of voting where benefits are usually collective in some form and the chances of casting a tiebreaking vote in a 500,000-person election are miniscule and therefore will never outweigh the costs. However, the reality of the situation is that people do vote— hence, the paradox. Why do people engage in "irrational" behaviors? Most famously, Rikker and Ordeshook (followed by a long lineage) realized the calculation must be missing something, because people vote in uncontested elections and people abstain even under the most liberal registration requirements or voting schemes. Instead, they argue, voters are socialized toward participation as a civic virtue through schooling and the media and this civic virtue or duty is inserted into the model to make voting rational.

My major concern with the calculus of voting and its lineage is that it is too voting-centered. The benefit of voting can be material or psychological, but is contingent on the differential between the benefit from your preferred candidate winning minus the challenger winning. For an African American in an 80 percent Anglo-congressional district and 65 percent African-American precinct, the chances of either candidate seriously addressing racial issues is negligible, so tangible benefits fall away. Psychologically, group reinforcement further lowers the potential benefits because one sees group members in the neighborhood but knows the most costless political expression, voting, will do nothing to help them as racial group members. In this instance, the probability of the

African-American voter participating in the election is lower than someone who feels better represented (even if only descriptively). Rational choice theorists would end the discussion there. Since voting is one of the least costly forms of participation and the perceived benefits do not outweigh the costs, there would be no need to look at their engagement in more costly forms of participation.

I argue that not doing so is a mistake. On the civic duty front, we should not expect an African American with high levels of income and education to have less civic duty than another voter *ceteris paribas*. However, we should expect high group identifiers to view the *duty* part differently. The duty will be less toward perpetuating the democracy and political culture and more toward advancing group aims. This is clear from years of surveys where most blacks score higher on group identification questions than questions linked to nationalism or civic duty (see for instance Eidelson and Lyubansky in this volume). Consequently, Blacks in predominantly Anglo CDs will transfer their participation from voting to acts deemed more beneficial to the race.

The rationality of alternative participation by affluent African Americans in high-SES neighborhoods can be seen from the cost side of the equation. I have said many times that voting is one of the most costless political behaviors. The very concept of precinct polling places is to cut the geographic distance one has to travel to vote. The spread of technology, including media Web sites and groups like the League of Women Voters, cut information costs beyond perennial candidate mobilization tactics. Institutions like early and straight-ticket voting all lessen the resource and information costs of voting, and though registration may be relatively difficult, once registered there is no recurring cost. Additionally, all of these "barriers" turn into mere anthills in the face of increasing income and education, which we find at higher levels in the very environments that are the target of this project. Alternative forms of participation (letter writing, donating money, volunteering time, etc.) come at higher resource costs than voting since at their least they receive less attention from elites and require the individual to expend more resources.

If one engages in an activity that comes at a higher cost, we can assume that they derive a larger benefit from it or attach a higher utility to it. If the data show that these particular African Americans choose the alternative behaviors over voting (when compared to other African Americans or other groups), we can plausibly attribute this difference to the higher salience of those behaviors.

A simple illustration may aid the point. Geographic distance has long been associated with costs in both the participation and social network literatures. Specifically, proximity is seen as one of the major cost cutters of political behavior; citizens register when they get drivers licenses, and social groups at work and home are the main movers of opinion. If one is headed to a grocery store and bypasses the store at the end of the block for one 15 miles away, the farther store must have something the other does not. All things being equal, we would expect a person to choose the closer store. Whatever extra item or service offered at the far store, rationality says it must be worth the extra cost in terms of time, gasoline, or even the potential to get in a car accident. Since both stores offer food, the *type* of food at the far store must be valued more than the closer store as the consumer must incur higher costs to attain it. The same can be said for a suburban African American living a drivable distance from a historic African-American central city community. Their immediate neighborhood has a church and restaurants, the local community has volunteer organizations, and the congressional district has candidates for office soliciting support through votes, time, and money. If their participatory choices take them away from the nearest church or campaign, and instead they devote more time, gasoline, and cognitive resources toward activities in the central city neighborhood we can assume that they value their racial identification more than other demographics that they have in common with other non-Black neighbors. In short, if you value your racial group contacts above your income or education group contacts then that group must be the most salient.

Motivated by my assumptions, this study will test three hypotheses:

H1: Majority African-American precincts in majority Anglo-congressional districts will have lower turnout rates because the local races do not speak to their issues.

H2: Majority African-American precincts in majority Anglo-congressional districts will have higher roll-off rates. The presidential election will discuss salient issues producing a psychic benefit from that vote, but issues in the local race will be deemed nonsalient and a certain proportion of voters will abandon the rest of their ballot.

H3: As the proportion of African Americans in a precinct rises, their proportion of voting for Gore will become more similar regardless of congressional district racial heterogeneity or demographics.

DATA AND DESIGN

The data come from the Federal Election Project by David Lublin of American University and Stephen Voss from the University of Kentucky. The authors traveled to all 435 congressional districts in the country compiling precinct-level vote shares and racial population information for the 2000 Presidential election between George W. Bush and Al Gore. In addition to presidential vote counts, the data include congressional, senate, state legislative, and in some cases school board, vote tallies as well as racial information for both the total and voting age population.

The present study will employ a multilevel model with individual precincts aggregated to the congressional district level. Data on the congressional districts come from the 2000 Census and were compiled via the University of Michigan library Web site. They include population, household, income, education, age, and mobility information for districts in Texas, Georgia, North Carolina, Illinois, and Michigan. After cleaning inconsistencies in the datasets, Texas had 7,674 precincts and 30 congressional districts; Georgia had 2,626 precincts and 11 CDs; North Carolina had 2,051 precincts and 12 districts; Illinois had 10,339 precincts and 20 congressional districts; and Michigan had 1,541 precincts and 16 congressional districts. A total of 23,376 precincts and 89 congressional districts were available for analysis. Campaign spending data come from the Federal Election Commission records of receipts and disbursements as of October 10, 2000.

The theoretical model will be estimated via a hierarchical linear modeling technique. This procedure is well-suited to questions where larger environments influence smaller or nested jurisdictions. The basic idea is that every precinct in the five state samples is not created equal but there are some similarities between precincts in the same congressional district. If we assume these precincts are more similar to each other than they are to precincts in other congressional districts, we can model this variability. The multilevel model uses maximum likelihood to estimate separate error terms for each level of the model. The result is analysis of effects between the dependent variable and covariates at level 1 (the precinct) and estimates of how level 2 (congressional district) variables affect the relationship between the first-level variables.

I ran two separate models, one for turnout and one for roll-off, each with the same independent variables:

Level-1 Model

$$\text{Turnout/Roll-off} = \beta_0 + \beta_1{}^*(\text{Black VAP\%}) + \beta_2{}^*(\text{Gore\%}) + \beta_3{}^*(\text{Anglo CD\%}) + r$$

Level-2 Model

$$\beta_0 = \gamma_{00} + \gamma_{01}{}^*(\text{Single mom}) + \gamma_{02}{}^*(\text{Unemployment}) + \gamma_{03}{}^*(\text{Income}) + \gamma_{04}{}^*(\text{Public assistance}) + \gamma_{05}{}^*(\text{Home value}) + \gamma_{06}{}^*(\text{Spending ratio}) + u_0$$

$$\beta_1 = \gamma_{10} + \gamma_{11}*(\text{Single mom}) + \gamma_{12}*(\text{Income}) + \gamma_{13}*(\text{Home value})$$
$$+ \gamma_{14}*(\text{Spending ratio}) + \gamma_{15}*(\text{Majority Anglo CD}) + u_1$$

$$\beta_2 = \gamma_{20}$$

$$\beta_3 = \gamma_{30} + \gamma_{31}*(\text{White collar}) + \gamma_{32}*(\text{Income}) + \gamma_{33}*(\text{Home value})$$
$$+ \gamma_{34}*(\text{Spending ratio}) + u_2$$

For the turnout model, all three slopes vary randomly so magnitudes and intercepts were estimated. In the roll-off model, only the slope for the level 1 intercept varies randomly. All other slopes were assumed to have the same magnitude but different intercepts. As stated earlier, the dependent variables are turnout and roll off for each model respectively. *Turnout* is compiled as the combined totals for Bush and Gore divided by the total voting age population of the precinct. *Roll-off* is calculated as the difference between presidential votes cast and congressional votes. Positive numbers indicate more people voting in the presidential race than the congressional contest. *Single mom* is the number of female-headed households with no male present and children under 18. *Unemployment* is the percent unemployed. *White collar* is a compilation of jobs deemed white collar from occupation questions on the census. *Income* is the number of voters with incomes between $100,000 and $150,000. *Public assistance* is the number of individuals on government subsidies. *Household value* is the number of households in the district valued at more than $100,000. *Spending ratio* is compiled as winner's disbursements divided by loser's disbursements. Higher numbers indicate larger gaps in spending between candidates. *Anglo CD%* is a four level categorical variable ranging from 1 (0–18.75 percent African Americans in the district) to 4 (56.25–75 percent African Americans in the district). *Black VAP%* is the proportion of the voting-age population that is African American. *Gore%* is Gore's vote share divided by the combined total of Gore and Bush votes. Alternative measures for median income and education were also used but were exchanged in the final models due to high correlations. Note that all of the variables are congressional-level variables except Black VAP%, Anglo CD%, and Gore %, which are precinct-level variables.

RESULTS

A look at the descriptive statistics shows the small number of majority African-American precincts and majority-minority congressional districts in these five states (that were selected by virtue of their large and compact African-American populations). Of the more than 23,000 precincts, only 4,000 can be classified as majority African American. Even the word majority is a misnomer because a threshold of 40 percent was actually the cut-point.[2] Of these 4,000 precincts, only 684 were located in a congressional district that was majority Anglo. Of the 89 congressional districts, only 11 can be considered minority opportunity districts for African Americans.[3] This extreme unbalance caused some models to fail to converge, most likely because there was too large a gap between the information in the control (Anglo-dominated precincts) and the actual population to be estimated (684 vs. 20,000). That said, preliminary descriptive evidence does confirm most of my hypotheses.

To show the relationship between Gore support, turnout, roll-off, precinct Black population, and district homogeneity, scatterplots (not shown) were run of samples from the entire dataset and individual states. The full sample had 2,376 precincts, the samples for Texas and Illinois also were 10 percent at 767 and 1033, respectively. The samples for Georgia, North Carolina, and Michigan were set at 500. As expected, support for Gore approached 100 percent as the African-American proportion in a precinct increased. The intercept for African-American population in heavily Anglo districts was higher than more heterogeneous districts but the slope was also much steeper. When the African-American population in a precinct reached about 80 percent support for Gore is the same no matter the racial make-up of the district, lending credence to the hypothesis of congruent opinion and the assumption that majority African-American precinct turnout can be seen as an expression of collective preferences. The relationship between Gore support and racial make-up was also parsed for each state in the dataset, with the results holding.

The relationship between turnout and black precinct population for each type of congressional district was also analyzed. In line with my hypothesis, majority African-American precincts in Anglo CDs had lower turnout, and the relationship was even negative in some states. Majority African-American congressional districts had stronger relationships between precinct composition and turnout, presumably because mobilization becomes more rational for congressional and presidential candidates and targeted messages have less chance of falling on unreceptive ears. The ballot roll-off measure showed the same relationship, just in different directions because of the variable's composition. Here, an increase in Black precinct population for the Anglo districts increases ballot roll-off as would be expected if the local race was nonsalient. For minority-majority districts, where voters are specifically mobilized for the congressperson and material and psychic ties are stronger than between the voter and the presidential candidate, we see less roll-off. The relationships held in turnout and roll-off relationships for each of the five states.

Table 12.1 shows the results from the hierarchical linear models. Again, each model has the same independent variables. Because the roll-off model

Table 12.1   Predictors of turnout and roll-off

Fixed effects	Explanatory variable	Turnout model	Roll-off model
Intercept (β_0)	Intercept (γ_{00})	0.483*	410.564
		(0.01)	(254.04)
	Single mom (γ_{01})	−0.000*	−0.037
		(0.00)	(0.07)
	Unemployment (γ_{02})	0.015	32.862
		(0.01)	(314.13)
	Income (γ_{03})	0.000*	0.052
		(0.00)	(0.03)
	Public assistance (γ_{04})	0.000	.35*
		(0.00)	(.17)
	Home values (γ_{05})	0.000*	.006
		(0.00)	(0.02)
	Spending ratio (γ_{06})	−0.092	−197.254
		(0.05)*	(1634.30)
Black VAP% (β_1)	Intercept (γ_{10})	−0.408*	−258.064*
		(0.06)	(114.55)
	Single mom (γ_{11})	0.000	0.026*
		(0.00)	(0.01)
	Income (γ_{12})	0.000*	−0.001
		(0.00)	(0.01)
	Home values (γ_{13})	0.000*	−0.028*
		(0.00)	(0.01)
	Spending ratio (γ_{14})	0.456	−260
		(0.29)	(390)
	Majority Anglo CD (γ_{15})	−0.426*	−20
		(0.13)	(160)
Gore% (β_2)	Intercept (γ_{20})	−0.406*	−27.586
		(0.03)	(64.90)
Anglo CD% (β_3)	Intercept (γ_{30})	0.140*	87.374*
		(0.02)	(35.41)
	White collar (γ_{31})	−0.000*	−0.001
		(0.00)	(0.00)
	Income (γ_{32})	0.000*	0.007
		(0.00)	(0.01)
	Home values (γ_{33})	−0.000*	0.010*
		(0.00)	(0.00)
	Spending ratio (γ_{34})	−0.133	46.606
		(0.08)	(146.48)
Random effects	Standard deviation		
	Intercept (u_{0j})	0.07	2393.50
	Black VAP% (u_{1j})	0.55	
	Anglo CD (u_{2j})	0.14	
	Level 1 residuals (e_{ij})	0.13	1074.49
Likelihood		13738	−196169.5
Level 1 N		23,376	23,376
Level 2 N		89	89

Note: Coefficients are maximum likelihood estimates. Standard errors appear in parentheses below coefficients. Starred coefficients are significant at the p < .05 level.
Source: Federal Election Project.

holds certain slope directions constant, it has fewer estimated parameters. The turnout model confirmed most of my hypotheses. The reliabilities for each of the slopes were high, well over 75 percent. This means that the variance of the estimated slopes between CDs is relatively small. Results for the turnout model were calculated with robust standard errors. The beta coefficients show us the results from the level 1 model. β_1 shows a negative relationship between African-American VAP and turnout, as would be expected with most majority African-American precincts coming from low resource areas. Gore support is negative (β_2), probably due to a lack of competitiveness in highly Democratic districts and majority African-American turnout in Anglo CDs (β_3) is positive, which seems to confirm the relationship between more resources and higher turnout found in the literature.

The second level results confirm the descriptive evidence and support my hypotheses. For the negative slope between African-American VAP and turnout (β_1), we see tentative evidence about the effect of Anglo CD on Black population as increases in Black population in Anglo CDs (β_{15}) make the relationship more negative, showing a depressing effect of Anglo political environment on turnout. If the story were all about resources we would expect the Anglo CD control to make the relationship more positive. β_{13} shows that higher home values increases turnout in African-American precincts and in an illusion to the roll-off model, more spending in African-American precincts increases turnout but is not statistically significant.

The pattern continues for African-American population in an Anglo CD (β_3). Higher spending gaps have a negative relationship, lessening the relationship between African-American proportion and turnout in Anglo CDs. As expected, more white-collar workers and higher home values also have negative relationships with turnout. These variables come as direct confirmation of the hypothesis that voters in majority African-American precincts in Anglo CDs will have lower turnout rates because the congressional races are less salient. Even as the number of white collar jobs or home values rises—situations that are expected to take average demographics and therefore political discourse away from racialized issues—voters in these precincts are turned off from the process and find other things to do. Individual-level surveys would be the best way to decipher whether these voters are choosing alternative avenues of participation or abstaining. But for now, we can at least see that higher resource levels in this case do not necessarily translate into higher turnout rates.

Interestingly, there may be cursory confirmation of a nonracial salience to the congressional race as the number of high-wage earners rises.

This variable is assumed to work the same way as home value and white-collar workers, driving political discourse to nonracial and therefore nonsalient areas. The high-income earners' strengthening of the turn-out-Anglo CD relationship shows certain types of political dynamics or certain demographics do increase the salience of local races.

The roll-off model also confirms the descriptive and turnout analysis. Unfortunately, robust standard errors could not be computed for this model despite the nonrandom specification of the level 1 independent variable slopes. As expected, the intercept for Black VAP (β_1) was negative, meaning majority African-American precincts are less likely to roll-off the ballot compared to all others. Amongst all majority African-American precincts, we also see from β_{13} that more high home values lessen roll-off as well. With most high African-American proportion precincts being in minority-majority congressional districts, we can expect this effect to describe how an increase in income for all Blacks makes them more likely to vote for the congressional representative. Yet, β_{33} shows us that for majority African-American precincts in Anglo CDs (β_3) higher home values produce more roll-off. Again, this provides tentative evidence (yet confirmatory of the scatter plots described earlier) that African-American precincts in Anglo congressional districts are less enthusiastic about their congressional contest compared to all other precincts. The intercept for all majority African-American precincts in Anglo congressional districts (β_{30}) is also positive indicating less salient and likely less receptiveness to campaign information from the local race overall.

CONCLUSION

The results seem to confirm all of my hypotheses. We have seen evidence that majority African-American precincts have similar opinions regardless of congressional district racial composition. With these racial composition districts also mirroring SES differences between districts, we can say that this opinion congruence occurs regardless of income or education levels in these precincts. These similarities would lead one to expect commiserate rates and stimuli to turnout for the precincts in each type of congressional district as well. This is not the case. Since the major difference between the two groups of majority Black precincts examined in this project was the political and electoral environments surrounding the precincts, we can attribute these turnout and roll-off differences to political environment. When voters with like opinion show different behaviors based on environment, it is safe to assume environment is what turns these voters off. The primary reasoning for this lack of enthusiasm is the (almost definitional) non-salience of campaign issues in majority Anglo districts.

Future research should test the results at the individual level. The validity of the current study is constrained by the use of aggregate data. While neighborhood effects are obvious motivators of political behavior, they clearly cannot tell the whole story. Nevertheless, I fully believe the relationship will hold at the individual level and will further illuminate the interaction between individual motivations and environmental dynamics, especially for minority communities. However, one must not discount the collective effects of group norms, mobilization, or racial threat perception, especially in the study of aggregative behaviors like elections.

NOTES

INTRODUCTION

1. For the purpose of these analyses, the discussion of race is confined to racial and ethnic politics within the United States and does not include articles or chapters about ethnic conflict in other parts of the world.

CHAPTER 1

1. We would be remiss if we did not also acknowledge the handful of psychologists housed in political science departments who have also contributed greatly to contemporary political psychology. This list includes but is not limited to Kathleen McGraw at The Ohio State University, Donald Kinder at the University of Michigan, Richard Lau at Rutgers University, and Jon Krosnick at Stanford University.

CHAPTER 3

1. We use "Black" and "African American" interchangeably throughout the article to refer to a socially constructed racial group or identity and recognize that this group, like all other racial groups in the United States, is ethnically heterogeneous.

2. Interestingly, while those subscribing to the color-blind approach may be well intentioned, there is growing evidence that even individuals who explicitly disavow prejudice may unconsciously hold negative attitudes and stereotypes about members of an outgroup (for a review, see Greenwald and Banaji 1995). Not surprisingly, there is also considerable evidence that a color-blind approach actually leads to a perpetuation of group inequalities (for a review, see Brewer and Brown 1998).

3. This subsample of Black Americans was used in a previously published study about Black double consciousness (Lyubansky and Eidelson 2005).

4. Of the Black participants, 29 percent were male and 71 percent were female; for the White sample, 47 percent were male and 53 percent were female. The average ages of the Black and White samples were 40.53 years (SD = 12.49)

and 39.71 years (SD = 12.38) respectively. The distribution on highest educational level attained for the Black participants was 18 percent graduate work, 17 percent college degree, 35 percent some college, 29 percent high school, and 1 percent no formal education; for the White sample these percentages were 24 percent graduate work, 24 percent college degree, 26 percent some college, and 26 percent high school. Family income distribution for the Black sample was 27 percent less than $30,000, 52 percent between $30,000-$75,000, and 21 percent greater than $75,000; the corresponding percentages for the White sample was 15 percent less than $30,000, 48 percent between $30,000 and $75,000, and 37 percent greater than $75,000.

CHAPTER 4

1. These datasets were made available through the Roper Center for Public Opinion Research.
2. Only in the 1950s and 1960s was voter turnout (as percent of voting age population) higher than 56 percent.

CHAPTER 5

1. See: Associated Press "NAACP: Bush 'playing race card' with Social Security and Fagan," Amy. "NAACP Fights Bush Social Security Plan." *Washington Post* April 12, 2006.
2. Priming as a mental process refers to the activation of particular associations in memory when making political evaluations (Price and Tewksbury 1997).
3. These numbers represent valid cases not individuals who completed only a portion of the experiment.
4. Subjects in the control condition read a story about the computer industry's efforts to gradually phase out 3¼-inch floppy disks in desktop computers. All subjects read two filler stories: one that dealt with advances in mp3 technology and another that discussed the injuries children face on playgrounds. These stories were exactly the same across all conditions.
5. To insure that differences in the distribution of students in each condition do not account for the differences in the results, I include a measure of student status as a control variable. Dummy variables for the baseline effects of each condition are also included in the model.
6. One alternative hypothesis might be that the accessibility of racial considerations is mediating the effects of racial frames for African Americans. Utilizing a procedure identical to that used by Valentino, Hutchings, and White (2001), I found no support for the idea that racial accessibility mediates the effect of the frames. These results are available upon request.

CHAPTER 6

1. The scant evidence supporting the notion that Black women exhibit a distinctive and separate consciousness that influences their political orientations is more a function of the relatively few studies devoted to the subject matter than the lack of findings among extant research (Gay and Tate 1998; Simien and Clawson 2004).

2. In these analyses as well as the analyses of the other two data sources, only Blacks and Whites are included in the sample because of the small number of respondents from other racial/ethnic groups. Likewise, we confine our examination to comparisons of Black and White candidates because of the difficulty associated with identifying and obtaining data for the relatively few elections featuring a female candidate who is also a racial/ethnic minority. Moreover, the complex (and sometimes divergent) intragroup histories of Latinos, Asian Americans, and Native Americans in the United States make it difficult to form theoretically grounded predictions of when, why, and how gender and racial/ethnic consciousness intersect.

3. This information was obtained from the Joint Center for Political and Economic Studies.

4. We restrict our analyses to only those cases in which the respondent voted in an election featuring a Black female candidate running for office, excluding those respondents that did not vote for a Black female candidate because they did not have that option.

5. Arguably, the description of the fictitious nonpartisan mayoral election might have been sending partisan cues. If this was the case, our results would be affected in a number of ways. For instance, the high levels of support exhibited by Blacks may be a result of their partisanship rather than their race. Likewise, the disproportionate number of White Democrats (44 percent, compared to about 30 percent in national random samples) in the experimental sample may be inflating the rate of support for Johnson among Whites. Note, however, that the differences between Blacks and Whites remain, even when controlling for party identification.

6. Two other candidates, G. B. Osborne and Trudy Kitchin, received less than 1 percent of the vote. Osborne, a Nigerian-American male, funded his own campaign. Kitchin, who also funded her own campaign, is a White female Republican and local political activist.

7. All of the marginal effects described in this paragraph were calculated by holding age, ideology, party identification, and income at their means and south and college constant at their modes.

8. All of the marginal effects described in this paragraph were calculated by holding age, ideology, party identification, and income at their means and south, college, Black, female, midterm election, incumbent, party match, held previous office, Black male opponent, and White female opponent constant at their modes.

9. A liberal significance test (p < .10 in a one-tailed test) indicates that there is a significant difference between Black women and Black men, as well as Black women and White women in their probability of voting for a Black female House candidate.

10. Support for this claim can be found in Conover's (1984) examination of group identification and political perceptions. In this study, Conover examines which considerations different groups bring to bear when evaluating candidates and parties. Her results suggest that individuals' perceptions of the political world are guided by a combination of objective group membership and psychological attachment to that group. Specifically, Conover found that using group-relevant criteria to evaluate candidates and parties is bolstered when the individual identifies with that group. However, objective group membership explains quite a bit of the decision to use group-relevant considerations.

CHAPTER 7

1. As suggested by Greenwald et al. (2003), trial response latencies less than 400 ms or greater than 10,000 ms were thrown out; in addition, participant response times that were less than 300 ms on more than 10 percent of the trials were excluded. Response artifacts threaten validity (i.e., random responding) and extremely slow mean response latencies may be due to biased responding, inattention, or some other response artifact (Greenwald et al. 1998). Participants were also excluded if they did not complete the study or if they left any part of the racial identity, demographic, or political questions unanswered.

CHAPTER 9

1. Loosely translated, the adjective "*idios*" describes a citizen who, through neglect or lack of training, is neither knowledgeable about nor skilled in the affairs of the state.

2. Like Bennett's (1986) Political Apathy Index, this composite measure gets an alpha reliability rating of 0.66. The data points before 1960 are for campaign interest only because the general interest item had yet to appear in the ANES.

3. All tests for significance are based on the p < .05 level.

4. The idea that societies have political atmospheres is an old one. Political socialization scholars often speak of the "social climate" when describing the intangible factors that guide the thoughts and actions of youths (see Giordano 2003 for a review). Lippmann (1922) uncovers a philosophical tradition dating back at least to the works of Jean-Jacques Rousseau (1762)—particularly, his discussion of the General Will—positing the existence of diffuse and overarching sentiments that are both the product and the basis of public opinion. Economists evoke a similar idea

when they refer to the phantom, macrolevel market processes that influence consumer preferences; this is what Adam Smith (1776) proposed when he spoke of "the invisible hand." Social movement scholars (e.g., McAdam 1982; Tarrow 1994) speak of "waves" or "cycles" of protest when they describe the rise and fall of conflict within a social system. More relevant to the study of race, Hanes Walton Jr. (1997) refers to the "political context variable" when he discusses the powerful but oftentimes-invisible effect of the racial environment on Black political behavior.

5. Debates over the exact dates aside, scholars often count the Civil Rights Movement as the ten or so years that started with the *Brown* decision in 1954 and culminated with the Voting Rights Act of 1965.

6. The Twenty-Fourth Amendment abolished the poll tax used in Southern states to discourage Black voters; civil rights organizations like C.O.R.E. (Congress of Racial Equality) and S.N.C.C (Student Nonviolent Coordinating Committee) took part in large voter-mobilization efforts during "Freedom Summer," and President Lyndon B. Johnson signed the Civil Rights Act, one of the most extensive pieces of antidiscrimination legislation since the Reconstruction.

CHAPTER 10

1. Mendelberg makes a distinction between "implicit" appeals--which rely on visual references to race and perhaps various code words—and "explicit appeals"—which specifically link particular policies to Black Americans.

2. Valentino et al. (2002) provide support for Mendelberg's claim that implicit racial messages can activate racial attitudes and that they do so on an unconscious level. Subsequent work by Hutchings and Valentino (2003), however, shows that explicit racial appeals can also succeed in priming racial attitudes.

3. Moreover, our earlier work in this area focuses exclusively on explicit, rather than implicit racial appeals.

4. We focus on attitudes concerning various social groups, as explained in more detail in the next section, because such perceptions represent one of the primary ways in which most citizens understand politics (Campbell, Converse, Miller, and Stokes 1960; Conover 1984; Converse 1964; Nelson and Kinder 1996).

5. The field period for the survey began on April 8 and ended on August 1st. Interviews were administered by a combination of trained graduate students and professional interviewers.

6. The sound track for the videos was played out loud over the laptops' speakers. The questions directly following the advertisements dealt with factual information contained in the ads and some relatively sensitive questions about social groups (e.g. racial and gender) in society. This portion of the survey was designed to be self-administered so that the respondent would be more likely to provide candid answers to these potentially

controversial questions. After answering a series of questions, the laptop was returned to the interviewer, who asked the questions in the final portion of the survey.

7. The response rate was calculated based on the American Association for Public Opinion Research's Response Rate 1 (RR1). Ineligible respondents were excluded either because the selected housing unit did not exist (n=72) or the occupant was under 18 years of age or a non-U.S. citizen (n=12).

8. The sample included 77 Blacks and 225 Whites.

9. The product ads were: Duralast Batteries, Staples Office Supplies, and Wallside Windows, in that order. In the treatment conditions, those who viewed the political spot did not see the Staples commercial.

10. For example, in this ad we show medical workers dressed in uniforms that completely obscure their racial characteristics.

11. We found similar effects when examining the effects of such cues on the gender gap (Hutchings et al. 2004).

12. The vote choice item is derived from two questions that ask respondents, first, which candidate they supported in the upcoming presidential contest and, second, how strongly they supported their candidate (e.g. "strong" or "not strong"). Combining these two measures results in a 5-point scale ranging from strong support for Al Gore to strong support for George W. Bush. Respondents who were unsure of their preference, or who selected a third-party candidate were coded to the middle category. This variable has been rescaled to range from 0–1. The feeling thermometer item ranges from 0, representing "cold" or more negative evaluations, to 100, representing more "warm" or more favorable impressions.

13. The control condition represents the excluded category. The analyses also include measures for party identification, education, gender, and race of interviewer to control for possible imbalances of these variables across conditions.

14. These groups seem to be obvious choices as two of the most salient cleavages in modern American politics involve race and economic issues (Campbell, Converse, Miller, and Stokes 1960; Carmines and Stimson 1989; Edsall and Edsall 1991). The questions on candidate responsiveness were worded as follows: "Now we would like to know which presidential candidate you think would do a better job representing the interests of particular groups in society. First let's take [Whites, or Blacks, or business groups]. Do you think George W. Bush or Al Gore would do a better job representing the interests of [Whites, or Blacks, or business groups]?" After indicating a preference for one of the two candidates, respondents were then asked if they believed this candidate would do "much better," or "somewhat better" than his opponent. The question on the economy followed a similar format. All responses were recoded to a 0–1 scale.

15. Again, all other variables in the model are held constant at their mean or median.

CHAPTER 11

1. Shortly after their arrest, it was determined that the suspects were active members in a White supremacist organization.
2. While the respondents in his study were certainly enraged by racist acts, they were not all angry at the perpetrators. They chalked up the offensive behavior to the person's background, considering them to be the victims of miseducation or lack of experience.
3. The film *Amistad* served to portray an event that was replicated many other times.
4. Because of technical problems, the data set has only 18 complete transcripts. Certain portions of the remaining three were not able to be heard or were too unclear to reproduce either manually or electronically.
5. This self-identification was not unusual, but clearly the participant could have identified himself as Caribbean American, Jamaican American, or some other reference.
6. None of the participants who were single reported having any children.
7. Names have been changed to protect the participants' identities.

CHAPTER 12

1. Unbeknownst to them, the convention would turn into the hottest ticket in town with the historic slugfest between Barack Obama and Hillary Clinton.
2. When drawing MMD, the 40 percent threshold is seen as enough for a homogeneous minority to elect a candidate of choice. As such, these districts are sometimes called minority opportunity districts. Scholars, most notably Canon et al. (1996), confirm that 40 percent is indeed a suitable plurality.
3. This does miss those districts that are minority-majority when African American and Latino populations are combined. Attaching a dummy variable to these districts would be difficult because it would also capture districts with very large Latino populations and few African Americans, a situation that is comparable but of a different dynamic than this study.

REFERENCES

Abelson, Robert P., Donald R. Kinder, Mark D. Peters, and Susan T. Fiske. 1982. Affective and semantic components in political person perceptions. *Journal of Personality and Social Psychology* 42(4): 619–30.

Abramson, Lyn, Martin E. P. Seligman, and John Teasdale. 1978. Learned helplessness in humans: Critique and reformulation. *Journal of Abnormal Psychology* 87: 49–74.

Abramson, Paul. 1972. Political efficacy and political trust among Black schoolchildren: Two explanations. *The Journal of Politics* 34: 1243–75.

Achen, Christopher, and W. Phillips Shively. 1995. *Cross-level inference.* Chicago: University of Chicago Press.

Adler, Jeffrey S. 2001. Introduction. In *African-American mayors: Race, politics, and the American city,* ed. David R. Colburn and Jeffrey S. Adler, 2–22. Urbana: University of Illinois Press.

Affigne, Tony. 1997. Black voters and urban regime: The case of Atlanta. In *Race and politics: New challenges and responses for Black activism,* ed. James Jennings, 67–81. London: Verso.

Alba, Richard D., and John R. Logan. 1993. Minority proximity to whites in suburbs: An individual-level analysis of segregation. *The American Journal of Sociology* 98(6): 1388–1427.

Allen, Richard L. 2001. *The concept of self: A study of Black identity and self-esteem.* Detroit, MI: Wayne State University Press.

Allen, Richard L., and Hatchett, Shirley. 1986. The media and social reality effects: Self and system orientations of Blacks. *Communication Research* 13(1): 97–123.

Allen, Richard L., Michael C. Dawson, and Ronald E. Brown. 1989. A schema based approach to modeling an African-American racial belief system. *American Political Science Review* 83(2): 421–41.

Almond, Gabriel, and Sidney Verba, eds. 1980. *The civic culture revisited.* Boston, MA: Little, Brown.

American national election study. 2008. Pre- and post-election survey [computer file].

American Psychological Association. 2010. http://www.apa.org/pubs/journals/psp/index.aspx.

Anderson-Bricker, Kristin. 1999. Triple jeopardy: Black women and the growth of the feminist consciousness in SNCC, 1964–1975. In *Still lifting, still climbing: Contemporary African American women's activism*, ed. Kimberly Springer, 49–69. New York: New York University Press.

Aptheker, Herbert. 1983. *American Negro slave revolts.* New York: International.

Association of Black Psychologists. 2010. http://www.abpsi.org/index.php/about-abpsi.

Azibo, Daudi Ajani Ya. 1997. African psychology in historical perspective and related commentary. Trenton, NJ: Africa World Press.

Baldwin, Joseph A. 1986. African (Black) psychology: Issues and synthesis. *Journal of Black Studies* 16(3): 235–49.

Banaji, Mahzarin R., Max H. Bazerman, and Dolly Chugh. 2003. How (un)ethical are you? *Harvard Business Review.* December.

Banks, James. 1981. Stages of ethnicity: Implications for curriculum reform. In *Multiethnic Education: Theory and Practice*, ed. James A. Banks, 129–139. Boston: Allyn and Bacon.

Barker, Lucius J., Mack H. Jones, and Katherine Tate. 1999. *African Americans and the American political system*, 4th ed. Upper Saddle River: Prentice Hall.

Barrett, Edith J. 1995. The policy priorities of African-American women in state legislatures. *Legislative Studies Quarterly* 20(2): 223–47.

Bartkowski, John. 1996. Beyond biblical literalism and inerrancy: Conservative Protestants and the hermeneutic interpretation of scripture. *Sociology of Religion* 57(3): 259–72.

Baxter, Sandra, and Marjorie Lansing. 1983. *Women and politics: The visible majority.* Revised Edition. Ann Arbor: University of Michigan Press.

Beck, Aaron T., Gary Emery, and Ruth L. Greenberg. 1985. *Anxiety disorders and phobias: A cognitive perspective.* New York: Basic Books.

Belgrave, Faye Z., and Kevin W. Allison. 2006. *African American psychology: From African to America.* Thousand Oaks, CA: Sage.

Bennefield, Robert. 1998. Dynamics of economic well-being: Health insurance, 1993 to 1995. Who loses coverage and for how long? U.S. Census Bureau Report. (August), http://www.census.gov/sipp/p70s/p70-64.pdf (accessed January 11, 2010).

Bennett, Stephen E. 1986. *Apathy in America, 1960–1984: Causes and consequences of citizen political indifference.* Dobbs Ferry, NY: Transnational.

Berelson, Bernard R., Paul F. Lazarsfeld, and William N. McPhee. 1954. *Voting: A study of opinion formation in a presidential campaign.* Chicago: University of Chicago Press.

Berger, Peter L. 1969. *The sacred canopy: Elements of a sociological theory of religion.* Garden City, NY: Doubleday.

Berger, Peter, and Thomas Luckmann. 1963. Sociology of religion and sociology of knowledge. *Sociology and Social Research* 47(4): 417–27.

Billig, Michael, and Henri Tajfel. 1973. Social categorization and similarity in intergroup behaviour. *European Journal of Social Psychology* 3(1): 27–52.

Billings, Andrew G., and Rudolf H. Moos. 1981. The role of coping responses and social resources in attenuating the stress of life events. *Journal of Behavioral Medicine* 4(2): 139–57.

Block, Ray, Jr. 2006. Racial cleavages in political interest. Ph.D. Dissertation: The Ohio State University.

———. 2007. "Usually, but not always": A report on the race gap in political interest, 1952–2004. *The Crisis: NAACP Special Edition* 114: 13–17.

———. 2009. "History voters" and their role in the 2008 presidential election. *Verj Magazine*, January.

Bobo, Lawrence, and Franklin D. Gilliam, Jr. 1990. Race, sociopolitical participation, and Black empowerment. *The American Political Science Review* 84(2): 377–93.

Bobo, Lawrence, and Vincent L. Hutchings. 1996. Perceptions of racial group competition: Extending Blumer's theory of group position to a multiracial social context. *American Sociological Review* 61: 951–72.

Bobo, Lawrence D., and Devon Johnson. 2004. A taste for punishment: Black and White Americans' views on the death penalty and the war on drugs. *Dubois Review* 1(1): 151–80.

Bobo, Lawrence, and James R. Kluegel. 1993. Opposition to race-targeting: Self-interest, stratification ideology, or racial attitudes? *American Sociological Review* 58: 443–64.

———. 1997. "Status, ideology, and dimensions of Whites' racial beliefs and attitudes: Progress and stagnation." In *Race Attitudes in the 1990's: Continuity and Change*, ed. Steven A. Tuch and Jack K. Martin, 93–120. Westport, CT: Praeger.

Bonilla-Silva, Eduardo. 2003. *Racism without racists: Color-blind racism and the persistence of racial inequality in the United States.* Boulder, CO: Rowman & Littlefield.

Boone, Kathleen C. 1989. *The Bible tells them so: The discourse of Protestant fundamentalism.* Albany: State University of New York Press.

Bositis, David A. 2000. *Black elected officials.* Washington, DC: Joint Center for Political and Economic Studies.

Brader, Ted. 2006. *Campaigning for hearts and minds: How emotional appeals in political ads work.* Chicago: University of Chicago Press.

Brader, Ted, Nicholas A. Valentino, and Elizabeth Suhay. 2006. Seeing versus feeling threats: Group cues, emotions, and activating opposition to immigration. Paper read at Annual Meeting of the Midwest Political Science Association, at Chicago, IL.

Branch, Taylor. 2008. *Parting the waters: America in the King years, 1954–63.* Bridgewater, NJ: Simon & Schuster.

Braumoeller, Bear. 2004. Hypothesis testing and multiplicative interaction terms. *International Organizations* 58 (Fall): 807–20.

Breckler, Steven J. 1984. Empirical validation of affect, behavior, and cognition as distinct components of attitude. *Journal of Personality and Social Psychology* 47(6): 1191–1205.

Brewer, Marilynn B. 1979. In-group bias in the minimal intergroup situation: A cognitive-motivational analysis. *Psychological Bulletin* 86(2): 307–24.

———. 1991. The social self: On being the same and different at the same time. *Personality and Social Psychology Bulletin* 17: 475–82.

Brewer, Marilynn B., and Rupert J. Brown. 1998. Intergroup relations. In *Handbook of social psychology*, ed. Daniel T. Gilbert, Susan T. Fiske, and Gardner Lindzey, 554–94. New York: McGraw-Hill.

Brody, Richard. 1978. The puzzle of political participation in America. In *The new American political system*, ed. Anthony King, 287–324. Washington, DC: American Enterprise Institute for Public Policy Research.

Broman, Clifford, Harold Neighbors, and James Jackson. 1988. Racial group identifications among Black adults. *Social Forces* 67(1): 146–58.

Brook, Judith S., and Kerstin Pahl. 2005. The protective role of ethnic and racial identity and aspects of an Africentric orientation against drug use among African American young adults. *Journal of Genetic Psychology* 166(3): 329–45.

Brown, Lisa M., and Gretchen E. Lopez. 2001. Political contacts: Analyzing the role of similarity in theories of prejudice. *Political Psychology* 22(2): 279–92.

Brown, Michael E. 1997. Ethnicity and violence. In *The ethnicity reader*, ed. Montserrat Guiberman and John Rex, 80–100. Malden, MA: Blackwell.

Brown, Rupert, Susan Condor, Audrey Mathews, Gillian Wade, and Jennifer Williams. 1986. Explaining intergroup differentiation in an industrial organization. *Journal of Occupational Psychology* 59: 273–86.

Bryce, Herrington J., and Alan E. Warrick. 1977. Black women in electoral politics. In *A portrait of marginality: The political behavior of the American woman*, ed. Marianne Githens and Jewel Limar Prestage, 395–400. New York: David McKay.

Bryce, James. 1909. The relations of political science to history and to practice: Presidential address, fifth annual meeting of the American political science association. *American Political Science Review* 3(1): 1–19.

Buchanan, Gregory M., and Martin E. P. Seligman, eds. 1995. *Explanatory style*. Hillsdale, NJ: Lawrence Erlbaum.

Buckingham, Justin T., and Mark D. Alicke. 2002. The influence of individual versus aggregate social comparison and the presence of others on self-evaluations. *Journal of Personality and Social Psychology* 83: 1117–130.

Burgess, W. Elaine. 1962. *Negro leadership in a southern city*. Chapel Hill: University of North Carolina Press.

Burke, Peter J. 1980. The self: measurement requirements from an interactionist perspective. *Social Psychology Quarterly* 43(1): 18–29.

Burns, Nancy, Kay Lehman Schlozman, and Sidney Verba. 2001. *The private roots of public action*. Cambridge: Harvard University Press.

Byrne, Donn, and Don Nelson. 1965. Attraction as a linear function of proportion of positive reinforcements. *Journal of Personality and Social Psychology* 1(6): 659–63.

Calhoun-Brown, Allison. 1996. African American churches and political mobilization: The psychological impact of organizational resources. *The Journal of Politics* 58(4): 935–53.

———. 1998. The politics of Black Evangelicals: What hinders diversity in the Christian Right? *American Politics Quarterly* 26(1): 81–109.

Campbell, Angus, Phillip E. Converse, Warren E. Miller, and Donald E. Stokes. 1960. *The American voter*. New York: Wiley.

Campbell, Angus, Gerald Gurin, and Warren E. Miller. 1954. *The voter decides*. Evanston, IL: Row, Peterson.

Campbell, Donald T. 1967. Stereotypes and perception of group differences. *American Psychologist* 22: 812–29.

Canon, David T. 1999. *Race, redistricting, and representation: The unintended consequences of Black majority districts*. Chicago: University of Chicago Press.

Canon, David, Matthew Schousen, and Patrick Sellers. 1996. The supply side of congressional redistricting: Race and strategic politicians, 1972–1992. *The Journal of Politics* 58: 846–62.

Carmines, Edward G., and James A. Stimson. 1989. *Issue evolution: Race and the transformation of American politics*. Princeton, NJ: Princeton University Press.

Carter, Robert T. 2007. Racism and psychological and emotional injury: Recognizing and assessing race-based traumatic stress. *Counseling Psychologist* 35(1): 13–105.

Cavendish, James C. 2000. Church based community activism: A comparison of Black and White Catholic congregations. *Journal for the Scientific Study of Religion* 39(4): 371–84.

Cavendish, James C., Michael R. Welch, and David C. Leege. 1998. Social network theory and predictors of religiosity for Black and White Catholics: Evidence of a "Black Sacred Cosmos?" *Journal for the Scientific Study of Religion* 37(3): 397–410.

CAWP. 2005. "Women in elective office 2005 fact sheet." New Brunswick: Eagleton Institute of Politics, Rutgers, State University of New Jersey.

Chaves, Mark. 2004. *Congregations in America*. Cambridge: Harvard University Press.

Chaves, Mark, and Lynn M. Higgins. 1992. Comparing the community involvement of Black and White congregations. *Journal for the Scientific Study of Religion* 31(4): 425–41.

Chong, Dennis, and Reuel Rogers. 2005. Racial solidarity and political participation. *Political Behavior* 27(4): 347–74.

Chunn, Sherri. 2001. Mayoral candidate Shirley Franklin files campaign disclosure report. *Atlanta Business Chronicle*, April 2, 2001.

Cialdini, Robert B., Richard J. Borden, Avril Thorne, Marcus Randall Walker, Stephen Freeman, and Lloyd Reynolds Sloan. 1976. Basking in the glory: Three (football) field studies. *Journal of Personality and Social Psychology* 34(3): 366–75.

Citrin, Jack, Donald Philip Green, and David O. Sears. 1990. White reactions to Black candidates: When does race matter? *Public Opinion Quarterly* 54(1): 74–96.

Clark, Kenneth B., and Mamie P. Clark. Racial identification and preference of Negro children. In *Readings in Social Psychology*, ed. Theodore M. Newcomb and Eugene L. Hartley, 169–78. New York: Holt.

Clayton, Dewey M., and Angela M. Stallings. 2000. Black women in Congress: Striking the balance. *Journal of Black Studies* 30(4): 574–603.

Cohen, Cathy. 1999. *The boundaries of blackness: AIDS and the breakdown of Black politics.* Chicago: University of Chicago Press.

Cohen, Marcia B. 1989. Social work practice with homeless mentally ill people: Engaging the client. *Social Work* 34(6): 505–9.

Cohen, Sheldon, and Thomas A. Wills. 1985. Stress, social support, and the buffering hypothesis. *Psychological Bulletin* 98(2): 310–57.

Cone, James H. 1997. *Black theology and Black power.* Maryknoll, NY: Orbis.

Cone, James H., and Gayraud S. Wilmore, eds. 1993. *Black theology: A documentary history.* 2nd ed. Maryknoll, NY: Orbis.

Conover, Pamela Johnston. 1984. The influence of group identifications on political perception and evaluation. *The Journal of Politics* 46(3): 760–85.

———. 1988. The role of social groups in political thinking. *British Journal of Political Science* 18: 51–76.

Conover, Pamela J., and Stanley Feldman. 1986. Emotional reactions to the economy: I'm mad as hell and I'm not going to take it anymore. *American Journal of Political Science* 30(1): 50–78.

———. 1989. Candidate perception in an ambiguous world: Campaigns, cues, and inference processes. *American Journal of Political Science* 33(4): 912–40.

Converse, Philip. 1964. The nature of belief systems in mass publics. In *Ideology and discontent*, ed. David Ernest Apter, 206–61. London: Free Press of Glencoe.

Corcoran, Carole Baroody, and Aisha Renée Thompson. 2004. "What's race got to do, got to do with it?" Denial of racism on predominantly White college campuses. In *The psychology of prejudice and discrimination: Racism in America*, vol. 1, ed. Jean Lau Chin, 137–76. Westport, CT: Praeger/Greenwood.

Cornell, Stephen and Douglas Hartman. 1998. *Ethnicity and race: Making identities in a changing world.* Thousand Oaks, CA: Pine Forge Press.

Cose, Ellis. 1993. *The rage of a privileged class.* New York: HarperCollins.

Crosby, Faye. 1984. The denial of personal discrimination. *American Behavioral Scientist* 27: 371–86.

Cross, William E., Jr. 1971. Discovering the Black referent: The psychology of Black liberation. In *Beyond Black and White: An alternative America*, ed. Vernon J. Dixon and Badi G. Foster, 95–110. Boston: Little, Brown and Company.

———. 1978. The Thomas and Cross models of psychological Nigrescence: A review. *Journal of Black Psychology* 5: 13–31.

———. 1991. *Shades of Black: Diversity in African-American identity.* Philadelphia, PA: Temple University Press.

Dahl, Robert A. 1961. *Who governs?: Democracy and power in an American city.* New Haven: Yale University Press.

Damasio, Antonio R. 2000. A second chance for emotion. In *Cognitive neuroscience of emotion*, ed. Richard D. Lane and Lynn Nadel, 12–23. New York: Oxford University Press.

Danigelis, Nicholas L. 1977. A theory of Black political participation in the United States. *Social Forces* 56(1): 31–47.

———. 1978. Black political participation in the United States: Some recent evidence. *American Sociological Review* 43(October): 756–71.

————. 1982. Race, class, and political involvement in the U.S. *Social Forces* 61(2): 532–50.

Davis, Darren W. 1997. The direction of race of interviewer effects among African-Americans: Donning the Black mask. *American Journal of Political Science* 41(1): 309–22.

Davis, Jessica, and Oscar Gandy. 1999. Racial identity and media orientations: Exploring the nature of constraint. *Journal of Black Studies* 29(3): 367–97.

Dawson, Michael C. 1994. *Behind the mule: Race and class in African-American politics*. Princeton, NJ: Princeton University Press.

————. 2001. *Black visions: The roots of contemporary African-American political ideologies*. Chicago: University of Chicago Press.

Dawson, Michael C., and Rovana Popoff. 2004. "Reparations: justice and greed in Black and White." *DuBois Review* 1(1): 47–91.

Dawson, Michael C., Ronald E. Brown, and Richard L. Allen. 1990. Racial belief systems, religious guidance, and African-American political participation. *National Political Science Review* 2: 22–44.

Delli Carpini, Michael X, and Scott Keeter. 1996. *What Americans know about politics and why it matters*. New Haven, CT: Yale University Press.

Dijker, Anton J. M. 1987. Emotional reactions to ethnic minorities. *European Journal of Social Psychology* 17(3): 305–25.

Doise, W., G. Csepeli, H. D. Dann, C. Gouge, K. Larsen, and A. Ostell. 1972. An experimental investigation into the formation of intergroup representations. *European Journal of Social Psychology* 2(2): 202–4.

Douglass, Frederick. 1999. Slaveholding religion and the Christianity of Christ. In *African American religious history: A documentary witness*, ed. Milton C. Sernett, 102–11. Durham, NC: Duke University Press.

Dovidio, John, and Russell Fazio. 1992. New technologies for the direct and indirect assessment of attitudes. In *Questions about questions: Inquiries into the cognitive bases of surveys*, ed. Judith M. Tanur, 204–37. New York: Sage.

Downs, Anthony. 1957. *An economic theory of democracy*. New York: Harper & Row.

Druckman, James. 2004. "Political preference formation: Competition, deliberation, and the (ir)relevance of framing effects." *American Political Science Review* 98(4): 671–86.

Du Bois, W. E. B. 1899. *The Philadelphia Negro: A social study*. Philadelphia: University of Pennsylvania Press.

————. 1903. *The souls of Black folk*. New York: Bantam Books (1989 reprint of the 1903 edition).

————. 1903. "The talented tenth," from *The Negro problem: A series of articles by representative Negroes of today*. New York: James Pott.

Duerst-Lahti, Georgia, and Dayna Verstegen. 1995. Making something of absence: The "Year of the woman" and women's representation. In *Gender power, leadership, and governance*, ed. Georgia Duerst-Lahti and Rita Mae Kelly, 213–38. Ann Arbor: University of Michigan Press.

Edsall, Thomas B., and Mary D. Edsall. 1991. *Chain reaction: The impact of race, rights, and taxes on American politics*. New York: Norton.

Eibach, Richard P., and Thomas Keegan. 2006. Free at last? Social dominance, loss aversion, and White and Black Americans' differing assessments of racial progress. *Journal of Personality and Social Psychology* 90(3): 453–67.

Eidelson, Roy J. 2002. Measuring Parallel Beliefs about Self and Group: Development and Validation of the Individual-Group Belief Inventory. Unpublished manuscript.

———. 2005. Assessing Order Effects with the Individual Group Belief Inventory. Unpublished data.

———. 2009. An Individual-Group Belief Framework: Predicting Life Satisfaction, Group Identification, and Support for the "War on Terror." *Peace and Conflict: Journal of Peace Psychology* 15: 1–26.

Eidelson, Roy J., and Judy I. Eidelson. 2003. Dangerous ideas: Five beliefs that propel groups toward conflict. *American Psychologist* 58: 182–92.

Eidelson, Roy. J., and Mary D. Plummer. 2005. Self and nation: A comparison of Americans' beliefs before and after 9/11. *Peace and Conflict: Journal of Peace Psychology* 11: 153–75.

Ekstrand, Laurie E., and William Eckert. 1981. The impact of candidate's sex on voter choice. *Western Political Quarterly* 34(1): 78–87.

Ellison, Christopher G. 1991. Identification and separatism: Religious involvement and racial orientations among Black Americans. *The Sociological Quarterly* 32(3): 477–94.

———. 1994. Religion, the life stress paradigm, and the study of depression. In *Religion in Aging and Health: Theoretical foundations and methodological frontiers*, ed. Jeff S. Levin, 78–124. Thousand Oaks, CA: Sage.

Ellison, Christopher G., and David A. Gay. 1990. Region, religious commitment, and life satisfaction among Black Americans. *The Sociological Quarterly* 31(1): 123–47.

Ellison, Christopher G., and Marc A. Musick. 1993. Southern intolerance: A fundamentalist effect? *Social Forces* 72(2): 379–98.

Ellison, Christopher G., and Darren E. Sherkat. 1997. The cognitive structure of a moral crusade: Conservative Protestantism and opposition to pornography. *Social Forces* 75(3): 957–82.

Enomoto, Carl E. 1999. Public sympathy for O. J. Simpson: The roles of race, age, gender, income, and education. *American Journal of Economics and Sociology* 58(1): 145–61.

Feagin, Joe R., and Melvin P. Sikes. 1994. *Living with racism: The Black middle-class experience*. Wilmington, MA: Beacon Press.

Fenno, Richard. 2003. *Going home: Black representatives and their constituents*. Chicago: University of Chicago Press.

Festinger, Leon. 1954. A theory of social comparison processes. *Human Relations* 7: 117–40.

Fish, Stanley. 1980. *Is there a text in this class? The authority of interpretive communities*. Cambridge: Harvard University Press.

Fiske, Susan T., and Shelley E. Taylor. 1991. *Social cognition.* 2nd ed. Reading: Addison-Wesley.

Foster, Kenneth. 2004. The relations between well being, attitudinal and behavioral factors across three Black identity orientations: Assimilated, Afrocentric, and Multicultural. PhD dissertation, City University of New York Graduate Center.

Fowers, Blaine J., and Frank C. Richardson. 1996. Why is multiculturalism good? *American Psychologist* 51: 609–21.

Franklin, Raymond S. 1991. *Shadows of race and class.* Minneapolis: University of Minnesota Press.

Frankovic, Kathleen A. 1982. Sex and politics: New alignment, old issues. *PS* 15(3): 439–48.

Frazier, E. Franklin. [1964] 1974. *The Black Church in America.* New York: Knopf. Original edition, 1963.

Freidrich, Robert J. 1982. In defense of multiplicative terms in multiple regression equations. *American Journal of Political Science* 1982(4): 797–833.

Frijda, Nico H. 1986. *The emotions.* Cambridge: Cambridge University Press.

Gaertner, Samuel, and John Dovidio. 1986. The aversive form of racism. In *Prejudice, discrimination, and racism,* ed. John F. Dovidio and Samuel L. Gaertner, 61–89. Orlando, FL: Academic.

Gamson, William A. 1992. *Talking politics.* Cambridge: Cambridge University Press.

Gay, Claudine. 2001. The effect of Black congressional representation on political participation. *American Political Science Review* 95(3): 589–602.

Gay, Claudine, and Katherine Tate. 1998. Doubly bound: The impact of gender and race on the politics of Black women. *Political Psychology* 19(1): 169–84.

Gay, David, and John Lynxwiler. 1999. The impact of religiosity on race variations in abortion attitudes. *Sociological Spectrum* 19: 359–77.

Gay, Geneva. 1985. Implications of selected models of ethnic identity development for educators. *Journal of Negro Education* 54(1): 43–55.

Gilens, Martin. 1996. "'Race coding' and White opposition to welfare." *American Political Science Review* 90(3): 593–604.

———. 1999. *Why Americans hate welfare: Race, media, and the politics of anti-poverty policy.* Chicago: University of Chicago Press.

Gilliam, Franklin D. Jr., and Shanto Iyengar. 2000. "Prime suspects: The influence of local television news on the viewing public." *American Journal of Political Science* 44(3): 560–73.

Gilliam, Franklin, Jr., and Karen M. Kaufmann. 1998. Is there an empowerment life cycle: Long term Black empowerment and its influence on voter participation. *Urban Affairs Review* 33(6): 741–67.

Gilliam, Franklin D., Jr., and Kenny J. Whitby. 1989. "Race, class and attitudes toward social welfare spending: An ethclass interpretation." *Social Science Quarterly* 70(1): 88–100.

Giordano, Peggy C. 2003. Relationships in adolescence. *Annual Review of Sociology* 29: 257–81.

Glaser, James M., and Martin Gilens. 1997. Inter-regional migration and political resocialization: A study of racial attitudes under pressure. *Public Opinion Quarterly* 61(1): 72–86.

Glick, Peter, and Susan Fiske. 2001. Ambivalent stereotypes as legitimizing ideologies: Differentiating paternalistic and envious prejudice. *The psychology of legitimacy: Emerging perspectives on ideology, justice, and intergroup relations,* ed. John T. Jost and Brenda Major, 278–306. New York: Cambridge University Press.

Gosnell, Harold. 1935. *Negro politicians.* Chicago: University of Chicago Press.

Green, Alexander R., Dana R. Carney, Daniel J. Pallin, Long H. Ngo, Kristal L. Raymond, Lisa Lezzoni, and Mahzarin Banaji. 2007. Implicit bias among physicians and its prediction of thrombolysis decisions for Black and White patients. *Journal of Internal Medicine,* 24(1): 1231–38.

Green, Donald, Bradley Palmquist, and Eric Schickler. 2002. *Partisan hearts and minds: Political parties and the social identities of voters.* New Haven: Yale University Press.

Greenstein, Fred. 1969. *Personality and politics.* Chicago: Markham.

Greenwald, Anthony, and Mahzarin Banaji. 1995. Implicit social cognition: Attitudes, self-esteem, and stereotypes. *Psychological Review* 102(1): 4–27.

Greenwald, Anthony, Debbie McGhee, and Jordan Schwartz. 1998. Measuring individual differences in implicit cognition: The implicit association test. *Journal of Personality and Social Psychology* 74(6): 1464–80.

Greenwald, Anthony G., Brian A. Nosek, and Mahzarin R. Banaji. 2003. Understanding and using the implicit association test: An improved scoring algorithm. *Journal of Personality and Social Psychology* 85(2): 197–216.

Gurin, Patricia. 1985. Women's gender consciousness. *Public Opinion Quarterly* 49: 143–63.

Grills, Cheryl, and Douglas Longshore. 1996. Africentrism: Psychometric analysis of a self-report measure. *Journal of Black Psychology* 22(1): 86–106.

Gurin, Patricia, Shirley Hatchett, and James S. Jackson. 1989. *Hope and independence: Blacks' response to electoral and party politics.* New York: Russell Sage Foundation.

Gurin, Patricia, Arthur Miller, and Gerald Gurin. 1980. Stratum identification and consciousness. *Social Psychology Quarterly* 43(1): 30–47.

Guth, James, John C. Green, Corwin E. Smidt, Lyman A. Kellstedt, and Margaret M. Poloma. 1997. *The bully pulpit: The politics of Protestant clergy.* Lawrence, KN: University of Kansas Press.

Guthrie, Robert V. 1980. The psychology of Black Americans: An historical perspective. In *Black psychology,* ed. Reginald L. Jones, 13–22. New York: Harper & Row.

Gutterbock, Thomas M., and Bruce London. 1983. Race, political orientation, and participation: An empirical test of four competing theories. *American Sociological Review* 48: 439–53.

Haire, Mason. 1950. Projective techniques in marketing research. *Journal of Marketing* 14(5): 649–56.

Hamilton, David L., and Diane M. Mackie. 1993. Cognitive and affective processes in intergroup perception: The developing interface. In *Affect, cognition, and stereotyping: Interactive processes in group perception*, ed. Diane M. Mackie and David L. Hamilton, 1–11. San Diego: Academic Press.

Hanes, Walton, Jr. 1997. *African American power and politics: The Political context variable*. New York: Columbia University Press.

Hardiman, Rita. 1982. White identity development: A process oriented model for describing the racial consciousness of White Americans. ProQuest Information & Learning.

Harding, Vincent. 1969. Religion and resistance among antebellum Negroes, 1800–1860. In *The making of Black America: Essays in Negro life and history*, ed. August Meier and Elliot Rudwick. New York: Atheneum.

Harris, Fredrick C. 1999. *Something within: Religion in African-American political activism*. New York: Oxford University Press.

Harris, Norman. 1992. A philosophical basis for an Afrocentric orientation. *The Western Journal of Black Studies* 16(3): 154–59.

Harris, Rafael S., Jr. 2009. Racial microaggression? How do you know?—Revisited. *American Psychologist* 64(3): 220.

Harris-Lacewell, Melissa V. 2003. The heart of the politics of race: Centering Black people in the study of White racial attitudes. *Journal of Black Studies* 34: 222–49.

———. 2004. *Barbershops, bibles, and BET: Everyday talk and Black political thought*. Princeton, NJ: Princeton University Press.

Hasenfeld, Yeheskel. 1987. Power in social work practice. *Social Service Review* 61(3): 469–83.

Hermann, Margaret G., ed. 1986. *Political psychology*. San Francisco: Jossey-Bass.

Herring, Mary, Thomas Jankowski, and Ronald Brown. 1999. Pro-Black doesn't mean anti-White: The structure of African-American group identity. *Journal of Politics* 61(2): 363–86.

Herrnstein, Richard J., and Charles Murray. 1994. *The bell curve: Intelligence and class structure in American life*. Riverside, NJ: Simon & Schuster.

Hetherington, Marc J. 1998. The political relevance of political trust. *American Political Science Review* 92: 791–808.

Highton, Benjamin. 2004. White voters and African American candidates for Congress. *Political Behavior* 26(1): 1–25.

Higgins, E. Troy. 1996. Knowledge accessibility and activation: subjectivity and suffering from unconscious sources. In *Unintended thought*, ed. James S. Uleman and John A. Bargh, 75–123. New York: Guilford.

Hinojosa, Victor J., and Jerry Z. Park. 2004. Religion and the paradox of racial inequality attitudes. *Journal for the Scientific Study of Religion* 43(2): 229–38.

Holloway, Harry. 1969. *The politics of the southern Negro: From exclusion to big city organization*. New York: Random House.

Homer-Dixon, Thomas F. 1999. *Environment, scarcity, and violence*. Princeton, NJ: Princeton University Press.

hooks, bell. 1981. *Ain't I a woman: Black women and feminism.* Boston: South End.

Horowitz, Donald L. 1985. *Ethnic groups in conflict.* Berkeley: University of California Press.

Horowitz, Irving Louis. 1979. Paradigms of political psychology. *Political Psychology* 1(2): 99–103.

Hsieh, Theodore T., John Shybut, and Erwin J. Lotsof. 1969. Internal versus external control and ethnic group membership: A cross-cultural comparison. *Journal of Consulting and Clinical Psychology* 33(1)(02): 122–24.

Huddy, Leonie, and Nayda Terkildsen. 1993a. The consequences of gender stereotypes for women candidates at different levels and types of office. *Political Research Quarterly* 46(3): 503–25.

———. 1993b. Gender stereotypes and the perception of male and female candidates. *American Journal of Political Science* 37(1): 119–47.

Huddy, Leonie, Stanley Feldman, Theresa Capelos, and Colin Provost. 2002. The consequences of terrorism: Disentangling the effects of personal and national threat. *Political Psychology* 23: 485–509.

Hughes, Michael, and Steven A. Tuch. 2000. How beliefs about poverty influence racial policy attitudes: A study of Whites, African Americans, Hispanics, and Asians in the United States. In *Racialized politics: The debate about racism in America,* ed. Donald O. Sears, Jim Sidanius, and Lawrence Bobo, 165–90. Chicago: University of Chicago Press.

Hunt, Matthew O. 2000. Status, religion, and the "belief in a just world": Comparing African Americans, Latinos and Whites. *Social Science Quarterly* 81(1): 325–43.

———. 2002. Religion, race/ethnicity, and beliefs about poverty. *Social Science Quarterly* 83(3): 810–31.

Hurwitz, Jon, and Mark Peffley. 2005. Explaining the great racial divide: Perceptions of fairness in the U.S. criminal justice system. *The Journal of Politics* 67(3): 762–83.

———. 2005. Playing the race card in the post–Willie Horton era: The impact of racialized code words on support for punitive crime policy. *Public Opinion Quarterly* 69(1): 99–112.

Hutchings, Vincent L. 2003. *Public opinion and democratic accountability: How citizens learn about politics.* Princeton, NJ: Princeton University Press.

———. 2009. Change or more of the same: Evaluating racial policy preferences in the Obama era. *Public Opinion Quarterly* 73(5): 917–42.

Hutchings, Vincent L., and Nicholas A. Valentino. 2003. Driving the wedge: The structure and function of racial group cues in contemporary American politics. Paper presented at the 2003 American Political Science Association, August 27–31, in Philadelphia, PA.

———. 2004. The centrality of race in American politics. *Annual Review of Political Science* 7: 383–408.

Hutchings, Vincent L., Nicholas A. Valentino, Tasha S. Philpot, and Ismail K. White. 2004. The compassion strategy: Race and the gender gap in campaign 2000. *Public Opinion Quarterly* 68(4): 512–41.

————. 2006. Racial cues in campaign news: The effects of candidate strategies on group activation and political attentiveness among African Americans. In *Feeling politics: Emotion in political information processing*, ed. David Redlawsk, 165–86. New York: Palgrave Macmillan.

Hyman, Herbert H. 1959. *Political socialization: A study in the psychology of political behavior*. Glencoe, IL: Free Press.

Iyengar, Shanto. 1986. Whither political information. NES Pilot Study Report, No. nes002253. Dataset(s): /1985 Pilot.

————. 1993. An overview of the field of political psychology. In *Explorations in political psychology*, ed. Shanto Iyengar and William J. McGuire, 3–8. Durham: Duke University Press.

Iyengar, Shanto, and Donald R. Kinder. 1987. *News that matters: television and American public opinion*. Chicago: University of Chicago Press.

Jackson, Bryan. 1987. The effects of racial group consciousness on political mobilization in American cities. *Western Political Quarterly* 40(4): 631–46.

Jacobson, Gary C. 1997. *The politics of congressional elections*. 4th ed. New York: Addison-Wesley Educational Publishers.

Jaret, Charles, and Donald Reitzes. 1999. The importance of racial-ethnic identity and social setting for Blacks, Whites, and Multiracials. *Sociological Perspectives* 42(4): 711–37.

JBHE Foundation. 1996. Almost no Black psychologists teaching at America's highly ranked universities. *Journal of Blacks in Higher Education* (12): 60–61.

Johnson, Guy B. 1937. Negro racial movements and leadership in the United States. *American Journal of Sociology* 43(6): 56–72.

Jones, James H. 1993. *Bad blood: The Tuskegee syphilis experiment*. Riverside, NJ: Free Press.

————. 1997. *Prejudice and racism*. 2nd ed. New York: McGraw-Hill.

Kahn, Kim Fridkin. 1996. *The political consequences of being a woman: How stereotypes influence the conduct and consequences of political campaigns*. New York: Columbia University Press.

Kaufmann, Karen M. 2004. The partisan paradox: Religious commitment and the gender gap in party identification. *Public Opinion Quarterly* 68(4): 491–511.

Kaufmann, Karen M., and John R. Petrocik. 1999. The changing politics of American men: Understanding the sources of the gender gap. *American Journal of Political Science* 43(3): 864–87.

Kay, Aaron C., Danielle Gaucher, Jennifer M. Peach, Kristin Laurin, Justin Friesen, Mark P. Zanna, and Steven J. Spencer. 2009. Inequality, discrimination, and the power of the status quo: Direct evidence for a motivation to see the way things are as the way they should be. *Journal of Personality and Social Psychology* 97(3): 421–34.

Kessler, Thomas, Amelie Mummendey, and Utta-Kristin Leisse. 2000. The Personal-group discrepancy: Is there a common information basis of personal and group judgment? *Journal of Personality and Social Psychology* 79: 95–109.

Key, V. O. 1949. *Southern politics in State and Nation*. New York: Vintage Books.

Kihlstrom, John. 2004. Implicit methods in social psychology. In *The Sage handbook of methods in social psychology,* ed. Carol Sansone, Carolyn Morf, and A. T. Panter, 195–212. Thousand Oaks, CA: Sage.

Kinder, Donald R., and Thomas R. Palfrey. 1993. On behalf of an experimental political science. In *Experimental foundations of political science*, ed. Donald R. Kinder and Thomas R. Palfrey, 1–39. Ann Arbor: University of Michigan Press.

Kinder, Donald R., and Lynn M. Sanders. 1996. *Divided by color: Racial politics and democratic ideals.* Chicago: University of Chicago Press.

Kinder, Donald R., and David O. Sears. 1981. Prejudice and politics: Symbolic racism versus racial threats to the good life. *Journal of Personality and Social Psychology* 40(3): 414–31.

Kinder, Donald R., and Nicholas Winter. 2001. "Exploring the racial divide: Blacks, Whites, and opinion on national policy." *American Journal of Political Science* 45(2): 439–56.

King, Mae C. 1975. Oppression and power: The unique status of the Black woman in the American political system. *Social Science Quarterly* 56(1): 116–28.

Kleiman, Michael B. 1976. Trends in racial differences in political efficacy. *Phylon* 37: 159–62.

Klinkner, Philip A., and Rogers M. Smith. 1999. *The unsteady march: The rise and decline of racial equality in America.* Chicago: University of Chicago Press.

Kluegel, James R. 1990. Trends in whites' explanations of the gap in Black-White socioeconomic status, 1977–1989. *American Sociological Review* 55: 512–25.

Knabb, Richard D., Jamie R. Rhome, and Daniel P. Brown. 2005. Tropical Cyclone Report, Hurricane Katrina, 23–30, August 2005, National Hurricane Center. Online at http://www.nhc.noaa.gov/pdf/TCR-AL122005_Katrina.pdf.

Knutson, Jeanne N., ed. 1973. *Handbook of political psychology.* San Francisco: Jossey-Bass.

Kobasa, Suzanne C. 1979. Stressful life events, personality, and health: An inquiry into hardiness. *Journal of Personality and Social Psychology* 37(1): 1–11.

Krosnick, Jon A. 2002. Is political psychology sufficiently psychological? Distinguishing political psychology from psychological political science. In *Thinking about political psychology*, ed. James H. Kuklinski, 187–216. Cambridge: Cambridge University Press.

Kuklinski, James H. 2002. Introduction: Political psychology and the study of politics. In *Thinking about political psychology*, ed. James H. Kuklinski, 1–20. Cambridge: Cambridge University Press.

Landrine, Hope, and Elizabeth A. Klonoff. 1996a. *African American acculturation: Deconstructing race and reviving culture.* Thousand Oaks, CA: Sage.

———. 1996b. The schedule of racist events: A measure of racial discrimination and a study of its negative physical and mental health consequences. *Journal of Black Psychology* 22(2): 144–68.

Lasswell, Harold. 1930. *Psychopathology and politics.* Chicago: University of Chicago Press.

———. 1948. *Power and personality.* New York: W.W. Norton.

Lau, Richard. 1989. Individual and contextual influences on group identification. *Social Psychology Quarterly* 52(3): 220–31.

Leavitt, David. 1998. The hate epidemic. *New York Times*, October 18, 15.

Leege, David C. 1993. Religion and politics in theoretical perspective. In *Rediscovering the religious factor in American politics*, ed. David C. Leege and Lyman A. Kellstedt, 3–25. New York: M. E. Sharpe.

Leege, David C., and Lyman A. Kellstedt, eds. 1993. *Rediscovering the religious factor in American politics*. New York: M. E. Sharpe.

Leighley, Jan E., and Arnold Vedlitz. 1999. Race, ethnicity, and political participation: Competing models and contrasting explanations. *The Journal of Politics* 61: 1092–114.

Lemm, Kristi, and Mahzarin R. Banaji. 1999. Unconscious attitudes and beliefs about women and men. In *Wahrnehmung and Herstellung von Geschlecht (Perceiving and performing Gender)*, ed. Ulla Pasero and Friederike. Braun, 215–33. Opladen: Westdutscher Verlag.

Lerner, Michael. 1971. *A source book for the study of personality and politics.* Chicago: Markham.

LeVine, Robert A., and Donald T. Campbell. 1972. *Ethnocentrism: Theories of conflict, ethnic attitudes and group behavior.* New York: John Wiley.

Lewis, Elsie M. 1955. The political mind of the Negro, 1865–1900. *Journal of Southern History* 21(2): 189–202.

Lincoln, C. Eric, and Lawrence H. Mamiya. 1990. *The Black church in the African American experience.* Durham, NC: Duke University Press.

Lippmann, Walter 1922. *Public opinion.* New York, NY: Free Press.

Locke, Mamie E. 1997. From three-fifths to zero: Implications of the Constitution for African American women, 1787–1870. In *Women transforming politics: An alternative reader*, ed. Cathy J. Cohen, Kathleen B. Jones, and Joan C. Tronto, 377–86. New York: New York University Press.

Lodge, Milton, Kathleen M. McGraw, and Patrick Stroh. 1989. An impression-driven model of candidate evaluation. *American Political Science Review* 83(2): 399–419.

Long, J. Scott, and Jeremy Freese. 2001. *Regression models for categorical dependent variables using Stata.* College Station, TX: Stata Press.

Lopez, Mark Hugo, and Paul Taylor. 2009. Dissecting the 2008 Electorate: Most Diverse in U.S. History. Pew Research Center. http://pewhispanic.org/files/reports/108.pdf.

Lublin, David. 2004. *The Republican South: Democratization and partisan change.* Princeton, NJ: Princeton University Press.

Luke, Douglas. 2004. *Multilevel modeling.* Thousand Oaks: Sage.

Lyubansky, Mikhail, and Roy J. Eidelson. 2005. Revisiting Du Bois: The relationship between African American double consciousness and beliefs about racial and national group experiences. *Journal of Black Psychology* 31: 3–26.

Macedo Stephen, Yvette Alex-Assensoh, Jeffrey M. Berry, Michael Brintnall, David E. Campbell, Luis Ricardo Fraga, Archon Fung, William A. Galston, Christopher F. Karpowitz, Margaret Levi, Meira Levinson, Keena Lipsitz,

Richard G. Niemi, Robert D. Putnam, Wendy M. Rahn, Rob Reich, Robert R. Rodgers, Todd Swanstrom, and Katherine Cramer Walsh. 2005. *Democracy at risk: how political choices undermine citizen participation, and what we can do about it.* Washington, DC: Brookings Institution Press.

Mackie, Diane M., Thierry Devos, and Eliot R. Smith. 2000. Intergroup emotions: Explaining offensive action tendencies in an intergroup context. *Journal of Personality and Social Psychology* 79(4): 602–16.

Mann, John H. 1959. The relationship between cognitive, affective, and behavioral aspects of racial prejudice. *Journal of Social Psychology* 49(2): 223–28.

Mansbridge, Jane, and Katherine Tate. 1992. Race trumps gender: The Thomas nomination in the Black community. *PS: Political Science & Politics* 25(3): 488–92.

Massey, Douglas S., and Nancy A. Denton. 1993. *American apartheid: Segregation and the making of the underclass.* Cambridge: Harvard University Press.

Matthews, Donald R., and James W. Prothro. 1966. *Negroes and the new southern politics.* New York: Harcourt, Brace, & World.

Mattis, Jacqueline S., Dwight L. Fontenot, Carrie A. Hatcher-Kay, Nyasha A. Grayman, and Ruby L. Beale. 2004. Religiosity, optimism, and pessimism among African Americans. *Journal of Black Psychology* 30(2): 187–207.

Maveety, Nancy, ed. 2003. *The pioneers of judicial behavior.* Ann Arbor: University of Michigan Press.

Mays, Vickie M., and Susan D. Cochran. 1993. The impact of perceived discrimination on the intimate relationships of Black lesbians. *Journal of Homosexuality* 25(4): 1.

McAdam, Doug. 1982. *Political process and the development of black insurgency, 1930–1970.* Chicago: University of Chicago Press.

McClain, Paula D., and John A. Garcia. 1993. Expanding disciplinary boundaries: Black, Latino, and racial minority group politics in political science. In *Political science: The state of the discipline ii*, ed. Ada Finifter, 247–79. Washington, DC: American Political Science Association.

McClerking, Harwood. 2001. We're in this together: The origins and maintenance of Black common fate perception. PhD dissertation, University of Michigan.

McClerking, Harwood K., and Tasha S. Philpot. 2008. Struggling to be noticed: The civil rights movement as an academic agenda setter. *PS: Political Science and Politics* 41(4): 813–17.

McConahay, John B. 1982. Self-interest versus racial attitudes as correlates of anti-busing attitudes in Louisville: Is it the buses or the Blacks? *Journal of Politics* 44(3): 692–720.

McDaniel, Eric L., and Christopher G. Ellison. 2008. God's party? Race, religion, and partisanship over time. *Political Research Quarterly* 61(2): 180–191.

McGuire, William J. 1993. The poly-psy relationship: Three phases of a long affair. In *Explorations in political psychology*, ed. Shanto Iyengar and William J. McGuire, 9–35. Durham: Duke University Press.

McIntosh, Peggy. 1998. White privilege: Unpacking the invisible knapsack. In *Re-visioning family therapy: Race, culture, and gender in clinical practice*, ed. Monica McGoldrick, 147–52. New York: Guilford Press.

Mendelberg, Tali. 1997. Executing Hortons: Racial crime in the 1988 presidential campaign. *Public Opinion Quarterly* 61(1): 134–57.

———. 2001. *The race card: Campaign strategy, implicit messages, and the norm of equality.* Princeton, NJ: Princeton University Press.

Milbrath, Lester W., and Madan Lal Goel. 1977. *Political participation: How and why do people get involved in politics.* Chicago, IL; Rand McNally.

Miller, Arthur, Patricia Gurin, Gerald Gurin, and Oksana Malanchuk. 1981. Group consciousness and political participation. *American Journal of Political Science* 25: 494–511.

Miller, Jill Young. 2001. Atlanta mayoral race: Meet the candidates: Gloria Bromell-Tinubu; driven by a people-first philosophy, long-shot hopeful challenges cronyism. *The Atlanta Journal-Constitution*, October 21, 2001, 3H.

Miller, Jill Young, and Alan Judd. 2001. Franklin clinches money-making reign. *The Atlanta Journal-Constitution*, November 3, 2001, 1.

Miller, Joanne, and Jon A. Krosnick. 2000. News media impact on the ingredients of presidential evaluations: Politically knowledgeable citizens are guided by trusted sources. *American Journal of Political Science* 44(2): 301–15.

Mink, Gwendolyn, and Alice O'Connor. 2004. *Poverty in the United States: An encyclopedia of history, politics, and polity.* Santa Barbara, CA: ABC-CLIO.

Moghaddam, Fatali M., Alison J. Stolkin, and Lesley S. Hutcheson. 1997. A generalized personal/group discrepancy: Testing the domain specificity of a perceived higher effect of events on one's group than on oneself. *Personality and Social Psychology Bulletin* 23: 743–50.

Moreland, Richard L., and Robert B. Zajonc. 1977. Is stimuli recognition a necessary condition for the occurrence of exposure effects? *Journal of Personality and Social Psychology* 35(4): 191–99.

Morris, Edward F. 2000. Assessment practices with African Americans: Combining standard assessment measures within an Africentric orientation. In *Handbook of cross-cultural and multicultural personality assessment*, ed. Richard Henry Dana, 573–603. Mahwah, NJ: Lawrence Erlbaum Associates.

Myrdal, Gunnar. 1944. *An American dilemma: The Negro problem and modern democracy.* New Brunswick: Transaction.

National Opinion Research Center. 2002a. General Social Survey: Study FAQs. http://www.norc.org/GSS+Website/FAQs/FAQs.htm (accessed January 11, 2010).

———. 2002b. America rebounds: A national study of public response to the September 11th terrorist attacks, preliminary findings. (October 25), http://www.norc.org/NR/rdonlyres/51AA73B5-EB68-4E2A-AC63-75D652AA7D41/0/pubresp.pdf (accessed January 11, 2010).

———. 2002c. America recovers: A follow-up to a national study of public response to the September 11th terrorist attacks. (August), http://www.norc.uchicago.edu/NR/rdonlyres/E80028D8-96BB-47EF-90A3-B69D253D8652/0/pubresp2.pdf (accessed January 11, 2010).

Nelson, Thomas E., and Donald R. Kinder. 1996. Issue frames and group-centrism in American public opinion. *The Journal of Politics* 58(4): 1055–78.

Nelson, Thomas, Rosalee Clawson, and Zoe Oxley. 1997. Media framing of a civil liberties conflict and its effect on tolerance. *American Political Science Review* 91(3): 567–83.

Newcomb, Theodore. 1957. *Personality and social change: Attitude formation in a student community*. New York: Dryden.

Nickerson, Kim J., Janet E. Helms, and Francis Terrell. 1994. Cultural mistrust, opinions about mental illness, and Black students' attitudes toward seeking psychological help from White counselors. *Journal of Counseling Psychology* 41(3): 378–85.

Nobles, Wade W. 1989. Psychological nigrescence: An Afrocentric review. *The Counseling Psychologist* 17(2): 253–57.

Norrander, Barbara. 1999a. The evolution of the gender gap. *Public Opinion Quarterly* 63(4): 566–76.

———. 1999b. Is the gender gap growing? In *Reelection 1996: How Americans voted*, ed. Herbert F. Weisberg and Janet M. Box-Steffensmeier, 145–61. New York: Chatham House.

Nosek, Brian A., Anthony G. Greenwald, and Mahzarin R. Banaji. 2005. Understanding and using the implicit association test: II. method variables and construct validity. *Personality and Social Psychology Bulletin* 31(2): 166–80.

Ogletree, Kathryn. 1976. Internal-external control in black and white. *Black Books Bulletin* 4: 26–31.

Olsen, Marvin. 1970. Social and political participation of Blacks. *American Sociological Review* 35(2): 682–96.

Omi, Michael, and Howard Winant. 1994. *Racial formation in the United States from the 1960s to the 1990s*. New York: Routledge.

Owen, Diana, and Jack Dennis. 2001. Trust in the federal government: The phenomenon and its antecedents. In *What is it about Government that Americans dislike?*, ed. John Hibbing, and Elizabeth Theiss-Morse, 209–26. Cambridge, UK: Cambridge University Press.

Paolino, Phillip. 1995. Group-salient issues and group representation: Support for women candidates in the 1992 Senate elections. *American Journal of Political Science* 39(2): 294–313.

Pape, Robert A. 2003. The strategic logic of suicide terrorism. *The American Political Science Review* 97(3): 343–61.

Parham, Thomas A. 1993. *Psychological storms: The African American struggle for identity*. 1st ed. Chicago: African American Images.

Paris, Peter J. 1985. *The social teaching of the Black churches*. Philadelphia: Fortress Press.

Pattilo-Mccoy. 1998. Church culture as a strategy of action in the Black community. *American Sociological Review* 63: 767–84.

Perez, Adela Garzon. 2001. Political psychology as discipline and resource. *Political Psychology* 22(2): 347–56.

Perkins, Margo V. 1999. Inside our dangerous ranks: The autobiography of Elaine Brown and the Black Panther Party. In *Still lifting, still climbing:*

Contemporary African American women's activism, ed. Kimberly Springer, 91–106. New York: New York University Press.

Philpot, Tasha S. 2004. A party of a different color? Race, campaign communication, and party politics. *Political Behavior* 26(3): 249–70.

———. 2007. *Race, republicans, and the return of the party of Lincoln*. Ann Arbor: University of Michigan Press.

Philpot, Tasha S., and Hanes Walton. 2005. An historic election in context: The 2001 Atlanta mayoral election. *National Political Science Review* 10: 43–53.

Phinney, Jean S. 1990. Ethnic identity in adolescents and adults: Review of research. *Psychological Bulletin* 108(3): 499–514.

Porter, Judith, and Robert Washington. 1979. Black identity and self-esteem. *Annual Review of Sociology* 5: 53–74.

Postmes, Tom, Nyla R. Branscombe, Russell Spears, and Heather Young. 1999. Comparative processes in personal and group judgments: Resolving the discrepancy. *Journal of Personality and Social Psychology* 76: 320–38.

Prestage, Jewel Limar. 1977. Black women state legislators: A profile. In *A portrait of marginality: The political behavior of the American woman*, ed. Marianne Githens and Jewel Limar Prestage, 401–18. New York: David McKay.

Price, Vincent, and David Tewksbury. 1997. News values and public opinion: A theoretical account of media priming and framing. In *Progress in communication sciences*, ed. Franklin.J. Boster and George Barnett, 173–212. Norwood: Ablex.

Priest, Ronnie. 1991. Racism and prejudice as negative impacts on African American clients in therapy. *Journal of Counseling & Development* 70(1): 213–15.

Rabbie, Jacob M., and Murray Horowitz. 1969. Arousal of ingroup-outgroup bias by a chance win or loss. *Journal of Personality and Social Psychology* 13(3): 269–77.

Raboteau, Albert J. 1978. *Slave religion: The "invisible institution" in the Antebellum South*. Oxford: Oxford University Press.

———. 2001. *Canaan land: A religious history of African Americans*. Oxford: Oxford University Press.

Ragsdale, Lyn. 1991. Strong feelings: Emotional responses to presidents. *Political Behavior* 13(1): 33–65.

Rahn, Wendy M., John L. Sullivan, and Thomas J. Rudolph. 2002. Political psychology and political science. In *Thinking about political psychology*, ed. James H. Kuklinski, 155–86. Cambridge: Cambridge University Press.

Rappaport, Julian. 1981. In praise of paradox: A social policy of empowerment over prevention. *American Journal of Community Psychology* 9(1): 1–25.

———. 1987. Terms of empowerment/exemplars of prevention: Toward a theory for community psychology. *American Journal of Community Psychology* 15(2): 121–48.

Reese, Laura A., and Ronald E. Brown. 1995. The effects of religious messages on racial identity and system blame among African-Americans. *The Journal of Politics* 57: 24–43.

Reeves, Keith. 1997. *Voting hopes or fears?: White voters, Black candidates & racial politics in America*. New York: Oxford University Press.

Riker, William H., and Peter C. Ordeshook. 1968. A Theory of the Calculus of Voting. *American Political Science Review* 62: 25–42.

Riley, Anna. 2000. The Quality of Work Life, Self-evaluation and Life Satisfaction among African Americans, African American Research Perspectives, 6(1). http://www.rcgd.isr.umich.edu/prba/perspectives/winter2000/ariley.pdf (accessed January 11, 2010).

Roccas, Sonia, and Marilynn B. Brewer. 2002. Social identity complexity. *Personality and Social Psychology Review* 6: 88–106.

Roseman, Ira J. 1984. Cognitive determinants of emotion: A structural theory. In *Review of personality and social psychology: Emotions, relationships, and health*, ed. Phillip Shaver, 11–36. Beverly Hills: Sage.

Roth, Benita. 1999. The making of the vanguard center: Black feminist emergence in the 1960s and 1970s. In *Still lifting, still climbing: Contemporary African American women's activism*, ed. Kimberly Springer, 70–90. New York: New York University Press.

Rousseau, Jean-Jacques. 1762. *The social contract, or principles of political right.* Trans. G. D. H. Cole, rendered into HTML and text by Jon Roland of the Constitution Society. http://www.constitution.org/jjr/socon.htm (Accessed 10 July 2007).

Rubens, Arthur J. 1996. Racial and ethnic differences in students' attitudes and behavior toward organ donation. *Journal of the National Medical Association* 88(7): 417–21.

Runyan, William McKinley. 1993. Psychohistory and political psychology: A comparative analysis. In *Explorations in political psychology*, ed. Shanto Iyengar and William J. McGuire, 36–69. Durham: Duke University Press.

Saegert, Susan. 1989. Unlikely leaders, extreme circumstances: Older Black women building community households. *American Journal of Community Psychology* 17(3): 295–316.

Sanbonmatsu, Kira. 2002. Gender stereotypes and vote choice. *American Journal of Political Science* 46(1): 20–34.

Sapiro, Virginia, and Pamela Johnston Conover. 1997. The variable gender bias of electoral politics: Gender and context in the 1992 U.S. election. *British Journal of Political Science* 27: 497–523.

Schacht, Thomas E. 2008. A broader view of racial microaggression in psychotherapy. *American Psychologist* 63(4): 273–79.

Scherer, Klaus R. 1988. Criteria for emotion-antecedent appraisal: A review. In *Cognitive perspectives on emotion and motivation*, ed. Vernon Hamilton, Gordon H. Bower, and Nico H. Frijda, 89–126. Dordrecht: Kluwer Academic Publishers.

Schuman, Howard, Charlotte Steeh, Lawrence Bobo, and Maria Krysan. 1997. *Racial attitudes in America: Trends and interpretations (rev. ed).* Cambridge, MA: Harvard University Press.

Sears, David O. 1989. The ecological niche of political psychology. *Political Psychology* 10(3): 501–6.

Sears, David O., and Carolyn L. Funk. 1991. Graduate education in political psychology. *Political Psychology* 12(2): 345–62.

Sears, David O., Leonie Huddy, and Robert Jervis, eds. 2003. *Oxford handbook of political psychology*. New York: Oxford University Press.

Sears, David O., John J. Hetts, Jim Sidanius, and Lawrence Bobo. 2000. Race in American politics: Framing the debates. In *Racialized politics: The debate about racism in America,* ed. David O. Sears, Jim Sidanius, and Lawrence Bobo, 1–43. Chicago: University of Chicago Press.

Segal, Steven P., Carol Silverman, and Tanya Temkin. 1995. Measuring empowerment in client-run self-help agencies. *Community Mental Health Journal* 31(3): 215–27.

Seligman, Martin E. P. 1975. *Helplessness: On depression, development, and death.* New York: W H Freeman/Times Books/ Henry Holt.

Sellers, Robert M., Mia A. Smith, J. Nicole Shelton, Stephanie Rowley, and Tabbye Chavous. 1998. Multidimensional model of racial identity: A reconceptualization of African American racial identity. *Personality and Social Psychology Review* 2(1): 18–39.

Shavers-Hornaday, Vickie L., C. F. Lynch, L. F. Burmeister, and J. C. Torner. 1997. Why are African Americans under-represented in medical research studies? Impediments to participation. *Ethnic Health* 2: 31–45.

Sherif, Muzafer, and Carolyn W. Sherif. 1966. *Groups in harmony and tension: An integration of studies on intergroup relations.* New York: Octagon Books.

Shuster, Rachel. 1993. Ashe legacy goes beyond sports, race. *USA Today*, February 8, 1C.

Sidanius, J. 1993. The psychology of group conflict and the dynamics of oppression: A social dominance perspective. In *Explorations in political psychology,* ed. Shanto Iyengar and William McGuire, 183–219. Durham, NC: Duke University Press.

Sidbury, James. 2003. Reading, revelation and rebellion: The textual communities of Gabriel, Denmark Vesey and Nat Turner. In *Nat Turner: A slave rebellion in history and memory*, ed. Kenneth S. Greenberg, 119–33. Oxford: Oxford University Press.

Sigelman, Carol K., Lee Sigelman, Barbara J. Walkosz, and Michael Nitz. 1995. Black candidates, White voters: Understanding racial bias in political perceptions. *American Journal of Political Science* 39(1): 243–65.

Sigelman, Lee, and Carol K. Sigelman. 1982. Sexism, racism, and ageism in voting behavior: An experimental analysis. *Social Psychology Quarterly* 45: 263–69.

Sigelman, Lee, and Susan Welch. 1984. Race, gender, and opinion toward Black and female presidential candidates. *Public Opinion Quarterly* 48(2): 467–75.

———. 1993. The contact hypothesis revisited: Black-White interaction and positive racial attitudes. *Social Forces* 71(3): 781–95.

Simien, Evelyn M., and Rosalee A. Clawson. 2004. The intersection of race and gender: An examination of Black feminist consciousness, race consciousness, and policy attitudes. *Social Science Quarterly* 85(3): 793–810.

Simon, Herbert A. 1985. Human nature in politics: The dialogue of psychology with political science. *American Political Science Review* 79(2): 293–304.

Sinclair-Chapman, Valeria, and Melanye Price. 2008. Black politics, the 2008 election, and (im)possibility of race transcendence. *PS: Political Science and Politics* 41(October): 739–45.

Singer, J. David. 1963. Inter-nation influence: A formal model. *American Political Science Review* 57(2): 420–30.

Smith, Craig A., and Phoebe C. Ellsworth. 1985. Patterns of cognitive appraisal in emotion. *Journal of Personality and Social Psychology* 48(4): 813–38.

Smith, Adam. 1776. *An inquiry into the nature and causes of the wealth of nations*, reprint. London: Methuen, 1904.

Smith, Eliot R. 1993. Social identity and social emotions: Toward new conceptualizations of prejudice. In *Affect, cognition, and stereotyping: Interactive processes in group perception*, ed. Diane M. Mackie and David L. Hamilton, 297–315. San Diego: Academic Press.

Smith, Elsie M. J. 1989. Black racial identity development: Issues and concerns. *The Counseling Psychologist* 17(2): 277–88.

Son Hing, Leanne S., Greg A. Chung-Yan, Leah K. Hamilton, and Mark P. Zanna. 2008. A two-dimensional model that employs explicit and implicit attitudes to characterize prejudice. *Journal of Personality and Social Psychology* 94(6): 971–87.

Speight, Suzette L., Elizabeth M. Vera, and Kimberly B. Derrickson. 1996. Racial self-designation, racial identity, and self-esteem revisited. *Journal of Black Psychology* 22(1): 37–52.

Spencer, Margaret B., and Carol Markstrom-Adams. 1990. Identity process among racial and ethnic minority children in America. *Child Development* 61(2): 290–310.

Stangor, Charles, Linda A. Sullivan, and Thomas E. Ford. 1991. Affective and cognitive determinants of prejudice. *Social Cognition* 9(4): 359–80.

Steeh, Charlotte, and Howard Schuman. 1992. Young White adults: Did racial attitudes change in the 1980s? *American Journal of Sociology* 98(2): 340–67.

Steele, Claude M. 1997. A threat in the air: How stereotypes shape intellectual identity and performance. *American Psychologist* 52(6)(06/01): 613–29.

Steele, Shelby. 1990. *The content of our character: A new vision of race in America*. Gordonsville, VA: St. Martin's Press.

Stephan, Walter G., and Cookie W. Stephan. 1996. *Intergroup relations*. Madison: Brown & Benchmark.

Stevenson, Howard C. 1994. The psychology of sexual racism and AIDS: An ongoing saga of distrust and the "sexual other." *Journal of Black Studies* 25(1): 62–80.

Stokes, Donald E., and Warren E. Miller. 1962. Party government and the saliency of Congress. *Public Opinion Quarterly* 26(4): 531–46.

Swain, Carol. 1993. *Black faces, Black interests: The representation of African Americans in Congress*. Cambridge: Harvard University Press.

———. 2002. *The new White nationalism in America: Its challenge to integration*. Cambridge: Cambridge University Press.

Swain, John, Stephen Borrelli, and Brian Reed. 1998. Partisan consequences of the post-1990 redistricting for the U.S. House of Representatives. *Political Research Quarterly* 51: 945–67.

Tajfel, Henri. 1970. Experiments in intergroup discrimination. *Scientific American* 223(5): 96–102.

———. 1982. *Social identity and intergroup relations.* Cambridge: Cambridge University Press.

Tajfel, Henri, and John C. Turner. 1986. The social identity theory of intergroup behavior. In *The psychology of intergroup relations*, ed. Stephen Worchel and William G. Austin, 7–24. Chicago: Nelson-Hall.

Tarrow, Sidney. 1994. *Power in movement: social movements, collective action and politics.* Cambridge, MA: Cambridge University Press.

Tate, Katherine. 1993. *From protest to politics: The new Black voters in American elections.* Cambridge, MA: Harvard University Press.

———. 2003. *Black faces in the mirror: African Americans and their representatives in the U.S. Congress.* Princeton, NJ: Princeton University Press.

———. 2003. Black opinion on the legitimacy of racial redistricting and minority-majority districts. *American Political Science Review* 97(1): 45–56.

Tatum, Beverly D. 1992. Talking about race, learning about racism: The application of racial identity development theory. *Harvard Educational Review* 62(1): 1–24.

Taylor, Robert Joseph, Linda M. Chatters, and Jeff Levin. 2004. *Religion in the lives of African Americans: Social, psychological, and health perspectives.* Thousand Oaks, CA: Sage.

Terkildsen, Nayda. 1993. When White voters evaluate Black candidates: The processing implications of candidate skin color, prejudice, and self-monitoring. *American Journal of Political Science* 37(4): 1032–53.

Terrell, Francis, Sandra L. Terrell, and Fayneese Miller. 1993. Level of cultural mistrust as a function of educational and occupational expectations among Black students. *Adolescence* 28(111): 573–78.

Thernstrom, Abigail M. 1987. *Whose votes count? Affirmative action and minority voting rights.* Cambridge, MA: Harvard University Press.

Thernstrom, Stephan, and Abigail Thernstrom. 1997. *America in Black and White: One nation, indivisible.* New York: Simon & Schuster.

———. 1999. *America in black and white: One nation, indivisible.* New York: Touchstone.

Thomas, Charles W. 1971. *Boys No more: A Black psychologist's view of community.* Beverly Hills: Glencoe Press.

Thompson, Suzanne C., and Shirlynn Spacapan. 1991. Perceptions of control in vulnerable populations. *Journal of Social Issues* 41(4): 1–21.

Tocqueville, Alexis de. 1835. *Democracy in America.* New York: Bantam Books.

Triandis, Harry C., and Earl E. Davis. 1965. Race and belief as determinants of behavioral intentions. *Journal of Personality and Social Psychology* 2(5): 715–25.

Tsitsos, William. 2003. Race differences in congregational social service activity. *Journal for the Scientific Study of Religion* 42(2): 205–15.

Tuch, Steven A., and Michael Hughes. 1996. Whites' racial policy attitudes. *Social Science Quarterly* 77(4): 723–45.

Tuch, Steven A., and Jack K. Martin. 1991. Race in the workplace: Black/White differences in the sources of job satisfaction. *Sociological Quarterly* 32: 103–116.

Tuch, Steven A., and Jack C. Martin, eds. 1997. *Racial attitudes in America: Continuity and change*. Westport, CT: Praeger.

Turner, John C. 1982. Towards a cognitive redefinition of the social group. In *Social identity and intergroup relations*, ed. Henri Tajfel, 15–40. Cambridge: Cambridge University Press.

Tversky, Amos, and Daniel Kahneman. 1974. Judgment under uncertainty: Heuristics and biases. *Science* 185(4157): 1124–31.

U.S. Census Bureau. 2002a. Table B-7. Standard Errors for Homeownership Rates by Race and Ethnicity: 2001. (October 1), http://www.census.gov/hhes/www/housing/hvs/annual02/ann02tb7.html (accessed June 1, 2003).

———— 2002b. Historical Tables on Income Inequality. (October 1), http://www.census.gov/hhes/income/histinc/ineqtoc.html (accessed June 1, 2003).

————. 2003. Table A-2. Percent of People 25 Years Old and Over Who Have Completed High School or College, by Race, Hispanic Origin and Sex: Selected Years 1940 to 2002. (March 21), http://www.census.gov/population/socdemo/education/tabA-2.pdf (accessed June 1, 2003).

Utsey, Shawn O. 1998. Assessing the stressful effects of racism: A review of instrumentation. *Journal of Black Psychology* 24(3): 269–88.

Valentino, Nicholas A. 1999. Crime news and the priming of racial attitudes during evaluations of the president. *Public Opinion Quarterly* 63(3): 293–320.

Valentino, Nicholas A., Vincent L. Hutchings, and Ismail K. White. 2002. Cues that matter: How political ads prime racial attitudes during campaigns. *American Political Science Review* 96(1): 75–90.

Valentino, Nicholas A., Vincent L. Hutchings, Tasha S. Philpot, and Ismail K. White. 2006. Racial cues in campaign news: The effects of candidate issue distance on emotional responses, political attentiveness, and vote choice. In *Feeling politics: Affect and emotion in political information processing*, ed. David Redlawsk, 165–86. New York: Palgrave Macmillan.

van Deth, Jan. 1990. Interest in politics. In *Continuities in political action: A longitudinal study of political orientations in three western democracies*, ed. Kent Jennings and Jan W. van Deth, 275–312. New York: De Gruyter and Aldine.

————. 2000. *Political involvement and apathy in Europe 1973–1998*. Arbeitspapiere—Mannheimer Zentrum für Europäische Sozialforschung [Papers Mannheimer Center for European Social Research]/No 33. Mannheim.

Vanman, Eric J., and Norman Miller. 1993. Applications of emotion theory and research to stereotyping and intergroup relations. In *Affect, cognition, and stereotyping: Interactive processes in group perception*, ed. Diane M. Mackie and David L. Hamilton, 213–38. San Diego: Academic Press.

Verba, Sidney, and Norman H. Nie. 1972. *Participation in America: Political democracy and social equality*. New York: Harper & Row.

Verba, Sidney, Kay Schlozman, and Henry E. Brady. 1995. *Voice and equality: Civic voluntarism in American politics*. Cambridge, MA: Harvard University Press.

Wagner, Peter. 2005. Incarceration is not an equal opportunity punishment. Prison Policy Initiative. (June 28), http://www.prisonpolicy.org/articles/notequal.html (accessed January 11, 2010).

Walters, Ron. 2007. Barack Obama and the politics of Blackness. *Journal of Black Studies* 38(1): 7–29.

Walters, Ronald W., and Robert C. Smith, eds. 1999. *African-American leadership*. Albany: State University of New York Press.

Walton, Hanes, Jr. 1973. *The study and analysis of Black politics: A bibliography*. Metuchen: Scarecrow Press.

———. 1985. *Invisible politics: Black political behavior*. Albany: State University of New York Press.

———. 1985. The recent literature on Black politics. *PS: Political Science and Politics* 18(4): 769–80.

———. 1989. The current literature on Black politics. *National Political Science Review* 1: 152–68.

———. 1997. *African American power and politics: The political context variable*. New York: Columbia University Press.

Walton, Hanes, Jr., and Robert C. Smith. 2000. *American politics and the African American quest for universal freedom*. New York: Addison-Wesley Longman.

———. 2003. *American politics and the African American quest for universal freedom*. 2nd. ed. New York: Addison Wesley Longman.

Walton, Hanes, Jr., Leslie Burl McLemore, and C. Vernon Gray. 1989. The pioneering books on Black politics and the political science community, 1903–1965. *National Political Science Review* 1: 197–218.

———. 1992. The problem of preconceived perceptions in Black urban politics: The Harold Gosnell-James Q. Wilson legacy. *National Political Science Review* 3: 217–29.

Walton, Hanes, Jr., Cheryl M. Miller, and Joseph P. McCormick, II. 1995. Race and political science: The dual traditions of race relations politics and African-American politics. In *Political science in history: Research programs and political traditions*, ed. James Farr, John S. Dryzek, and Stephen T. Leonard. New York: Cambridge University Press.

Walton, Hanes, Jr., Marion E. Orr, Shirley Geiger, and Mfanya Tryman. 2001. The literature on African-American politics: The decades of the nineties. *Politics and Policy* 29: 753–82.

Ward, Janie Victoria. 1996. Raising resisters: The role of truth telling in the psychological development of African American girls. In *Urban girls: Resisting stereotypes, creating identities*, ed. Niobe Way, 85–99. New York: New York University Press.

Washington, James Melvin. 2004. *Frustrated fellowship: The Black Baptist quest for social power*. Macon, GA: Mercer University Press.

WebCASPAR. 2010. www.webcaspar.nsf.gov

Weis, Lois, Michelle Fine, Tracey Shepherd, and Kenny Foster. 1999. "We need to come together and raise our kids and our communities right": Black Males Rewriting Social Representations, *The Urban Review* 31(2): 125–52.

West, Cornel. 1993. *Race matters.* New York: Beacon Press.

Wilcox, Clyde, and Leopoldo Gomez. 1990. Religion, group identification, and politics among American Blacks. *Sociological Analysis* 51(3): 271–85.

Williams, Linda. 1989. White/Black perceptions of the electability of Black political candidates. *National Political Science Review* 2: 45–64.

———. 2003. *The constraint of race: Legacies of White skin privilege.* University Park, PA: Pennsylvania State University Press.

Wills, Garry, ed. 1982. *The federalist papers by Alexander Hamilton, James Madison, and John Jay.* New York: Bantam Books.

Wilson, Ernest J., III. 1985. Why political scientists don't study Black politics, but historians and sociologists do. *PS* 18(3): 600–607.

Wilson, William J. 1978. *The declining significance of race: Blacks and changing American institutions.* Chicago: University of Chicago Press.

Winant, Howard. 1997. Behind blue eyes: Whiteness and contemporary U.S. racial politics. *New Left Review* (September-October): 73–88.

Wirls, Daniel. 1986. Reinterpreting the gender gap. *Public Opinion Quarterly* 50(3): 316–30.

Whaley, Arthur L. 2004. A two-stage method for the study of cultural bias in the diagnosis of schizophrenia in African Americans. *Journal of Black Psychology* 30(2): 167–86.

White, Clovis, and Peter Burke. 1987. Ethnic role identity among Black and White college students: An interactionist approach. *Sociological Perspectives* 30: 310–31.

White, Ismail K. 2007. When race matters and when it doesn't: Racial group differences in response to racial cues. *American Political Science Review* 101(2): 339–54.

White, Ismail K., Tasha S. Philpot, Kristin Wylie, and Ernest McGowen. 2007. Feeling the pain of my people: Hurricane Katrina, racial inequality, and the psyche of Black America. *Journal of Black Studies* 37: 523–38.

Wolfenstein, E. Victor. 1967. *The revolutionary personality.* Princeton, NJ: Princeton University Press.

———. 1981. *The victims of democracy: Malcolm X and the Black revolution.* Berkeley, CA: University of California Press.

Woodard, Maurice, and Michael B. Preston. 1985. Black political scientists: Where are the new PhDs? *PS* 18(1): 80–88.

Woodmansee, John J., and Stuart W. Cook. 1967. Dimensions of verbal racial attitudes: Their identification and measurement. *Journal of Personality and Social Psychology* 7(3): 240–50.

Wu, Chung Li. 2003. Psycho-political correlates of political efficacy: The case of the 1994 New Orleans mayoral election. *Journal of Black Studies* 33: 729–60.

Young, Stephanie L. 2007. A review of speaking power: Black feminist orality in women's narratives of slavery. *Howard Journal of Communications* 18(2): 193–95.

Zajonc, Robert B. 1980. Feeling and thinking: Preferences need no inferences. *American Psychologist* 35(2): 151–75.

Zimmerman, Marc A. 1990. Taking aim on empowerment research: On the distinction between individual and psychological conceptions. *American Journal of Community Psychology* 18(1): 169–77.

Zipp, John F., and Eric Plutzer. 1985. Gender differences in voting for female candidates: Evidence from the 1982 election. *Public Opinion Quarterly* 49(2): 179–97.

Index